National Institute of Economic and Social
Research
Policy Studies Institute
Royal Institute of International Affairs

Joint Studies in Public Policy 3

INDUSTRIAL
POLICY AND
INNOVATION

Edited by
CHARLES CARTER

Heinemann · London

Heinemann Educational Books Ltd

LONDON EDINBURGH MELBOURNE AUCKLAND TORONTO
HONG KONG SINGAPORE KUALA LUMPUR NEW DELHI
NAIROBI JOHANNESBURG IBADAN
KINGSTON

Cased edition ISBN 0 435 83115 1
Paper edition ISBN 0 435 83116 X

315993

Published by Heinemann Educational Books Ltd
Filmset and printed in Great Britain by Richard Clay (The Chaucer Press) Ltd
Bungay, Suffolk

Contents

Foreword by *Sir Arthur Knight*   vii

Contributors and Participants   ix

1   **Introduction** by *Charles Carter*   1

2   **Innovation: Does Government have a Role?** by *Andrew Shonfield*   4

3   **Reasons for Not Innovating** by *Charles Carter*   21

Comment on Chapters 2 and 3 by *S. J. Prais*   32

4   **Industrial Policies in Britain 1960–80** by *Aubrey Silberston*   39

5   **Government Support for Innovation in the British Machine Tool Industry: a Case Study** by *Anne Daly*   52

6   **Industrial Policy and Innovation in Japan** by *G. C. Allen*   68

7   (I) **Technology in British Industry: a Suitable Case for Improvement** by *Keith Pavitt*   88

(II) **The Case for Government Support of R and D and Innovation** by *D. K. Stout*   116

(III) **Industrial Innovation and the Role of Bodies like the National Enterprise Board** by *W. B. Willott*   129

(IV) **Catching up with Our Competitors: the Role of Industrial Policy** by *D. T. Jones*   146

(V) **The Adoption and Transfer of Technology and the Role of Government** by *G. M. White*   157

Comments on Chapter 7: (I) by *P. D. Henderson*; (II) by *R. W. Archer*   170

8   **Institutions and Markets in High Technology: Government Support for Micro-electronics in Europe** by *Giovanni Dosi*   182

9   **The NEB Involvement in Electronics and Information
     Technology** by *W. B. Willott*   203
10   **Policies for Micro-electronic Applications in Industry**
     by *Jim Northcott*   213
11   **Report of the Discussion** by *Charles Carter*   225

Index   237

Foreword

The conference which provided the subject matter for this volume took place on 9 and 10 December 1980, and was the sixth in the series initiated by the National Institute of Economic and Social Research with a grant from the Nuffield Foundation for three studies. In 1978 it was decided to re-launch the series under the aegis of the National Institute of Economic and Social Research, the Policy Studies Institute and the Royal Institute of International Affairs. This decision followed a wide debate, in part in public, about the need in this country for a more concerted approach to the consideration of questions of public policy, drawing upon a wider range of expertise than might be available to any one of the existing institutes. This particular study, on industrial policy and innovation, was sponsored and financed by the Social Science Research Council.

This volume is a timely contribution to an issue of public policy which has not generally received the comprehensive treatment which its continuing importance deserves. The papers, circulated in advance of the conference, are reprinted here and include new insights into the subject. The two-day discussion gave those taking part full opportunity both to express and to re-assess their views. Sir Charles Carter's concluding chapter gives his personal summing-up, drawing upon both the papers and the discussion which developed from them. It will doubtless lead others also to search for some coherent formulation of principle and measures which might guide action in this area.

No one, in either the papers or the discussion, sought to argue that it was desirable, or even possible, for government to do nothing in this field; there was general agreement that further action is needed. Of course, there were differences of opinion about the form this action should take. One of the purposes of this series of policy studies is to bring such differences into the open, and to array the arguments for and against particular policy choices.

Those responsible for the new tripartite series were clear that there is hardly a single policy issue without its international dimension. This was reflected at the conference in Professor Allen's paper on Japan and in Giovanni Dosi's paper on government support for micro-electronics in Europe, as well as in the discussions.

The first paper in this volume is by Andrew Shonfield, and it sets out with his usual clarity the main questions of principle which arise in any discussion of industrial policy and innovation. It is one more contribution to add to the very large number of contributions which he made to the study of the problems of the western industrial world. I record a sense of great loss at his death.

London   Arthur Knight
January 1981

Contributors and Participants

Contributors

G. C. Allen, Emeritus Professor of Political Economy, University of London

R. W. Archer, Finance Director, Unilever Ltd

Sir Charles Carter, Chairman of Research and Management Committee, Policy Studies Institute

Ms A. Daly, Research Officer, National Institute of Economic and Social Research

G. Dosi, Sussex European Research Centre, University of Sussex

P. D. Henderson, Professor of Political Economy, University College, London

D. T. Jones, Senior Research Fellow, Sussex European Research Centre, University of Sussex

J. Northcott, Policy Studies Institute

K. Pavitt, Senior Fellow, Science Policy Research Unit, University of Sussex

S. J. Prais, Senior Research Fellow, National Institute of Economic and Social Research

Sir Andrew Shonfield, Professor of Economics, European University Institute, Florence

A. Silberston, Professor of Economics, Imperial College, London

D. K. Stout, Professor of Economics, University of Leicester

G. M. White, Senior Economic Adviser, Department of Industry

W. B. Willott, Chief Executive, National Enterprise Board

Other Participants

F. T. Blackaby	D. J. Morris
J. C. Cain	Sir Richard Powell
T. Forester	G. F. Ray
Lord Kearton	T. M. Rybczynski
D. King	J. R. Shepherd
Sir Arthur Knight (*Chairman*)	J-C. Tourret

1 Introduction

by Charles Carter

Britain, in the postwar period, has not had any settled industrial policy; it is a matter on which there has been no consensus. This makes it an appropriate subject for this series of studies, whose objective is to explore some of Britain's main policy problems. 'Industrial policy' is potentially, a broad term – since virtually any economic policy measure has some industrial impact. Here it is narrowed in two ways: first, to exclude what might be called general macroeconomic policies; secondly, to concentrate on policies which are concerned in some way with economic innovation – with research and development, with new technologies and their diffusion. That is, it is not concerned to discuss policies appropriate for those older industries which need large subsidies to survive. It rather asks the question: 'What, if anything, should the government do to help British industry (or parts of British industry) to keep at (or near) the technological frontier?'

The structure of the book is as follows. There are two chapters (followed by a comment) on the general rationale for government intervention in this matter. Then British experience is reviewed, first in general, and then specifically in the policies adopted towards the machine tool industry. A chapter follows on Japan's success. Next, five authors were asked to address themselves to the question: 'What, if anything, should the government do?' There are two discussants of this set of papers. Lastly, there are three chapters on the specific problems of industrial policies towards micro-electronics.

What is the rationale for any government intervention? Shonfield points out, first, that innovation 'requires that the rules governing the model of perfect competition be systematically negated', and also cites Arrow's conclusion that market forces will not lead to an optimal allocation of resources to invention. Further, he presents Mansfield's evidence which suggests that the private rate of return on inventions is generally much lower than the social rate of return

– and that the divergence between the two tends to be particularly marked for major innovations. He points to the evidence which suggests that it is the 'upper-middle size firms' which are best at innovating, and suggests that firms organised in a 'multi-divisional' way have a particular advantage. He comments in particular on the deleterious effects of increased uncertainty. Shonfield accepts that the fact of 'market failure' does not necessarily imply that governments will be able to do better; he suggests various safeguards against arbitrary or consistently wrong decisions on these matters by governments. Carter, in his chapter, asks why firms do not innovate enough. He provides a long list of possible reasons which firms might give for not innovating, and concludes: 'We thus come back from the immediate reasons given by businessmen for not innovating, first to a series of external disadvantages or internal inadequacies which may lie behind the reasons given; and then to the problems of the distribution of ability, of education and training, and of the habits and attitudes of management . . .' Prais, in his comment on these chapters, cites international comparisons of the numbers of engineering graduates, and also of technicians and skilled workers; he also suggests that the social rate of return for those with degrees in engineering and technology is lower than it is for those with degrees in the arts, science and social science.

The chapters on British and Japanese experience follow. Silberston chronicles the changes in industrial policies since 1960; Daly addresses herself in particular to the policies tried on the machine tool industry, and asks the question: 'Could the £100 million spent by the government on this industry have been spent more effectively – for example on special grants or loans for engineering students, or on establishing departments within universities to specialise in engineering research for industry?' Allen reviews Japan's successful experience and disputes the proposition 'that the British would have to become Japanese before they could accept Japan as a model'. He points out that 'many of the qualities and practices that are considered peculiarly Japanese today were not conspicuous until recently'.

In the five sections of Chapter 7, five authors discuss what the government should do. Pavitt documents the extent to which Britain appears to have fallen behind in research and development, and has various suggestions in this field. Stout puts forward some general guidelines for industrial policy, and again has a list of specific proposals. Willott argues for the role of a body on the lines of the National Enterprise Board. White is particularly concerned with government incentives for the diffusion of new technology, and recommends a diversity of approaches. Jones cites French as well as Japanese experience, and would like to see, *inter alia*, an Industrial Structure Commission. In comment on these papers, Archer is impressed particularly by Japanese experience. Henderson sees particular weaknesses in some of the more ambitious suggestions: 'the belief in manifest destiny, the neglect of uncertainty, the bias towards centralised decision, and the lack of concern for results, assessment and accountability'. His own suggestions are primarily concerned with 'influencing in various ways the underlying culture'.

In the first of three chapters on government support for microelectronics, Dosi reviews the policies which have been followed in Germany, France, Italy and the UK. He suggests that 'it is very difficult for public institutions to set and implement objectives that do not correspond to tendencies already existing in the private sector. However, "market mechanisms" do not lead towards convergence of technological capabilities and industrial strength amongst different countries which started from different technological levels.' Willott describes the background to the NEB's involvement in electronics, and explains in particular the reasons for its decision to support Inmos. Northcott reviews the government's Microprocessor Application Project and makes various suggestions for its improvement – suggestions which would involve a greater degree of discrimination between one proposal and another.

These papers were discussed at a conference held at the National Institute of Economic and Social Research in December 1980, and there is a report of that discussion in Chapter 11. As editor, I am grateful to Frank Blackaby for commissioning the papers, organising the conference and doing much to make my task simple, and to Gillian Little of the National Institute for her expert and expeditious work in preparing the book for the printer.

2 Innovation: Does Government have a Role?

by Andrew Shonfield

A useful point of entry is to postulate that public policy-makers need not, or more strongly should not, be concerned with economic innovation, and then to ask what conditions have to be fulfilled by market processes to secure an optimum outcome. This is only a first step in the argument: even if it could be shown that the market process was deficient, it would not follow that intervention by public authorities would produce a better answer.

If markets are to manage the business of innovation successfully, with no help from outside, they will have to perform the following functions. First, they must provide innovators with an environment which both stimulates their entrepreneurial activity, and minimises the time interval between the formulation of a viable scheme and its realisation. Second, they must select efficiently among the various proposals, so that they are ranked in an appropriate order, in terms of the timing of investment and the allocation of scarce resources, in order to maximise the total return from this activity. Stating the desired outcome in this extreme way makes it clear that it would not be possible to apply precise measurement to the performance of any given market in this regard. One could only hope to identify a possible bias tending to make the outcome deviate from the optimum. Such a bias would exist if, for example, the discounted present value of the anticipated benefits from investments as measured by the market differed from the value that would be placed upon them by applying a time discount which corresponded to the collective preferences of the society affected by the innovation.

We have still not escaped from the problems of measurement: calculating social preference presents particular difficulty. But it is important to establish the point that market rates of discount may well differ from social rates of discount, especially for long-term investments. This is partly because market signals are necessarily limited to expressing the preferences of contemporaries. The limitation cannot be entirely overcome by any other form of signal. But it is possible to devise a means of giving greater weight to the imputed desires of future generations than the market provides. This matters particularly when a proposed innovation involves changes in the environment, or in the provision of public goods, which will be difficult or impossible to reverse in the future. Such consequences grow increasingly common as the pressure of economic activity on space and other natural resources rises.

This leads to a third requirement: markets must be able to *regulate* the effects of economic innovation on public goods. This could be done, in principle, if appropriate charges were levied for the use, or destruction, of public goods on the producers of private goods and services (Schultze [8]). But the identification of public goods is not always a simple matter. It may not be too difficult to defend parts of the natural environment by introducing charges which the polluter has to pay. But what about the effect of innovation on public goods which are less tangible?

The fact is that the volume of man-made social capital installed in the past half century or so has vastly increased with the advance of the Welfare State. Much of it consists of long-term capital investment. Innovations which have the effect of destroying employment in particular localities and causing emigration are in consequence more costly than they would have been half a century ago. One of the factors which made the exodus from European agriculture in the postwar period relatively painless was that the social infrastructure provided for peasant communities was relatively modest. A comparable movement of population out of well-endowed urban centres would surely have caused a more worried reaction among governments and taxpayers.

This is, of course, not a reason for preventing innovations which require large-scale changes of employment. The destruction of old industries and occupations is the very stuff of material progress. But it is a reason for governments to be concerned about the long-term consequences of innovations which have this effect, and to make plans to protect the welfare of communities which are threatened by the process. The social and personal disturbance caused by innovations of this type cannot be treated as a pure external cost by those responsible for making the relevant investment decisions when these decisions involve a net addition to public expenditure which is borne by the taxpayer.

It would be logical to impose some tax on the beneficiaries of the innovative investment – if they could be identified – which would pay for part at least of the cost of disturbance. The reason for making it a part rather than the whole is that it is assumed that there will be compensating benefits from the innovation, which will be enjoyed by consumers in the form of cheaper or better goods and services, or by other producers. The calculation of the balance between local costs and general benefits will be very difficult. The argument is not that the precise calculation needs to be made; it is rather that innovation involving social disturbance requires that public authorities be involved at an early stage as planners. Markets do not make spontaneous provision for the secondary consequences of their decisions on the supply of public goods.

A fourth requirement is that market forces should cause an optimal allocation of resources to the innovative activity. To some extent this requirement is subsumed under the first of the criteria of market efficiency above. I mention it separately to emphasise the difference between the process of invention, which may be adequately stimulated by the market, and the further stage of the diffusion of new knowledge and its widespread embodiment in the process of production. In perfect markets, of course, competition ensures maximum diffusion consistent with minimum irreducible costs. In practice, however, the process of converting a new idea into a piece of property which is capable of commercial exploitation is not compatible with these conditions. As Schumpeter puts it: 'Perfectly free entry into a *new* field may make it impossible to enter it at all. The introduction of new methods of production and new commodities is hardly conceivable with perfect – and perfectly prompt – competition from the start' ([9], p. 104).

The Limits of Competition

Here we touch upon a fundamental problem of innovation in the capitalist system, which Schumpeter was, so far as I know, the first to subject to systematic examination. On the one hand, the traditional justification for competitive capitalism is that it tends to approximate to the model of perfect competition under which producers, consumers, sellers and buyers, achieve maximum satisfaction. On the other hand the essence of the long history of economic growth which is the characteristic feature of the capitalist system is the *routine* of innovation. And routinised innovation requires that the rules governing the model of perfect competition be systematically negated. It is true that the monopolistic behaviour and the restriction of free entry which go with product innovation are transient phenomena which continue only so long as a patent or some unique technical advantage lasts. But the act of innovation is both so commonplace and so eagerly sought after, especially by large firms which have already captured a substantial portion of the market, that a style of corporate behaviour which is wholly unlike that of the seller under conditions of perfect competition must be regarded as characteristic of a major segment of successful business enterprise.

Antitrust legislation is, as Schumpeter observed rather contemptuously, no answer to the problem. He thought that big firms which made a habit of capturing innovative positions of transient monopoly were often benign in their price and production behaviour – though he offered no satisfactory explanation for the fact that many of them did not exploit the advantages of market dominance to the full. Accordingly, he conceded the case for public regulation of these firms – so long as it was not 'indiscriminate "trust busting" ' [9].

In an interesting variation on Schumpeter's theme Kenneth Arrow argues that the system of perfect competition is positively damaging to the optimal allocation of resources for 'inventions' [1]. Of the three reasons which he advances for this conclusion, one is the point already made about the impossibility of appropriating the new idea as a piece of private property under these conditions. He goes on to give particular emphasis to the uncertainty of new inventions; Schumpeter tended to take this for granted as part of the small change of capitalist entrepreneurship. But Arrow quite rightly argues that investment in the purchase of untried inventions, or in the research leading to them, presents the kind of risk for which, unlike the normal risks of capitalist enterprise, it is difficult to obtain adequate insurance. The only way to cope with the problem is to be a large corporation with a number of different research projects, each of them comparatively small in relation to net income, so that the risks are spread. This factor combines with another – that a firm with an established dominant market position will be better able than a small competitor to appropriate to itself the full benefits of the innovation – to favour the large enterprise with monopolistic features.

Arrow's concluding observation takes the argument a step

beyond Schumpeter: '... for optimal allocation to invention it would be necessary for the government or some other agency not governed by profit-and-loss criteria to finance research and invention' [1]. Contemporary adherents of 'free market' doctrines would no doubt regard as highly paradoxical this formal statement of what competition can and cannot do, even when the market is perfect, to make the most of the resources of innovation. Moreover, it is not only in the rather special ideological climate of Tory Britain in 1980 that the Schumpeter–Arrow analysis requires attention. The view to which they put a major question mark continues to be part of the received wisdom in a much larger area of the western world. The OECD, which has a deserved reputation for careful examination of policy issues, concluded in a recent report that governments could most usefully 'fortify' the process of innovation by three types of activity. These were: 'financial aid, promotion of "technical culture", and measures to maintain or stimulate competition between enterprises' [6].

No doubt the stimulation of competition would perform a useful function in a society dominated by a number of monopolies with no interest in lowering costs or improving the quality of their products. Invention, like other risky activities, is likely to be reinforced by the existence of a competitive market for its output. But there is nothing either in economic theory or in the empirical evidence to sustain the view that measures applied generally to raise the tempo of competition are likely to result in more resources being devoted to innovation or in the reduction of the time interval between the formulation of a new idea and its realisation in practice. The kindest thing one can say is that this is an uncharacteristic piece of knee-jerk economics.

Social and Private Returns

It is probably an error to expect that macroeconomic analysis will provide many clues about the way in which the innovative process might be speeded up. Such analysis mainly serves to clear the ground of some common errors and to focus attention on the key unsolved questions. In the remainder of this chapter I consider some of the evidence about the way in which the process of innovation operates in advanced industrial societies; how it might be affected by changes in the rate of economic growth; and what effect non-market factors deliberately introduced to aid the process might be expected to have.

In the first place it is worth asking whether there is a significant difference between the private and social rates of return on industrial innovations. If there were indications that the private rate of return tends to be lower, then there would be a prima facie case for supplementing market incentives by some form of general financial inducement to firms to innovate. Mansfield's pioneering investigation of a varied sample of US innovations in the early 1970s compared the additional profits appropriated by the innovating firm with the social benefits in the form of both the added consumer surplus and the resources saved [4]. He avoided the familiar pitfalls in any comparison between the hypothetical situation in which the innovation was not undertaken and the results which actually occurred, including for example an allowance for the R and D costs incurred by firms engaged in the pursuit of roughly the same kind of innovation which proved to be *un*successful. He tried to make his estimate of input costs as comprehensive as possible and to apply conservative measures to the returns.

The results indicated that the private rate of return was generally much lower than the social rate of return. (It is to be noted that the resource saving, included in the additional profits figuring in the private rate of return, constitutes part of the social return on innovation.) The median social rate was 56 per cent compared with a private rate of return of 25 per cent. More important was the evidence of large variations in the private return, with nearly one third of the cases showing a rate which was so low that no business would have invested in the innovation if it had known the outcome in advance. In almost all of these cases the social rate of return was so high that 'from society's point of view the investment was well worthwhile' [4].

Mansfield's sample was a non-random one because a number of the firms which had been selected at random for investigation refused to answer the questionnaire. However, subsequent investigations in the US commissioned by the National Science Foundation, using more extensive samples, showed a similarly large, or larger, gap between private and social rates of return. That there should be a gap between the two is not surprising, in view of the problems for the innovator (referred to earlier) in appropriating the full benefits of his venture. But the order of magnitude of the *additional* social return provides a prima facie case for a generous policy in making public funds available to support investment in R and D, even where the marginal expected rate of private return is low. Modest private returns are not an argument for public abstention. Whether such support can be provided on a discriminating basis, so that public funds are not used to support R and D which would have been conducted in any case, is an important administrative question which I shall not try to examine here. The answer depends in part on the type of administrative apparatus available to a government; on its capacity to discriminate; and on the extent to which it can participate in the investment decisions of private firms.

The results of Mansfield's method are necessarily limited by the need to consider relatively simple and separate cases of innovation, where measurable inputs and outputs can be identified. They are no more than indicative of certain features of the innovative process in industry. One such indication is that, as a proportion of the social rate of return, the private rate of return on major innovations tends to be lower than on minor product or process improvements. The reason is largely that major advances are particularly subject to rapid imitation, so that the original innovator has greater difficulty in holding on to his gains. He must reckon that the ownership of his intellectual property will probably be diffused quickly – which is good for society but may well reduce the incentive to undertake the special risks attendant on major innovations. The point has some bearing on public policy during a period of slower economic growth. If during such a period the criteria applied to business budgets for new ventures become more severe, it may well be that spending on major innovations – as on basic research – becomes particularly vulnerable. The OECD, in its latest report summing up the conclusions of a two-year study of innovation policy, is concerned with precisely this danger when it urges that 'basic research must be shielded from the consequences of recession' (Salomon [7]). How is not made clear.

Industrial Organisation
What matters especially is the complex process by which innovation at one point in the system influences the rate of advance elsewhere and, if successful, creates an epidemic effect. This does not lend itself to measurement by Mansfield's method or any of the variations on it. An alternative approach is to ask what types of industrial organisation appear to be conducive to the process of innovation, and most likely to maximise the social return. Small firms operating in conditions which approximate to those of perfect

competition are doubtful instruments for this purpose. This argument does not in any way controvert the findings which have shown that many important inventions derive from the ideas of individuals or very small groups of people (Jewkes *et al.* [3]). But this is only the starting-point of the chain of effects which determines whether improvements thought up by inventive people are absorbed fast or slowly into the process of production. Britain is perhaps the outstanding example of a nation with a long record of rapid invention and of slow improvements in production.

It is also clear, at the other extreme, that unchallenged monopoly is unlikely to promote rapid innovation. There is, however, strong presumptive evidence that a small number of firms of substantial size operating in an oligopolistic situation, with some elements of competition and some public regulation, do provide a favourable environment. Size is useful. The work done in the United States, employing 'research and development intensiveness' as a measure (i.e. the ratio of R and D expenditures to total sales) indicates that big firms tend to be more research-intensive than small ones. The US National Science Foundation's study in 1967 divided firms into three categories on the basis of numbers employed – under 1000; 1000 to 5000; over 5000 – and showed a clear progression in the proportion of research expenditure between categories.

However, within the last group there was no correlation between the size of the individual firm and its degree of research intensity. A detailed examination of this group led Williamson to conclude that the most innovative and progressive performance tends to come from 'upper-middle size firms' [11]. His evidence suggested that when firms got beyond a certain very large scale they showed a propensity to devote their effort to the improvement of established products and were less likely to achieve major innovations than businesses of rather smaller size.

Williamson's general argument about firm and industry structures is more directly relevant to the possible use of public policy as a means of encouraging innovation. He starts from empirical evidence about the relative inefficiency of market mechanisms as a means of managing the introduction and employment of new ideas by firms. This is chiefly because transaction costs, which are a significant item of business expenditure (generally ignored in traditional economic models), increase when the parties to a complicated transaction are compelled to draw up formal contracts which try to cover all future relevant contingencies. That is most obviously so

when two or more firms conducting their businesses at arm's length
are involved in some collaborative endeavour to exploit new ideas,
deriving from their respective research efforts, which they acquire
from one another. To use Williamson's language, relationships
within the 'hierarchy' of a well-organised firm, in which the power
to make many decisions is effectively decentralised, are a more efficient instrument of innovation than a market relationship between
independent actors ([11], pp. 206, 253 and *passim*).

Williamson has in mind a particular type of industrial organisation, the 'multi-divisional' firm, which through its combination of
decentralised management and centralised strategic decisions
achieves something approaching the optimal allocation of resources, in a manner which is supposed to be performed by competitive markets, but at lower transaction costs. This type of firm,
he avers, has become widely established first in the United States,
and later on in Western Europe after industrial tariffs on intra-
European trade were minimised and then abolished in the late
1960s. Without subjecting this argument to systematic scrutiny, it
is at least intuitively plausible that firms approximating to the
model which he describes – a model which can only be realised by
a conscious effort of corporate organisation of a radical kind –
would be extremely well adapted to the business of exploiting the
opportunities for innovation.

One of the policy conclusions suggested by this research into the
changing structure of firms and its effect on innovation is that the
current fashion for treating the 'small firm' as a kind of universal
aunt of the western economy may be diverting attention from the
rôle of other, less glamorous, entrepreneurs. The notion that big is
ugly (to vary Schumacher's powerful slogan) has now been joined
by the conviction that the big are slow – slower than others to
respond to new ideas. There is no hard evidence to support the
latter contention. Big firms are generally more able to obtain oligopolistic profits out of the exploitation of new ideas. They have a
capacity for collusion not generally given to small firms – which
have to fall back on organised restrictive practices to collect their
additional rent from a collective monopoly. But the large firms are
generally more visible – and also more usable as·instruments of
public policy. The Japanese experience exemplifies most obviously
the benefits that can be drawn from a policy which starts from the
proposition that big is malleable.

At the far end of the scale of size and market power, the publicly owned monopoly constitutes a special problem. The fact of public ownership tends to inhibit the impulse to press awkward questions about the extent to which management innovates, which a private monopoly like American Telegraph and Telephone has to face as a matter of routine. The constant threat to some part of the monopoly position enjoyed by ATT is almost certainly a factor in keeping it at the forefront of innovative activity. What the company would most dislike is to face a credible accusation that it had delayed the introduction of some new product or process because this delay had served to maintain, or increase, its profits. There are considerable advantages to American telephone users from having a standardised national service provided by a single firm, so long as it is a monopoly which feels itself to be under constant public scrutiny.

In Britain the Conservative government has been especially preoccupied by the commercial performance of nationalised undertakings. However, the dominant concern has not been to ensure that these enterprises are placed under pressure to exploit opportunities for useful innovation. The breaking up of such monopolies into separate profit centres with a limited degree of competition between them could serve this purpose, if each centre were given the freedom to exercise entrepreneurial initiative. The coal industry might lend itself to this device. But it is not an arrangement which could be easily applied to other publicly owned utilities, where it is geographical location that produces monopoly conditions, so that entirely new enterprises would have to be created in order to subject the existing public undertaking to some degree of competition.

Other, less costly means need to be sought to induce a locational monopoly to engage in a more active policy of innovation. There is no evidence that selling its shares to private investors would serve this end. Some form of audit of industrial performance, such as is commonly applied to those large American enterprises which attract the attention of the Antitrust Division of the Department of Justice would probably be useful. This, it should be noted, is a quite different kind of process from routine Parliamentary investigation of the activities of nationalised undertakings as at present practised here. The proposed audit would mean that the management of these enterprises would be investigated in depth by experts in the field – experts who would be likely to know about the opportunity costs of specific innovations forgone.

Measures of the kind taken by the Conservative government since 1979, which largely consist of applying a more severe financial squeeze on management, are of doubtful relevance. Strapping the railways for the cash required for technological innovation, or inducing the electricity industry to raise its prices during a recession in order to pay for more of its investment out of its own earnings, tend to hinder, rather than help, the process of innovation. Even more obviously, the government's general policy of restricting the access of British public undertakings to private capital markets, international as well as national, to finance their investment programmes does the reverse of stimulating risk-taking.

Business in Conditions of Increased Uncertainty
The general question of how, or indeed whether, it is possible to offset the disincentive to innovate in conditions of increased uncertainty is central to public policy now. The increase in uncertainty takes a variety of forms. One obvious aspect is the prospect of more frequent and wider fluctuations in economic activity, with the timing of the ups and downs and their duration more indeterminate. For example, will the downswing of the second business cycle of the past decade, which began in 1979, have similar or different characteristics to the 1974–5 recession? Some optimists argue that consumers, having now got used to the prospect of continuing inflation, will this time spend more of their income and save less (OECD [5]). But who knows? The common expectations of governments and economists about consumer behaviour in the inflationary slump of 1975 proved wrong.

The contrast with the confident and, on the whole, accurate short-term forecasts of domestic demand in the 1960s is striking. Expectations about the behaviour of key economic variables carried much more assurance during the period of sustained high pressure of demand before 1973. It will take some time before the old assurance returns – assuming that variables such as consumer spending do in fact show a similar consistency in conditions of slower economic growth to that displayed in the years of rapid advance. Even so, the degree of variance of most, or all, of the variables relevant to investment decisions – prices and interest rates, as well as consumer and investment demand – is likely to be greater than in the past. It may be that the *anticipated* variance will increase further, at least for a time, until the underlying forces determining the pattern of behaviour (including the behaviour of governments) become clearer.

On the (favourable) assumption of a once-and-for-all increase in the degree of variance, there would be a rise in the market rate of discount, because the preferred time horizon of investors would be shortened. That is the rational response to a loss of assurance about the future. Long-term investment, especially investment based on new ideas, subject to the usual uncertainties about the timing of the conversion of a product or a process from the laboratory stage to full-scale production, is likely to be disfavoured.

This development will take effect at a time when the great change in the cost and supply of energy points to the need for much investment of a long-term character. The need applies not only to the production side, where lead-times are often long because of the indivisibility of large-scale capital inputs, but also to the social and private infrastructure serving the users of energy. In the latter case small piecemeal adjustments are certainly feasible; the economies in the use of oil which have already occurred show that to be so. But after the first flush of economies, which are to a large extent a modest correction of the extravagant use of energy to which our societies had become accustomed, further significant progress will almost inevitably require massive inputs of capital.

What is needed is an extensive adaptation of much of our existing equipment to the change in relative factor costs. New processes and inventions are crucial for this purpose. Thus, in addition to the argument for measures to subsidise innovative investment in general, there is a particular need to prevent the postponement of long-term investment decisions in energy-related fields during the prospective economic slow-down. It is a sound instinctive response which has prompted several governments in the late 1970s – Germany and Japan markedly, but also the US, France and others – to offer increased financial support for R and D in private business.

These separate actions by a great variety of governments in different political circumstances have probably not been consciously designed to meet a commonly perceived economic problem. None the less, the general trend towards increased provision of public funds for business R and D is clear. Britain is, however, a notable absentee. Indeed in the 1970s the proportion of British GNP devoted to civilian R and D expenditure declined, when it was rising in other major industrial countries such as Japan, Germany and France (Salomon [7]). Apart from the recent special measures to stimulate more industrial research in these countries, there was already a longer-term rising trend – possibly prompted by the declining scope for imitating American innovations as these countries narrowed the gap in industrial performance between themselves and the US.

Market Failures versus Political Failures

As I said at the start, the evidence that market forces when left to themselves are not able to respond to the opportunities for innovation in a satisfactory manner does not necessarily imply that governments will be able to do better. There is a considerable body of contemporary economic literature which sets out to show that market failures are transcended, both in number and in magnitude, by political failures. I want here to consider the general arguments which underlie the assertion that, however bad a showing the market may make, there is an overwhelming probability that centralised decisions by a public authority will make a bigger mess of it.

A brief summary of the key argument runs as follows. The power of public agencies whose task is to supervise the activities of a small group of producers with the aim of promoting the interest of consumers will generally be captured in whole, or in part, by the constituency under their surveillance. This is because small groups which are efficiently organised to influence political decisions have greater bargaining strength than is possessed by the diffused consumer interest. Thus, political power in elected systems of government flows towards small groups with narrow and well-defined interests. The process is reinforced by a second factor, which is the desire of persons and organisations endowed with public authority to increase their activity and their expenditure. This leads to a preference for spending on public goods over spending on private goods. The interest-group constituencies are natural allies in presenting a case for increased spending of taxpayers' money on their behalf as a public good. This combination of political forces leads to an allocation of economic resources which is a random deviation from the optimum.

The foregoing is a highly truncated account of some elaborate reasoning on the mechanics of public choice: its purpose is solely to indicate the crucial steps in an argument which leads to the rejection of any increase in public expenditure designed to repair market failures of almost any kind. Since it is an argument about political processes and about probabilities, the outcome will be different in different times and places. Even if the argument were accepted at its full face value, it would, accordingly, be worth trying to devise political counter-measures which would reduce the risk of systematic frustration of the aims of legislators who authorise the allocation of funds for a public purpose. A first step is to ensure that the objects to be served by any public expenditure programme and the criteria for the selection of its beneficiaries are set out in a highly explicit form. Secondly, the actions of officials in furthering these objects should be subjected to systematic examination *ex post* by bodies of experts, known to be independent of the constituency of likely beneficiaries. This is a similar formula to that mentioned earlier for by-passing representative institutions in favour of quasi-judicial forms of inspection.

Judging whether or not any particular branch of R and D expenditure offers a reasonable prospect of generating useful innovations is by its very nature subject to a high degree of uncertainty. The efficient allocation of resources for research, where the capacities of individual firms vary enormously in ways not subject to measurement, requires the exercise of some measure of discretionary authority by officials. Probably the best that can be done to secure discretionary judgements of high quality is to make those concerned aware that their decisions may be examined after the event by a jury of their peers, equipped with expert knowledge of the subject matter, whose views are of sufficient weight to affect an individual official's personal and professional reputation. The technique is to mobilise a professional constituency to constrain the pressures exercised by the interest-group constituency. It is a familiar formula from other fields, including that of the judiciary.

The alternative course would be to subject the provision of public finance for business R and D to rigorous regulation which would eliminate administrative discretion altogether. But if the application of simple and uniform rules of entitlement were the sole means of distributing public funds for this purpose, it would be wasteful to the extent that R and D expenditures which would in any case have been incurred would now be publicly financed. And it is by no means inevitable that the corporate funds thus saved would be applied by the firms concerned to additional R and D.

In practice the subsidisation of R and D has been directed, as Arrow has pointed out, to certain traditional objectives where a public interest has been assumed to exist – like agriculture and medicine [1]. I do not find that an unsuitable way of using public money in pursuit of public goods which private initiatives would be less likely to provide or provide quickly. In medicine, as in agriculture, inventions have often produced widely diffused benefits. The assertion of a public interest, either through state research establishments or by means of conditions attached to the provision of finance to private researchers, helps to ensure that the diffusion of useful results is delayed less than it would be in conditions of pure private enterprise by the (legitimate) demand of the innovator to appropriate some measure of monopoly profit.

These objects of selective public concern may sometimes be ill-chosen, or excessively influenced by some powerful group like the farm lobby. However, farmers are hardly typical of the politics of the distribution of public funds. In recent times, aircraft, nuclear power and computer technology have been favoured objects of publicly financed R and D. Such priorities can be, and are, changed – despite the doubts of public choice theorists – as a result of a debate in which the voices of scientific experts, economists and elected Parliamentary representatives co-mingle. This is not more difficult to achieve than other decisions of a quasi-technical character which are arrived at by reasonably well-conducted democracies. Whether one happens to like the results or not, monetary policy in most western countries has been subject to just such a process during the past decade. The interest-groups most seriously affected do not seem to have been uniformly successful in pre-empting government decisions.

There is an interesting British variation on the theme of the inadequacies of government as a promoter of useful innovative research, which criticises public agencies for being captured by the scientists. This was Lord Rothschild's argument in 1971, when he proposed that government departments' relations with researchers should be strictly governed by a 'contractor–customer relationship' (Central Policy Review Staff [2]). This relationship, whose essential feature was that it would be at arm's length, was to ensure that the powerful interest-group of scientists, with their well-known lack of concern for the practical applications of additions to pure knowledge, would be kept in check.

The fallacies of the simple market model underlying the Rothschild proposals have been analysed elsewhere (Shonfield [10]). The main point here is that the organisation of research for which a government department is a potential customer must be regarded as a *joint* product of customer and contractor. The strict separation of the two in the process of developing new ideas is likely to prove inefficient. To this extent the critique of Rothschild's scheme for the conduct of research on behalf of government is a variation on Oliver Williamson's analysis of the inadequacies of traditional market relationships as a device for promoting innovation.

Apart from the issues of scientific and political organisation, there remains the question of what criteria might be applied to the size of the contribution from public funds to further the process of innovation. Plainly there is no standard answer, since it depends in large part on the degree to which private funds are readily available; the appropriate allocation of public funds may thus vary widely over time. When the marginal efficiency of capital for domestic investment is low – because of high interest rates, prospects of low profits, or generally increased economic uncertainty – public spending should be deliberately pushed above the long-term average. It would thus have a markedly anti-cyclical character.

Even with the various safeguards against arbitrary or consistently wrong decisions on the promotion of R and D by governments, there will almost inevitably be misallocation. And to the extent that it occurs taxes will be higher than they otherwise would be. Public agencies cannot avoid such mistakes, any more than private firms investing their own funds in R and D. But the fact that *some* public money will be wasted, on purposes for which private money might have been ventured and wasted instead, seems a poor reason for resigning oneself to the prospect of a slower rate of innovation during the early 1980s – at a time when the process most especially needs to be speeded up.

References

[1] Arrow, K., 'Economic welfare and the allocation of resources for invention' in NBER, *The Rate and Direction of Inventive Activity*, Princeton University Press, 1962, pp. 602 ff.

[2] Central Policy Review Staff, *A Framework for Government Research and Development*, Cmnd 4814, London, HMSO, 1971.

[3] Jewkes, J., Sawers, D. and Stillerman, R., *The Sources of Invention* (2nd edn), London, Macmillan, 1969.

[4] Mansfield, E., 'Measuring the social and private rates of return on innovation' in *Economic Effects of Space and Other Advanced Technologies*, Strasbourg, Council of Europe, 1980.

[5] OECD, *Economic Outlook*, July 1980, p. 40.

[6] —, *Observer*, September 1980, pp. 15 ff.

[7] Salomon, J-J., 'Technical change and economic policy', OECD, *Observer*, May 1980.

[8] Schultze, C., *The Public Use of Private Interest*, Washington DC, Brookings Institution, 1977.

[9] Schumpeter, J. A., *Capitalism, Socialism and Democracy*, New York, Harper, 1942.

[10] Shonfield, A., 'The social sciences in the great debate on science policy', *Minerva*, July 1972.

[11] Williamson, O. E., *Markets and Hierarchies*, New York, Free Press, 1975.

3 Reasons for Not Innovating

by Charles Carter

This chapter is primarily concerned with manufacturing industry, though the word 'innovation' can, of course, be used also for new systems in service industries. The word carries a presumption of virtue; and it is therefore wise to begin this discussion with a reminder that a refusal to seek or to adopt new products or processes may be a perfectly sensible business decision. The choice of process depends on the expected relative prices and availability of factors of production, so the technology appropriate to the United States will certainly be, in many industries, different from that appropriate to (say) China. It is perfectly possible that a British businessman, fully apprised of a new and more sophisticated method of production, and both willing and financially able to innovate, may nevertheless decide that the new process would not pay at the prices of labour and capital thought likely to prevail, and within the time horizon which he thinks appropriate. The choice of product depends on a judgement of the markets to be served; and here there is indeed some presumption that, in many cases, innovation will be desirable, since (in addition to the marketing appeal of novelty for some products) the average consumer, worldwide, is no doubt becoming more sophisticated. But again it may be perfectly proper for a British businessman to decide to continue to supply an 'old-fashioned' product to a market which he judges likely to continue to appreciate it. Indeed, he may rightly judge that the old-fashioned product is more robust and trouble-free, and will do its job just as well as its successors. Nevertheless, the decision not to seek new products is a dangerous one; the market for the traditional product often turns out to be static or contracting (for even less developed countries find an appeal in sophisticated products), and we can all think of cases in which an inferior innovation (for instance, kitchen ware made of plastic instead of metal), has nevertheless driven the older products off the shelves.

There are many other variations of local circumstance which rightly affect the degree of attention given to particular innovations. Thus, the development of engine management systems in United States automobiles is greatly affected by government regulations on exhaust emissions. British manufacturers may judge that, for a particular model, the American market is worth sacrificing in order to allow freedom to pursue a different line of innovation. The development of new processes in the nuclear industry has become dominated by judgements about likely local reactions from environmentalists, who are often quite unbalanced in their assessment of the alternative risks. Fashions in clothing, food, furniture, style of living vary, and by doing so cause the pressures to innovate to be different in different places.

It follows from all this that the fact that a particular innovation can be found in use in other countries, but not in Britain, proves nothing at all – not even if it arises from British fundamental research or invention. However, the broad judgement that the British economy has, in recent times, shown an undesirable sluggishness in innovation is correct. Indeed, it is a truism: however great our economic success had been, we could no doubt have done even better by a more ingenious use of our brains to devise and introduce even more appropriate products and processes. The fact that the British economy has in reality been markedly unsuccessful merely adds urgency to the search for ways of removing blockages in the innovatory process.

The causes of failure to innovate when innovation is desirable are to be found at different levels, so I begin from a list of some of the reasons for inaction which might be given by a businessman, or deduced from his answers, in the course of a case study of an innovation which (it is thought) ought to have been adopted.

(1) He was ignorant of the possibility of the particular innovation because:

    (a) the firm is too small to do research and development, and suppliers, customers or others did not bring the innovation to his attention;

    (b) research and inquiry were concentrated in other directions;

    (c) research and inquiry failed to turn up this possibility.

(2) He knew of the possibility, but further development and adaptation seemed too difficult because:

(a) they are too costly;
(b) they require skills which are not available;
(c) they go too far outside the firm's existing product range or process experience;
(d) there is difficulty over patents;
(e) there is difficulty over possible terms of licensing; or (in a multinational company) markets desirable for success have been allocated to another subsidiary.

(3) For a product innovation: the market is judged to be too small or uncertain or slow to develop. Since I am discussing innovations which are *not* properly rejected on these grounds, this implies:

(a) that market research was insufficient;
(b) that the assumptions about competitors' actions or general market trends were wrong.

(4) For a process innovation: the advantage in cost or quality is judged inadequate or non-existent. Since I am discussing innovations which are *not* properly rejected on these grounds, this implies:

(a) an inadequate system for appraising investment;
(b) that the assumptions about prices, availability of factors, or the appropriate time horizon were wrong.

(5) Problems of timing – the 'Yes but not yet' decisions, made because:

(a) further change in technology or cost is expected to make the innovation much more attractive if adopted later;
(b) the innovation requires capital investment which must await a proper time for the replacement of existing equipment (this is a problem when industrial growth is slow, and new equipment cannot be installed in the process of expansion);
(c) the innovation must await cheaper terms for borrowing money, or more favourable exchange rates, or other improvements in the economic environment.

(6) Problems of scale and finance:

(a) the innovation is too large for the firm to tackle, or requires an unacceptably great change of structure;
(b) no lender on appropriate terms can be found (and the firm cannot generate the required finance internally).

(7) The firm is unable to obtain essential skills.

(8) There is difficulty in getting around government regulations, or planning restrictions, or there are environmental problems.

(9) There is opposition from the existing labour force or some essential part of it.

(10) There are internal structural problems in the firm – the decision-making process has seized up.

(11) There is lack of cooperation from related industries, e.g. suppliers of machinery, components, special materials, or distributors of the product.

(12) The firm cannot compete because other countries subsidise or assist the innovation to a greater degree, or prevent access for it to their markets.

These reasons for not acting, or for not acting now, are not, of course, exclusive. If (as sometimes happens) an innovation has an identifiable sponsor in the firm, many of these problems may face the sponsor as successive obstacles to be overcome, each consuming time and managerial energy in its solution. The horse may fall at the final fence, but it will have been weakened and slowed down by its exertions in jumping the earlier ones; or perhaps the innovation will eventually take place, but after so long a delay in overcoming the difficulties that its place in the market has been taken by foreign competitors. (The reference to an identifiable sponsor reminds us that success may depend on the personality of a particular individual.)

However, a number of the items on the list are problems of innovation liable to arise in any part of the world. The United States, for instance, suffers more than Britain from delays due to government regulation and the influence of pressure groups. Certain problems can plausibly be regarded as acute in Britain: for instance, a bad distribution of research effort, slow growth, the high cost of borrowing, an exchange rate unfavourable to exports. But some of these begin to look more doubtful or complex on closer examination. It is true that industrial R and D in Britain has been declining, and is heavily concentrated in a few industries which are not necessarily those most appropriate for overall economic success; but the links between the amount of R and D and the effectiveness of innovation are not easily determined – it may be that our true fault is to be inefficient in picking other people's brains. The high cost of borrowing can only be interpreted by reference to an expected rate of increase of prices; those who produce for the home market must sometimes, in recent years, have been borrowing at a negative real rate, while suffering no disadvantage from high exchange rates. For the 'burden' of the high exchange rate is an advantage to a firm which imports materials and sells at home, and is in any case too recent a phenomenon to explain Britain's failures in innovation.

Examples of innovations prevented by workforce or trade union obstruction are much more difficult to find than is commonly supposed; few industries are like newspaper publishing. Where this is a reason for abandoning or delaying an innovation, or not daring to try it out, it may simply be evidence at the next level of analysis of a fault in management. The idea that the conservatism of financial institutions is a major problem was never very plausible for a country with a financial system as varied and well developed as that of Britain, and in repeated investigations has never been clearly established; the fact that would-be borrowers are disappointed is more probably evidence of their lack of that combination of qualities which are necessary for the successful management of innovation.

If, in fact, one takes the first list of problems and asks who or what has to be changed in order to put things right, the result is another list which is more helpful in getting to the essentials of the matter. This list suggests that inaction may be due, not to the immovability of obstructions, but to the absence of a sufficient motivation to overcome them.

(1) An unfavourable economic environment for innovation:

    (a) slow growth implying few opportunities to embody new ideas in expansion: but, of course, slow growth may be the consequence as well as the cause of a failure in innovation;

    (b) the wrong balance of competition and safety – too little competition leading to complacency in accepting old ideas, and too much to short views unfavourable to a planned innovation policy;

    (c) persistently depressed profits, making ventures more difficult to launch;

    (d) exaggerated uncertainty about the pay-off on projects produced by high and varying rates of inflation;

    (e) inadequate personal expectation of reward from taking the risk of innovation.

(2) An unfavourable social and educational context:

It is appropriate to treat the educational defects, allowing shortages of essential skills, as subsidiary to social attitudes. Any major innovation is liable to create demands for skills for which adequate training facilities did not previously exist. This is a problem for all countries – a delaying factor for a few years while industry and the educational system take steps to put it right. But it is much more serious if social attitudes (as in Britain) tend to be rather unfavourable to wealth creation in industry and to particular professions which serve it, such as engineering. In these circumstances, the men and women of the quality required for key functions in the innovatory process may be difficult to find, even after allowing a period for adjusting educational provision.

(3) An insufficiently supportive government:

The interventions of government in advanced economies are so numerous and complex that it is almost impossible to assess whether, on balance, one government is better than another in its effect on innovation. But there may be a chance that, even within present budgets, the British government's interventions could be made more effective in supporting innovation.

(4) Inadequate management:

    (a) inability to understand what an innovation is about;
    (b) lack of a policy to draw in relevant information;
    (c) unwillingness to take new knowledge on licence from outside;
    (d) lack of resolution in developing an idea;
    (e) poor assessment of markets, and of needs for customer service;
    (f) poor assessment of investment opportunities;
    (g) tendency to run machines for too long a life;
    (h) undue caution, and readiness to seize excuses for delay;
    (i) unwillingness to alter structures or to seek cooperative arrangements to deal with problems of scale;
    (j) lack of resolution in overcoming difficulties of government regulation, material supply, skill availability, etc.;
    (k) poor labour relations policy;
    (l) sluggish internal decision-making systems.

This long list is, for the most part, the obverse of the description of a typical technically progressive firm given in Chapter 16 of Carter and Williams [2]. The point made in that chapter was that technical progressiveness is related to all-round quality: that, to succeed in innovation, a firm must seek to be good in all the main areas of management responsibility. So the heading 'inadequate management' may imply that British management is good in parts, but too seldom achieves all-round quality.

Hindrances to innovation produced by the economic and social environment, or by inadequacies of government, are difficult to evaluate because they are to some extent subjective: that is, what matters is not just the factual situation in Britain relative to other countries, but the way in which the facts are interpreted by decision-makers. Thus, whatever may be the data revealed by international comparisons of the rates of taxation of personal income and capital, what matters is the way in which the burden and structure of taxation is felt by people in different countries; their reactions to the same weight of taxation may be very different. It is possible that British management is in a phase of pessimism and apathy, in which doubts and unfavourable factors are given great emphasis, and stimuli have to be unusually strong to produce action. Such attitudes of pessimism would be self-justifying; and it is easy to think of plausible reasons for their occurrence, such as the absence of a settled consensus about the places of private and public enterprise, the long years of (comparative) ill-success in managing the economy under both Labour and Conservative governments, or even the loss of Empire and the decline to being a second-rate power.

Such matters of attitude tend to get little attention from scholars, because their existence is a matter of conjecture. But this does not prove them to be unimportant. It is not enough to point to external hindrances to innovation; we have also to explain why those which are in principle capable of removal are not removed. Thus, if innovation is held back by a lack of engineers, technologists or technicians of appropriate skill and quality, and if this is caused by a lack of status which discourages able people from entering such employment, why does not industry take steps to alter that status? As Austen Albu writes [1]:

It has been the historical lack of demand by the engineering and allied industries that has been the main cause of the low level of status, pay and, in particular, education of British engineers . . . The engineer will have the status of his perceived importance to industry and society will accept the judgement of those who employ him. If British industry does not recognise the danger of failure to maintain a technically competitive world stance, then it will not employ and adequately reward the best-qualified men and women the educational system can provide.

The most plausible of the objective external factors which might depress innovation in Britain are slow growth, depressed profits, uncertainty produced by a high rate of inflation, and social attitudes which abridge the supply of ability to industry. No doubt there are particular industries which suffer from too much or too little competition, but it does not seem likely that a rather general weakness in innovation can be attributed to so variable a factor. There is no clear evidence on the effect of personal reward, and no consequence to innovation has yet been observed from the major reductions in high rates of taxation made in 1979 – perhaps because insufficient time has passed. The effects of government support are, as suggested above, difficult to assess (and, of course, too much public support may lead to lassitude in those supported, who feel sure of rescue whatever their real deserts): I know of no studies which prove this to be a matter on which Britain has made more errors than other countries.

But, of course, the British economy is not uniformly unsuccessful. Faced by the same problems of low growth and uncertainty produced by high inflation, but with the advantage of a much greater attraction to those of ability, the financial sector – for instance – has on the whole remained strong and innovative (though the innovations are commonly in ideas and methods rather than hardware). This suggests that the problems external to the firm may be an explanation of inadequate innovation only because they interact with management which is insufficiently able, uneven in performance, not sufficiently vigorous in overcoming its difficulties, and prone to pessimism. I turn, therefore, to consider how it could be that fundamental faults exist in British management.

Part of the problem is that the educational system has (as suggested above) acquired an ideological bias against productive industry, the effects of which are no doubt strengthened by the greater security offered by many non-industrial occupations, and (until recently, at least) by the high pay, good security and generous pensions thought to be available in a prodigal public sector. This is likely not only to have deprived industry of a full share of ability in general (though there are very recent signs of change on this matter), but also to have made it difficult to create a management team of consistent quality. Thus, it is still true that far more able people seek training in accountancy (which has non-industrial uses) than in engineering. The faults in innovation which are sometimes ascribed to the dominance of finance over science in British board-rooms may simply be a result of the existence of more ability in finance than in applied science and technology.

Conceivably, however, the problem is not just one of misdirection of available ability, but of failure to stimulate and develop ability in sufficient amounts. Perhaps the British are too stupid to prosper in the present world for some genetic or environmental reason not yet disclosed: but this does not seem likely to be a testable hypo-thesis. It is potentially of greater interest that for a generation we have been developing an educational system which is far more pre-occupied with improving opportunities for the disadvantaged and those of low ability than with seeking out the gifted and giving them special opportunities. Furthermore, it is an educational system which is 'soft' in terms of the effort required of students, notably so in comparison with Japan (for instance). It would not be sur-prising if these trends left us with a supply of vigorous ability ade-quate only for a part of the economy.

On the other hand, there have been in the last twenty years con-siderable developments of initial and in-service management educa-tion, and – though it takes time for those trained to reach positions of senior responsibility – it might be expected that by now some effect on innovation would be visible. However, other countries have also advanced in management education, and Britain has never attempted (or seen the need to attempt) a 'crash programme' to enable us to catch up with others. Nor, indeed, would such a catching-up exercise have been at all easy, because several of our major rivals have the advantage of a culture much more strongly orientated towards the practical applications of science and tech-nology. We could do more to teach managers sophisticated tech-niques of management, but this is not an assurance of innovation if those managers are technologically illiterate.

Possibly, too, the management education which we have de-veloped has been insufficiently tough and demanding, infected by the general softness of the educational system. The British tradition of 'muddling through', the high regard paid to pragmatism and commonsense, the suspicion of glossy precision in management techniques, all have their good side; on the whole we do not suffer the extremes of bureaucratic nonsense which are sometimes found in large enterprises elsewhere. But readiness to proceed by commonsense applied to partial (but timely) information is one thing: sloppy analysis of problems, with decisions made in an ill-argued way, ignoring information which is readily to hand and obviously relevant, is another. The deficiencies listed above under the head of 'inadequate management' are, taken broadly, symptoms of an unwillingness or inability to do a thorough job. Perhaps, if the standards of management education were more demanding (which probably implies a greater emphasis on specialist rather than general courses), it would be easier to attain high standards of management practice.

However, the most relevant formative influence on managers is bound to be their own industrial experience, rather than their initial education or the special training given to some of them. The standards, habits and attitudes which (as I suggest) hold back innovation are acquired in the process of acceptance into the culture of British management. Furthermore, managers are predominantly selected by managers, who are not likely to take or retain people seen as radically unlike themselves. We thus face a sociological problem which is just as difficult as the problem of the 'two cultures' (the lack of understanding between scientists and non-scientists), or the problem of the lack of interest in technology. We can observe the existence of a self-perpetuating state of inadequacy, but it is far from clear that we know what measures of social engineering will be effective in breaking the chain by which bad habits and attitudes are passed on. Indeed, history provides a number of uncomfortable examples of civilisations which acquired unbreakable habits of mind inconsistent with their economic success.

We thus come back from the immediate reasons given by businessmen for not innovating, first to a series of external disadvantages or internal inadequacies which may lie behind the reasons given; and then to problems of the distribution of ability, of education and training, and of the habits and attitudes of management, which may explain why the internal inadequacies persist and why the external disadvantages are viewed pessimistically as impossible to overcome. Operating at the first and second levels, we can no doubt find measures which will lead to some marginal improvement; but, to obtain a radical change, we need to go to the fundamental problems of quality and attitude, and at this level it is far from clear what can best be done. If once we could begin to be more successful in innovation, attitudes would no doubt change in a way which would encourage further success; it is the first step of improvement which is most difficult.

References

[1] Albu, A., in K. Pavitt (ed.), *Technical Innovation and British Economic Performance*, London, Macmillan, 1980.

[2] Carter, C. F. and Williams, B. R., *Industry and Technical Progress*, London, Oxford University Press, 1957.

Comment on Chapters 2 and 3

by S. J. Prais

The subject of this volume is close to the heart of Political Economy: what is it that a government can do – and should do – in order to promote the use of better methods of production, and thereby advance the welfare of its citizens? The two chapters before us provide admirably general treatments of this very broad topic. In the time allotted I can do little more than comment on a few details, based in part on recent work at the National Institute on comparative productivity.

A distinction is now often drawn between invention – that is, the discovery of a new product or method of production, including the development of prototypes – and the subsequent application of that invention in routine commercial production, which is termed 'innovation,' and which may well take place in a different country. Particularly important in our present-day world of shrinking distances has been the incorporation of innovations in the mass-production of goods for sale to worldwide markets. Irrespective of the rate of invention, it is an inadequate rate of innovation that may lead not only to a relative decline in our national income in comparison with other countries – but also to an absolute decline. For, as other countries catch up in their technology, they remove the justification for the continued existence on this island of those industries pioneered here, and the accumulated expertise and embodied technology for which the rest of the world has in the past been prepared to pay us highly.

Sir Charles Carter's chapter is entitled 'Reasons for Not Innovating'; but should we not consider – as a separate matter – whether there may be sound Reasons for Not Inventing – or for not inventing so much? It has often been observed that Britain's failings lie particularly at the innovatory stage, while its record in inventions has been good; on the other hand, the success of the Japanese, to take the outstanding example, lies particularly in innovating – in their ready adaptation of the inventions of others to the methods of mass-production. A misallocation of our intellectual resources – the devotion of too much activity to invention at the expense of innovation – is not a mere forgivable variant in national tastes, but can become a national curse; other nations then reap the main benefit of seeds planted here at great cost. As was written: 'Thou shall plant a vineyard and shalt not gather the grapes thereof ... The fruits of thy land, and all thy labours, shall a nation which thou knowest not eat up.' (Deut. 28: 30,33.)

Of the many contributory factors mentioned in these two chapters, two seem to me of particular importance: (i) the direction and control of resources absorbed by our education and training systems; and (ii) the issues surrounding industrial relations in large production units in this country.

With inadequate numbers of engineers one can hardly expect to be in the forefront of innovation; the recent Finniston Report [2] has drawn attention to our deficiencies in this respect. It has to be remembered that by international standards we produce an exceptionally large number of pure scientists, but we seem very clearly to be deficient in producing graduate engineers. For example, the United States produced 47,000 engineering graduates (first degrees) in 1975, and Germany produced 21,000 graduates (including 6000 diploma engineers) in 1978: these numbers are roughly proportional to the total numbers employed in manufacturing in the two countries. In view of its size, Britain might be expected to produce a similar number of graduate engineers to the Germans; but in fact it produced only about half as many: 8000 graduates in engineering and technology from universities in 1977, plus another 2000 from polytechnics – and about a fifth of these were students from overseas. (These figures come from national statistical sources; they differ from those quoted in the Finniston Report which were taken from a not wholly adequate table in the UNESCO yearbook; see [2], p. 83, and cf. p. 204.) There is the further deficiency – from the point of view of the present discussion – that those graduating in this country as engineers tend to have too theoretical a background, and are lacking in the practical element which forms a large part of the German graduate engineer's longer training course. Lower down the occupational ladder, at the level of technician and skilled worker, the available statistics are more difficult to interpret, but they seem to suggest a greater relative deficiency; for example, our Engineering Industry Training Board has about 10,000 a year completing their recently developed two-module 'apprenticeship-type' (and unexamined) training, while the Germans have over 30,000 a year passing their final craft examination as various types of fitters, mechanics and toolmakers on completing their obligatory period of vocational schooling (the discrepancies in the numbers passing their electrical and electronic craft examinations appear even greater). However, this is not the occasion to go into this in further detail.

Why are we short of engineers? Lack of status and lack of demand, says Carter quoting Albu. Notional calculations of rates of return to education point in the same direction. Recent studies based on the incomes and costs of training of graduates in various subjects in this country in 1971 show the social rate of return to those with degrees in engineering and technology to be lower than in the three other main subject groups considered – arts, science and social science – [1]. In other words, the contribution of engineers to production is relatively low – at least in the circumstances in which British industry at present finds itself.

In looking for reasons we must go beyond simply referring to 'managerial inadequacies' in appreciating their value. I would suggest that the lack of complementary trained personnel – technicians and skilled workers – reduces the value of the work that the trained engineer can achieve; he is too often obliged to carry out work that others with less training could do for him, and consequently has less time to carry out his highly skilled functions. (He is like a skilled surgeon trying to work without adequate nursing help.) It is significant that the study of incomes just mentioned [1] shows the *social* rate of return in 1971–8 to the HNC – which is based on part-time training – exceeding that to a degree (confirming the results for 1966–7 reported by Morris and Ziderman [4] p. XXVIII); this is in conformity with there being – at least at present in Britain – a greater shortage of people with qualifications below that of graduate engineer. Unfortunately incentives to training have been distorted by the relatively greater subsidies given to university education; the study shows that the *private* rate of return is higher for graduates than for HNCs. We consequently have too few in part-time technical education; young men who would make perfectly good practical craftsmen and engineers are bribed by our educational policies into the study of liberal arts – or at best into pure science.

Errors in educational policy are one part of the story. The second part relates to the difficult industrial relations in large manufacturing plants in Britain; this inhibits the introduction of improved working methods, stultifies the work of the innovating engineer, and reduces his value to management below that of the man who concerns himself simply with keeping production going. 'Few industries are like newspaper publishing', says Carter; and perhaps equally few are quite like large-scale motor car assembly. But it is becoming increasingly apparent that many sections of even medium-scale industry are approaching that state. To give just two examples. Following its investigations into the production of car parts, which is typically carried out in plants with 1000–2000 employees, the Price Commission noted that improvements in production methods were often not introduced: 'difficulties of negotiating such changes with the workforce, combined with the risk of more stoppages, tended to discourage management attempts to secure improvements' ([6], p. 62). Similarly, the Price Commission re-

Table 3.1   Average number of strikes per plant per year by size of plant, as shown in official statistics and in Warwick survey

Plant size (employees)	Official statistics[a]	Warwick survey[b]
50–99	0.02[c]	0.26
100–199	0.03	0.26
200–499	0.08	0.42
500–999	0.21	0.98
1000–1999	0.37	1.26
2000–4999	0.83	2.86
5000+	2.48	7.62
Average[d]	0.08	0.43

Sources: Officially recorded strikes: *Department of Employment Gazette*; Prais [5], p. 370. All strikes: from Warwick survey as reported in Edwards [3], p. 150 (calculated from table 1, cols. 2 and 5, after grouping).

[a]Official recorded statistics are based on voluntary returns of strikes lasting at least one day and involving at least ten workers, or at least a total of 100 man–days. The data presented here relate to the average of 1971–3.
[b]Based on an interview survey in 1977–8 requesting the number of *all* strikes in the past two years, for a sample of approximately 1000 manufacturing plants.
[c]Interpolated estimate.
[d]Weighted average for all plants with more than 50 employees.

ported on attempts by the Metal Box company to introduce a new labour-saving method of production (two-piece instead of three-piece cans) which met with substantial 'industrial relations problems'; output on the new production lines had been restricted by the unions to half capacity for three years (see Karin Wagner's recent article [8], p. 33).

The full burden of Britain's difficult industrial relations problems has recently become clearer as a result of the Warwick sample survey of strikes in 1000 manufacturing plants; this asked for the number of *all* strikes, and not merely those above the threshold criteria of the Department of Employment (the results were published recently by Edwards [3]). Table 3.1 compares the results of the survey with the available official figures of the number of strikes a year for various plant sizes. We see that: (a) throughout the range of plant sizes the official statistics cover only a small fraction of all strikes – for plants with more than 50 employees, the weighted average is only approximately one in six; and (b) the largest plants – those with over 5000 employees – experienced an *average* of eight strikes a year. (The periods covered by the two sets of figures is not the same, but an adjustment based on the slight difference between the numbers of strikes shown in the official figures in the two periods would only further emphasise the shortcomings of the official returns.) It is thus particularly where we are engaged in large-scale production, and where the engineer should be using his innovatory skills to reap scale economies, that he is opposed by difficulties in industrial relations. The Department of Employment seems apparently content to make its annual remark that official figures show Britain's strike experience to be about average by international standards; regrettably it has done nothing to compile comprehensive returns to give a realistic count of the total number of strikes.

All this should help us attain a proper sense of priorities in considering policies to advance Britain's rate of innovation. It is very tempting to say, let us provide subsidies of various sorts for the production of robots, or grants to selected industries on which we shall concentrate our innovative resources. Sir Andrew Shonfield has reminded us that the good that men do lives on after them; that it brings a benefit to the world that may be incalculable in terms of social rates of return; and that it should therefore be encouraged in various ways. I will not quarrel with him here on the technicalities of whether the comparisons he mentions related to *average* or *marginal* rates of return; or whether the samples investigated were adequately representative also of the many attempted innovations that turned out to be costly failures; or whether those that were subsidised did better than those that were not. For even if we accept that society should intervene in the market process and encourage innovative activities, the question still arises of the most effective point of intervention.

Rather than subsidise a businessman to undertake more innovative activity than he would otherwise judge wise, I suspect we would do better to concentrate on the sources of his difficulties. A re-ordering of educational priorities and subsidies seems well overdue, with the aim of encouraging a more practical slant in education throughout – from primary schooling to universities. Once we have a more technically competent labour force, I suspect business will not be slow in moving in a more technically innovative direction. But without a more technically competent labour force, the provision of subsidies is a little like encouraging someone to make omelettes without giving him eggs.

In so far as we nevertheless subsidise innovations, the lesson to be drawn from strike statistics must be that we should favour those that have application in medium-sized rather than giant industrial plants. Just over a decade ago Shonfield pointed the path towards more orderly industrial relations in his well-known Note of Reservation to the Donovan Report [7]; I believe he was entirely right in what he then said. I fear that until all concerned are prepared to follow that path, the future for large-scale industry in this country remains bleak; and policies of subsidising innovation in large-scale industry will provide little more than disappointing palliatives for our Conscience.

References

[1] Adamson, A. D. and Reid, J. M., 'The rate of return to post-compulsory education during the 1970s: an empirical study for Great Britain' (mimeo.), Department of Education and Science, 1980.

[2] Department of Industry, *Engineering Our Future* [Finniston Report], Cmnd 7794, London, HMSO, 1980.

[3] Edwards, P. R., 'Size of plant and strike-proneness', *Oxford Bulletin of Economics and Statistics*, vol. 42, May 1980.

[4] Morris V. and Ziderman A., 'The economic return on investment in higher education in England and Wales', *Economic Trends*, May 1971.

[5] Prais, S. J., 'The strike-proneness of large plants in Britain', *Journal of the Royal Statistical Society* (series A), vol. 141, part 3, 1978.

[6] Price Commission, *Prices, Costs and Margins in the Manufacture and Distribution of Car Parts*, London, HMSO, 1979.
[7] Royal Commission on Trade Unions and Employers' Associations, 1965–1968, *Report* [Donovan Report], Cmnd 3623, London, HMSO, 1968.
[8] Wagner, K., 'Competition and productivity: a study of the metal can industry in Britain, Germany and the United States', *Journal of Industrial Economics*, vol. 29, September 1980.

4 Industrial Policies in Britain 1960–80

by Aubrey Silberston

Industrial policies during the last twenty years can be divided broadly into those which were well established before 1960 and those which were introduced during the period. Among the former were regional policy, antitrust policy, policies to stimulate investment and provide funds for industry, and policies to encourage the exploitation of inventions. Among the latter were the setting up of the National Economic Development Council (NEDC), which is concerned with industrial strategy, the creation and abolition of the Industrial Reorganisation Corporation (IRC), and the creation of the National Enterprise Board (NEB), both concerned with industrial reorganisation. Another notable event was the production in 1965 of the *National Plan* [2], the successor of which, in much watered down form, is the current 'Industrial Strategy'.

In addition, a number of bodies have been concerned with pay and prices since 1960; the National Board for Prices and Incomes (NBPI) was the best known. These bodies certainly affected industry, although whether they can be said to have been concerned with industrial policies is perhaps a matter for argument.

The creation or abolition of particular institutions has tended to mirror changes in policy, possibly stemming from changes in government. But policy changes have also taken place within the existing structure of institutions, partly arising from changes of government and partly from changes in policy by the same government. If told in detail, the story would be long and complex. The present chapter attempts to cover it under broad headings.

Investment Incentives and Regional Policy

Investment incentives of various types have been in existence since 1945. These have often been linked with regional policies, in that the level of incentives has been higher in certain regions than in others.

A system of initial allowances, instituted in 1945, enabled firms to accelerate depreciation for tax purposes. Investment allowances, introduced in 1954, could be added to the initial allowance without reducing depreciation in later years; an investment allowance of 25 per cent, for example, made the total depreciation allowance for tax purposes 125 per cent, which by reducing total tax was in effect a subsidy. Both initial and investment allowances varied over time, but were generally at lower rates on buildings than on plant and machinery. They both suffered from the drawback that firms had to have sufficient profits to benefit from them, and there were also inherent delays in the system.

Partly because of such objections, investment grants were introduced in 1966, generally equal to 20 per cent of the cost of plant and machinery (buildings still received initial allowances). They were paid in cash, irrespective of whether the firm earned profits or not, and supposedly within six months. Depreciation allowances were however reduced by the amount of the grant, so that with a 20 per cent grant tax was remitted only on 80 per cent of the cost.

This system also was criticised, mainly because it subsidised investment in loss-making firms, and led to a high level of payments. Further, it involved much administrative detail and was slower than had been expected. It was brought to an end in 1970, with a return to initial allowances; in 1972 the rate was raised to 100 per cent on plant and machinery (still in force) and 40 per cent on buildings. Since the system again depends on profits being sufficient in the early years of investment, in present circumstances of low profits the incentive must be small.

Regional policy has depended partly on incentives of this type and partly on other measures. In general, investment incentives have been higher in relatively depressed regions than elsewhere, and at times have applied (for example, investment grants from 1963 to 1966) in these regions only. Regional policy has, however, had a longer history. It began in its modern form with the Special Areas Act of 1934, which was succeeded in 1945 by the Distribution of Industry Act. The policy aimed to help parts of the country where unemployment was persistently above average, generally because of a concentration of 'old' industries subject to long-term decline; since the war these areas have been called 'development areas', 'development districts' and a number of other titles. Their boundaries have varied from time to time, and the provisions of the policy have changed frequently. Its essence has, however, remained the same – to provide incentives for investment and new plants in the development areas, and to discourage them in prosperous and congested areas. The main instrument for discouragement has been industrial development certificates, which are granted more readily in development areas than elsewhere. The main incentives have included not only investment incentives, but also the provision of roads, industrial estates, government-owned factory buildings, cheap loans and outright grants.

During the period 1960–80 these policies have been pursued with varying intensity. The most dramatic innovation was the introduction by the Labour government in 1967 of the regional employment premium. This was a direct employment subsidy to all firms in development areas, with different rates for men, women and minors. It was introduced partly as an incentive for new investment and partly to encourage existing labour-intensive firms. The Heath government decided to phase it out, but payments were made during much of the 1970s. Another measure of the previous Labour government was the Selective Employment Tax, introduced in 1965, which was a levy per head on nearly all firms in the country rebated back to manufacturing; thus, in effect, it taxed services and distribution. It included a subsidy for manufacturing in development areas between 1968 and 1970, but was terminated by the Heath government.

At present the traditional regional incentives continue to apply. They have been supplemented (where the doctrine of non-additionality allows) by EEC aid to depressed industries, many of them in development areas. The latest British measure, in 1980, has been the creation of 'enterprise zones' in large cities, where incentives are in the form of special tax allowances for capital expenditure on the construction or improvement of industrial and commercial buildings. Offices qualify also, in contrast to discrimination against office building in some past years.

It is not easy to assess the impact of investment incentives or of regional policies. Their effectiveness clearly varies with the state of the economy. At times like the present they are likely to be comparatively ineffective. It must be doubted how far general investment incentives have ever been effective, partly because they have changed so often that many businessmen have discounted them in their investment planning. Regional policy has probably had more impact. It has been suggested by Moore and Rhodes [9] that after 1963, for example, the strengthening of regional policy caused an

increase in investment and employment in development areas above
the level that would otherwise have occurred.

Competition and Merger Policy
The first British legislation dealing specifically with monopolies and
restrictive practices was in 1948, when the Monopolies and Mergers Commission (its current name) was set up. This was followed
by the Restrictive Trade Practices Act of 1956, which set up the
Restrictive Practices Court and a register of restrictive trading
agreements. In the period under review, the principal acts were the
Resale Prices Act 1964, the Monopolies and Mergers Act 1965, the
Restrictive Trade Practices Act 1968, the Fair Trading Act 1973,
the Restrictive Trade Practices Acts 1976 and 1977, the Resale
Prices Act 1976 and the Competition Act 1980.

The 1956 Act made its major impact in 1959, when the Restrictive
Practices Court judged the Cotton Yarn Spinners' agreement to be
against the public interest. In the years following a large number of
restrictive agreements were abandoned. The present position is that
comparatively few agreements on the register contain significant
restrictions unless these have been permitted by the Court. To some
extent the merger wave of the late 1960s and early 1970s may have
been a reaction to the collapse of restrictive agreements. In addition,
information agreements have grown in importance, no doubt partly
as a consequence. They were brought within the scope of the legislation in 1968.

The 1964 Resale Prices Act had a considerable effect. It was
worded in such a way as to make it difficult for resale price maintenance agreements to get through the Restrictive Practices Court.
So it proved, and after the first few cases resale price maintenance
virtually came to an end, except in cases such as the net book
agreement which had already been blessed by the Court.

The position has been different with the 1965 Monopolies and
Mergers Act, which introduced the control of mergers for the first
time. Prospective mergers, or mergers less than six months old,
may be referred by the Secretary of State for Trade to the Monopolies and Mergers Commission if the assets being transferred
exceed £5 million in value, or if more than 25 per cent (formerly
33.3 per cent) of the relevant market in the United Kingdom is
involved. Newspaper mergers are dealt with separately. In practice
relatively few mergers have been referred to the Commission: excluding newspaper mergers, only about 3 per cent of those eligible

[6]. The Act requires the Commission to say whether mergers are in their opinion against the public interest, which is weaker than if they were required to say that mergers were positively in the public interest. Nevertheless, roughly three fifths of mergers referred to the Commission have been stopped or abandoned. The Green Paper [6] suggested that the presumption on public interest should be made neutral, but in July 1980 the government announced that it was not to be changed, although a rather more sceptical view than previously would be taken of mergers which reduced competition and were unlikely to contribute to efficiency. The impression given was that a higher proportion of mergers than in the past might be referred to the Commission.

The 1980 Competition Act was linked with the abolition of price control and introduced powers to investigate 'anti-competitive' practices by firms. It also provided for investigations into the efficiency of, or possible abuse of market power by, public bodies with state-endowed monopolies. It is too early to see how this Act will operate in practice.

Since accession to the EEC in 1973, the EEC rules of competition also apply. Article 85 of the Treaty of Rome prohibits most restrictive agreements which affect trade between member states, while Article 86 prohibits the abuse of dominant positions. These rules are principally designed to prevent the economic integration of the Community from being hindered by cartels and monopolies. Their enforcement is in the hands of the European Commission, which under Article 85 has power to exempt individual restrictive practices, or to make block exemptions, where the restriction improves production or distribution or promotes technical or economic progress, provided that consumers receive a fair share of the resulting benefits. Articles 85 and 86 do not directly apply to mergers, but the Commission has been seeking powers to exercise prior control over large-scale EEC mergers, though it has not yet succeeded in this.

The EEC rules are both more absolute in prohibition and yet more flexible in operation than UK legislation. Their interpretation is continually evolving as decisions are made by the Commission and judgements are handed down by the European Court of Justice. If a conflict should arise between UK and EEC law, the latter would in theory take precedence. As pointed out in the Restrictive Trade Practices Green Paper [7], it is possible for agreements permitted under the Restrictive Trade Practices Act to be condemned under the Treaty of Rome and vice versa; although clashes of this sort are not thought likely, nevertheless they could occur. The Green Paper expresses the view that the differences between the two sets of legislation should be reduced, and it notes that a significant step would be for UK law to concentrate more directly on *effects* on competition.

Price Control

Some form of price control was in operation for much of the period under review, usually in conjunction with an incomes policy. The most notable body concerned was the NBPI, set up in 1965 by a Labour government and abolished by the Heath Conservative government in 1971. The Board was required to inquire into matters referred to it by Ministers, and to have regard to the current White Paper on prices and incomes policy; it had no power to initiate investigations itself. A large number of references was, however, made, and it published 170 reports in all [11]. Of these 67 were concerned solely with prices, 79 with pay and the remainder with both pay and prices or with general matters. In 1967 the Labour government decided to refer to it all major price increases in nationalised industries, so that about one third of the reports concerning prices in 1969–71 dealt with the public sector. In practice, the NBPI could not separate the problems of prices and incomes, because it was asked to look also at productivity and efficiency. It did not automatically conclude, therefore, when a wage increase was given, that this would justify a price increase. It investigated in some detail the scope for efficiency gains (employing consultants to advise it on many occasions), and was not prepared to recommend price increases if it considered efficiency could be improved.

The NBPI produced its reports quickly and did not mince its words. It was not universally loved, especially by the objects of its censure, but given its remit it was an effective and valuable body, and when it was abolished an important source of pressure for increased efficiency in British industry was removed.

The Labour government had planned to bring together the Monopolies Commission and the NBPI in a new body, but this was not proceeded with by the Heath government, which not only abolished the NBPI but abandoned prices and incomes controls altogether. However, a pay standstill with legal backing was introduced in November 1972; there was also a price freeze initiated by the CBI. In 1973 two new bodies, the Pay Board and the Price

Commission, were created. The Price Commission had to work to rules clearly laid down by the government, and had far less scope for discretion than the NPBI. Price control, which continued under the Labour government, consisted of two main elements – price increases were restricted to changes in allowable costs, and profit margins were limited by reference to earnings prior to 1973. Allowable costs were automatically adjusted to take account of notional productivity increases, thus tending to squeeze profit margins. Legislation in 1977 abolished the 'allowable cost' provisions, and gave the Price Commission permanent powers to investigate the 'reasonableness' of prices. The more rigid features of the previous rules were therefore removed, but there was not much time for the new arrangements to work, since the Price Commission was abolished by the Competition Act of 1980.

Economists generally have been sceptical of the effects of price control in reducing inflation and regard it as a cosmetic addition to incomes policy [1]. A study in the *National Institute Economic Review* [8] concluded that by the summer of 1976 the average price level was little different from what it would have been in the absence of the 1973 controls. These were, however, blamed by many manufacturers and distributors for imposing low profit margins, particularly in the period before the present recession, which made it difficult for firms to earn profits as high as those permitted by the price controls.

National Planning
In its fourth and final report in 1961, the Council on Prices, Productivity and Incomes had urged that a planning institution should be set up on French lines to coordinate the plans of the main sectors of the economy. It was hoped that this might lead to faster economic growth and to a more assured level of investment. This report heralded the setting up of the NEDC, consisting of representatives of government, management and labour at a very high level. It was based on a considerable supporting staff (NEDO). The Council first considered a feasibility study of faster growth, prepared by NEDO, and then a set of recommendations concerned with overcoming obstacles to faster growth. At the same time, Economic Development Committees (EDCs) for individual industries were set up, also with a tripartite composition, plus independent members. These were to consider the problems of their particular industries, with special reference to growth and efficiency.

In 1964 work on indicative planning was transferred to the Department of Economic Affairs, which prepared, in conjunction with the EDC's, a plan based on a growth target of 25 per cent between 1964 and 1970 (approximately 4 per cent per annum). This was embodied in *The National Plan* [2]. Its credibility was, however, soon destroyed by the restrictive measures taken to deal with the sterling crisis of July 1966. Indicative planning has never recovered from this setback. The next plan, published in 1969, after the 1967 devaluation of sterling, was a good deal more modest [3]. It was not so much a plan as a survey of the possible use of resources from 1967 to 1972, based on two alternative growth rates, and went into far less industry detail than its predecessor.

Further reviews of the economy have taken place since then, under the aegis of the NEDC. The trend has, however, been towards investigating the fortunes of individual sectors of the economy, and towards a detailed study of the reasons for low productivity or poor competitiveness in those sectors. This has been accompanied by selective intervention, in the form of help to particular firms and industries.

In 1966 the IRC was set up to encourage concentration and rationalisation in industry, in order to promote greater efficiency and international competitiveness. It was given wide powers, much freedom from government control, and £150 million to be used as a revolving credit. It helped to bring about a number of mergers, for example, those in the electrical industry where GEC absorbed several other leading companies, and that which created British Leyland. It gave support to companies in difficulties, such as Rolls-Royce and Cammell Laird. It also made loans to companies in need of modernisation (as in the Textile Re-equipment Scheme). It succeeded in reducing the population of small firms in the textile industry, while still leaving a reasonably competitive structure, but in other sectors it definitely encouraged monopoly.

The IRC was an expression of Harold Wilson's belief that, in the context of European integration and rapid technical progress, what was needed was a large scale of output in industry, allied to investment in modern methods and products. This philosophy was at times fundamentally at war with that behind the various monopoly and merger Acts, and there was undoubtedly conflict in individual cases between the IRC and the government departments concerned with antitrust policies. The IRC was, however, useful as an instrument through which government could deal with individual industrial firms at arm's length. It was an early casualty of the Heath government of 1970–4, but in 1975 the NEB was formed as a similar body, and has, significantly, been kept in existence by the Thatcher government of 1979. The NEB was set up amid fears on the political right that it would be used as an instrument to take over successful private firms, but in practice it has used most of its resources in supporting lame ducks such as British Leyland and Rolls-Royce. It has now given up responsibility for Rolls-Royce (after a furore which involved the resignation of the entire board) and is about to give up British Leyland, thus leaving itself free to concentrate on smaller firms and the encouragement of promising ventures.

The latest manifestation of planning has been the 'Industrial Strategy', which was launched by the publication of a White Paper in 1975 [5]. This followed the controversial White Paper of August 1974 on the regeneration of British industry [4], which had proposed the creation of the NEB and a system of planning agreements. The 1975 White Paper was a good deal less controversial, proposing an agreed long-term Industrial Strategy. The aim was to provide a framework in which the prospects of the most important sections of industry could be considered over a period of five or more years, an analysis would be made of the past performance of individual sectors of manufacturing industry, and the implications of alternative medium-term growth assumptions would be worked out. Those sectors most important for achieving the government's economic objectives (the 'winners') would be selected as follows:

(i) industries intrinsically likely to be successful judged by past performance and current prospects;
(ii) others which had the potential for success if appropriate action was taken;
(iii) industries whose performance has most effect on the rest of industry.

An attempt would then be made to tackle the problems affecting their performance.

Tripartite committees were to discuss in detail the problems and opportunities of particular sectors. The government would help to see that these committees were set up and would try in various ways to promote their main recommendations; it also made two important commitments. The first was to give priority to industrial development and to see that its own policies were consistent with this. The second was to help ensure that industry was able to earn sufficient profits on its investment (this was a brave commitment from a Labour government, although the rapid fall in the real rate of return in manufacturing industry during the 1970s was causing widespread concern).

The notion of picking 'winners' was never actually put into practice. The attempt to diagnose problems was spread across a wide range of industries, and the Industrial Strategy became, in effect, a general one.

The basic mechanism of the present Industrial Strategy is the Sector Working Party, which is a tripartite body for a particular sector of industry set up under the aegis of NEDO, to supplement the EDCs. (There are now 11 EDCs and 29 SWPs.) Each has looked in detail at the problems and performance of its own sector, and has tried to bring about improvements. The government claims that many SWP requests have been met quickly and effectively, for instance through improvements in export financing arrangements, increases in selective financial assistance, tax changes, and so on; also that it has made extensive use of all its schemes to increase the competitiveness of manufacturing industry. Under the Market Entry Guarantee Scheme, for instance, assistance totalling over £1 million was offered in 1979 to launch 17 market-entry projects; £57 million was offered in 1979 under the Selective Investment Scheme, and industry schemes generated 1326 offers of assistance towards projects worth £558 million. Under the Product and Process Development Scheme the government supported 90 projects at a cost of nearly £8 million. In the autumn of 1978 a micro-electronics support programme was announced greatly exceeding the scope of earlier schemes. Some £70 million was made available to encourage microprocessor-based developments, and £55 million was provided for increasing awareness of micro-electronics and the speeding-up of training. The NEB gave backing of £50 million for the Inmos project, while other government agencies embarked on programmes to stimulate relevant training and education.

Clearly a good deal of activity has been going on, but it is difficult not to feel some doubts about the effectiveness of the SWPs. Tripartite working parties covering individual industries have been at work in Britain in one form or another since Sir Stafford Cripps set up his Working Parties in 1945–6. They have produced many excellent surveys, but it would be difficult to say that their practical effects have been substantial. A fundamental problem is that, although they may not find it difficult to agree on the factors making for poor performance as compared with competitive firms overseas, it is likely to be much more difficult to agree on remedies. The union side is likely to wish for more investment in modern equipment, while the management side advocates more flexible working practices. The old conflicts arise, therefore, and cannot easily be resolved.

Old and New Industries

In the measures mentioned so far, there is no doubt that the weight of policy has been directed at helping old industries to survive rather than encouraging new products and new technology. Regional policy in its various forms has absorbed very large resources. Specific interventions by the NEB, and earlier by the IRC, have used up large sums. In addition, direct support for nationalised industries has been very expensive, notably recently in the case of British Steel.

In several instances losses have been incurred partly because of other government action, for example, the imposition of price controls, or the refusal to allow outdated factories to be shut down. Losses have occurred also as a result of British entry into the EEC, since this greatly sharpened competition which was already accentuated by the worldwide recession. But whatever the reason, the subventions by British governments to old and ailing industries have undoubtedly been very large.

Subventions for old industries are not of course unconnected with plans for modernisation. Investment in old industries is likely to be in modern equipment, as in BL's Mini Metro plant at Longbridge, or the BSC's new blast furnaces at Llanwern and Lackenby. The scope for both product and process innovation in 'old' industries should not be underestimated.

As far as new departures are concerned, the first postwar encouragement to invention was the setting up of the National Research Development Corporation (NRDC) in 1948. This body was intended to help exploit inventions not taken up by the private sector, or arising in universities or government research centres. At first it devoted itself solely to development, but more recently it has undertaken manufacture also. In total, however, it disposes of modest resources (some £15 million per annum at present).

Very large sums of government money have been made directly available for several years for limited areas of industrial innovation – some £300 million per annum at 1975 prices (Morris [10],

p. 469) – but these have gone mainly to the space or aircraft industries, or to nuclear power. The computer industry in the shape of ICL has received more modest support, and more recently (as noted above) some money has been provided for micro-electronics, but the sums involved have not been large.

It is not perhaps surprising that capital-intensive old industries should have in general absorbed more attention and resources than newer industries, apart from aircraft and nuclear power. Old industries tend to be in vulnerable areas of the country, and with their scale and degree of capital intensity they can easily swallow up vast sums. Newer industries, on the other hand, always excepting aircraft and nuclear power, tend to need sums which are small in comparison. There is no reason to believe that these have been starved of desirable government support (at least in the past) because of resource problems. It is more likely that government hesitation, as in the Inmos project recently, has been concerned with doubts about viability and competitive strength rather than with the funds required. Similar doubts have hindered new developments in private industry, especially during the recession of recent years, and even more so now, when the exchange rate is so strong.

It may be that if the prospects for British manufacturing industry as a whole looked brighter, there would be little need for concern about the readiness of investors, whether public or private, to support innovation. The market situation would encourage innovation in private firms and in nationalised industries. Government help might be needed for projects with long-term rather than short-term prospects, but this could be made available, on the comparatively small scale generally needed, if there were a stable background for manufacturing industry as a whole. Policies to support British manufacturing generally seem likely, therefore, to be the precondition for effective policies to support innovation.

References

[1] Cairncross, A., Kay, J. A. and Silberston, A., 'The regeneration of manufacturing industry', *Midland Bank Review*, Autumn 1977.
[2] Department of Economic Affairs, *The National Plan*, Cmnd 2764, London, HMSO, 1965.
[3] —, *The Task Ahead: economic assessment to 1972*, London, HMSO, 1969.
[4] Department of Industry, *The Regeneration of British Industry*, Cmnd 5710, London, HMSO, 1974.
[5] —, *An Approach to Industrial Strategy*, Cmnd 6315, London, HMSO, 1975.
[6] Department of Prices and Consumer Protection, *A Review of Monopolies and Mergers Policy*, Cmnd 7198, London, HMSO, 1978.

[7] —, *A Review of Restrictive Trade Practices Policy*, Cmnd 7512, London, HMSO, 1979.

[8] Evely, R., 'The effects of the Price Code', *National Institute Economic Review*, no. 77, August 1976.

[9] Moore, B. and Rhodes, J., 'Evaluating the effects of British regional economic policy', *Economic Journal*, vol. 83, March 1973.

[10] Morris, D. J., 'Industrial policy' in D. J. Morris (ed.), *The Economic System in the United Kingdom*, Oxford University Press, 1977.

[11] National Board for Prices and Incomes, *Fifth and Final General Report, July 1969 to March 1971*, Cmnd 4649, London, HMSO, 1971.

5 Government Support for Innovation in the British Machine Tool Industry: a Case Study

by Anne Daly*

International competition in the machine tool industry has long been significant, and official concern has been expressed in Britain over the ability of its machine tool producers to compete with foreign suppliers for over a hundred years (Floud [6]). Active government measures began in the 1930s, when the industry received protection against imports, allowing only those machine tools deemed to be necessary and unobtainable in Britain to be admitted duty-free. In the postwar period, as successive governments have become more involved in the structure, conduct and performance of this industry, there has been growing concern over the relatively poor performance of British manufacturing as a whole, and particularly the relatively slow rate of innovation. Included in a range of schemes aimed at promoting innovation, that is the development and marketing of new products and processes, were a number designed specifically for the machine tool industry. This chapter will outline these schemes in the context of general industrial policies directed towards encouraging innovation. It concludes with an assessment of the effects of these policies and of the performance of the machine tool industry over the relevant period.

The Rationale for Government Intervention in the Process of Innovation
The government has an important role in establishing the general framework in which business operates, and this has obvious implications for the rate of innovation. For example, the type of patent laws established, the taxation concessions granted for capital

* I would like to thank members of staff at NIESR, especially Professor S. J. Prais, for their helpful comments on earlier drafts.

investment, and legislation affecting labour costs (for instance minimum wage laws and compulsory national insurance) will all influence the demand for and supply of new types of machinery. The government also may have a significant influence over the supply of technically competent personnel; for example, schools might be encouraged to include more technical subjects in their curricula or legislation introduced to make vocational training for school leavers compulsory. However, apart from this general role for government, its intervention in a specific industry must rest on the belief that net positive social benefits would arise from a greater investment in that industry than is likely to be undertaken by private entrepreneurs if left to themselves. These potential additional benefits might include defence considerations, the development of a pool of skilled labour, the production of a more technically advanced mix of products, or the encouragement of alternative sources of employment in declining regions. If these social benefits are of substance, the question then arises as to the most effective form which government intervention should take.

Successive British governments have intervened in the machine tool industry mainly by providing financial support for innovation. The implicit argument appears to have been that a shortage of physical capital, or too high a cost of capital, has retarded the rate of innovation, and that by subsidising the cost of innovation (and reducing the cost to the buyer of experimenting with these new products) some of the barriers to innovation would be overcome. There is some evidence that, while the capital market operates relatively efficiently for large-scale British industry, small and medium-sized firms in Britain are less well served than their German counterparts (Prais [17]); and, given the relatively small scale on which machine tool manufacturing is undertaken, this provides some justification for public support.

It is, however, arguable that a shortage of technical expertise has been the real impediment to progress in this industry and that an inadequate supply of risk capital to the industry is merely a symptom of underlying weakness. We shall return to this issue at the end of the chapter; first, we shall examine how the main schemes to promote innovation have operated in practice.

Background to the Government Schemes
Shortages of certain types of machine tools had created critical difficulties in the first and second world wars, but there was no

detailed official study of the industry until the 1950s, when the Anglo-American Council on Productivity published its report [1] emphasising the need to establish standards and rationalise design (pp. 46–53). In the late 1950s an unpublished study by the Department of Scientific and Industrial Research (DSIR) emphasised the role of R and D and the importance of engineering education; it also proposed placing government contracts with firms to encourage them to develop new machine tools. The theme of the importance of technical excellence was further developed in the Mitchell Committee's study in 1960 [2], which concluded that the British industry suffered from an 'over-concentration on the production of standard machine tools' arising from 'the lack of a sufficiently intensive development effort' (p. 33). The Mitchell Committee outlined two roles for government: first, the supply of public funds to promote R and D and, secondly, the extension (in both quality and quantity) of engineering education.

The existing administrative machinery for the first of these roles, chiefly the DSIR and the NRDC, came under the control of the newly established Ministry of Technology in 1964. The new Ministry had been set up by the Labour government – under Mr Wilson's famous 'white heat of technology' theme – to 'guide and stimulate a major national effort to bring advanced technology and new processes into British industry' [14]; the machine tool industry was selected as one of its first four sponsored industries (the other three were computers, electronics and telecommunications).

The expansion of engineering education, the second possible role for government, fell within the ambit of the Department of Education and Science. Although the growth of tertiary education following the Robbins Report [13], and the development of the Industry Training Boards, may be regarded as essential parts of any general policy designed to increase the supply of qualified personnel, they will not be considered further in this chapter. This is not meant to deny the importance of education, but rather to focus the discussion here on policies designed specifically for the machine tool industry. We shall therefore now turn to an examination of the relevant policies in the period 1965–78 devised by the Ministry of Technology (and its successors).

The Ministry of Technology Schemes
Two major schemes were introduced under the Ministry of Tech-

nology aimed at reducing the costs and risks of innovation to producers of machine tools; the pre-production order scheme and the numerically controlled machine tools trial-period scheme (administered by the NRDC).

The first of these schemes was introduced in 1965 and was aimed at encouraging the development of technologically advanced machine tools and at overcoming user-conservatism. The government ordered and paid for pre-production models of newly developed British machine tools, and then gave them free of charge to selected users for a trial period. At the end of this period the users had the option of buying, renting or returning the machine. The scheme underwent a number of modifications, and in 1971 it was extended to cover all types of equipment (for example textile and printing machinery, and mechanical handling and scientific equipment), although the machine tool industry continued to be the major beneficiary. There was no detailed assessment of firms before they were given support under the scheme, and problems sometimes arose through companies being unable to accommodate the new types of machines in their production schedules past the prototype stage. A further drawback was that the 100 per cent subsidy encouraged the development of new machine tools without reference to product demand. It was estimated that about £5.5 million was spent on the machine tool industry under this scheme.

The numerically controlled machine tool trial-period scheme, the responsibility of the NRDC and introduced in 1966, required users to pay a premium to participate but gave them the option of reselling numerically controlled (NC) machines to the suppliers at a government-guaranteed repurchase price. The NRDC also undertook to pay the manufacturer any reconditioning or re-selling costs. In its 1967–8 annual report [16] the NRDC noted that, although the range available to users included 49 different models from thirteen suppliers, only five machines had been sold to users by July 1968; in April 1970 the scheme was withdrawn. Over the four years of its operation, £1 million had been allocated to the scheme (but it appears that not all of this sum was taken up). The NRDC was also involved in the promotion of NC machine tools via its financial support for BSA Tools (later part of Alfred Herbert) for the development of NC turning machines.

Other sources of the machine tool industry's difficulties were also examined by the Ministry of Technology; among them was an analysis of the problems resulting from the cyclical pattern of machine tool orders [15]. The report compared the size of fluctuations in output among British capital goods industries and among the machine tool industries of different countries; but it concluded that 'it would clearly be wrong to suggest that the machine tool industry as a whole had been uniquely, or even exceptionally, affected by cyclical fluctuations' (p. 11). It was therefore decided that there was no basis for financial assistance on this account. The Ministry of Technology also briefly introduced a stock insurance scheme but there was little demand.

Another government agency active at this time was the IRC, established in 1966. In line with the argument (see Galbraith [7], pp. 89–99) that large firms tend to be more innovative than small ones, the IRC aimed at encouraging 'structural reorganisation' – chiefly via mergers – to 'eliminate wasteful duplication and permit economies of scale in production, marketing and research' (*First Annual Report* [10], p. 6). The IRC encouraged the then largest British machine tool company, Alfred Herbert, to take over a number of other companies in the industry; during the 1960s, the firm's employment rose to a peak of 15,000 from about 6000 in the late 1950s. Alfred Herbert prided itself on being 'the largest machine tool organisation in the world'. However, machine tools are generally produced on a small scale; the median plant producing metalworking machine tools in the 1970s had about 400 employees in Britain, Germany and America. Significant economies of scale in marketing and research must therefore have been expected from the formation of such a relatively large company, but the arguments for public support of this expansion were never spelt out. In 1970 the IRC gave financial support to Herbert in a joint venture with the American company Ingersoll for the development of specialist transfer machinery. £2.5 million was committed to this, but the newly formed joint subsidiary was unsuccessful and within two years had gone into receivership.

The IRC made loans to a number of other companies in its attempt to promote the development of NC machine tools. A loan of £1.5 million was made to Marwin in 1970–1 for the development of NC machine tools, and in 1971 £300,000 was invested in the British subsidiary of the American company Kearney & Trecker for a similar purpose. Neither of these ventures proved viable and, in 1973, with the aid of additional government finance (£1.25 million) under the Industry Act of 1972, these two firms merged (*Annual Report 1972–73* [19]); in 1974 Vickers, the engineering group, took over managerial responsibility for the company and in 1976 a further reconstruction of Kearney & Trecker Marwin resulted in Vickers holding 86 per cent of voting shares and Kearney & Trecker, Milwaukee, 14 per cent (*Annual Report 1975–76* [19]); the Department of Industry held an equal number of non-voting shares. Despite early difficulties, the company has become a relatively successful producer of NC machine tools. A third loan, of £3 million, was made to the Plessey company in 1969 to accelerate the development of Plessey Numerical Controls; Plessey, in 1979, sold this part of their activities to the American company Allen Bradley. A final, if not entirely direct, attempt in 1970 to assist the machine tool industry was the loan of £10 million to British Leyland for modernising its machines; the IRC proposed discussions with British machine tool manufacturers on the development of new machine tools so that British Leyland would not have to rely on foreign machinery.

Following the election of a Conservative government, the IRC was disbanded in 1971, and the Ministry of Technology was absorbed by the Department of Trade and Industry. In 1972 the Industry Act was passed, under which financial assistance could be made available to the private sector, but apart from aid to Kearney & Trecker Marwin and Alfred Herbert there was no general assistance offered to the machine tool industry until 1975.

The next major programmes directed towards innovation began after a Labour government had been re-elected; they were administered under the auspices of the Department of Industry and the NEB. Apart from the nationalisation of Alfred Herbert, one feature of these schemes was that they offered only partial assistance. The argument appears to have been that if the company provided a substantial part of the investment funds, better commercial decisions would be made.

The Department of Industry's Machine Tool Industry Scheme
The Machine Tool Industry Scheme (MTIS) was announced in August 1975, with the objective of encouraging the development of new products and processes. Applications were possible under two headings; a loan for both manpower and equipment necessary for the design, development and marketing of a new machine tool and, secondly, grants or loans for the modernisation of production facilities (plant, machinery and buildings). In 1976 the scheme was extended to include manufacturers of one-off tooling and assembly

machines, and a third category of assistance was created for under-taking studies of efficiency in small and medium-sized companies. A 50 per cent loan allowed under the original scheme for the de-velopment of new machine tools was replaced by a 25 per cent grant from August 1976. Applications for the scheme closed at the end of 1977 with the full £30 million budget allocated; however, with the recession, the full allocation was not subsequently taken up. At the British machine tool exhibition in May 1980, 38 com-panies exhibited machine tools which had been built with MTIS support. The German government has adopted a similar scheme for firms with an annual turnover of less than £35 million. Grants of 25 to 30 per cent are made towards R and D personnel costs and a further scheme offers support for capital projects.

A second scheme launched in 1977 by the Department of Indus-try, under the Science and Technology Act, was aimed at promoting innovation throughout manufacturing industry. Financial assist-ance came in the form of either a 50 per cent shared-cost contract with the government, which in turn received a levy from commercial sales, or a grant of up to 25 per cent. £20 million was made available under this Product and Process Development Scheme, and by June 1980 27 machine tool projects had been approved.

The National Enterprise Board and Alfred Herbert
The financial assistance given to the machine tool industry by the NEB after 1975 should perhaps not be classified as money spent directly to promote innovation, as the major share was invested in Alfred Herbert with a view to overcoming the company's liquidity crisis. In 1974 Alfred Herbert applied for government assistance and received a government guarantee of the company's overdraft facilities. Following further investigations, the government, under the Industry Act 1972, formed a holding company to purchase the existing ordinary shares in Alfred Herbert at a cost of £1.2 million (*Annual Report 1975–76* [19]). An additional £25 million was made available in the form of equity and loan capital and the holding company was transferred to the NEB, which proposed replacing the company's range of low-value conventional machine tools with new high-technology products. Considerable rationalisation took place and an additional £18.5 million of public funds was invested between 1976 and 1980. The group, nevertheless, was unable to maintain sales and continued to make losses; employment had fallen from 15,000 in the 1960s to 6700 in 1975 and to 5400 in

1978, and in 1979 the company began to sell off its subsidiaries. In July 1980 the final closure of Alfred Herbert was announced.

In addition to its investment in Alfred Herbert, the NEB provided finance for the building of machine tools for stock during 1976–7. Three machine tool companies besides Alfred Herbert took advantage of this scheme, but it has been suggested that the scheme was mainly a further form of loan to Alfred Herbert.

Other Forms of Aid to Innovation

The other two major forms of government assistance to innovation which existed throughout the 1960s and 1970s were direct government funding of research in its own laboratories (for example the National Engineering Laboratory) and in collective research institutions (for example the Machine Tool Industry Research Association (MTIRA)) and, secondly, government purchasing of technically advanced products, as was proposed by the DSIR in the late 1950s.

The government research laboratory which could be expected to have had the closest ties with the machine tool industry is the National Engineering Laboratory, but it has done only a small amount of work directly for the industry and has been criticised for being too academic. An example of related research was the automated small-batch production programme begun in 1978 and sponsored by the Department of Industry.

The industry's own research association, MTIRA, has been of greater importance, especially to smaller firms lacking the resources necessary for their own R and D. The research association has been mainly funded by membership subscription and, until the mid-1960s, by a grant from government. Following the Rothschild Report on government-funded research [4], the responsibility for allocating government funds has fallen to the Research and Development Requirements Boards established in 1973. There are now twelve of these Boards covering specific industries (for example the Mechanical Engineering and Machine Tools Board) and they are responsible for assessing projects put forward by government laboratories, research associations and private industry [5]. Of the £44 million allocated to mechanical engineering and machine tools over the period 1973–4 to 1978–9, 17 per cent went to the research associations, 64 per cent to government laboratories, 13 per cent to the UK Atomic Energy Authority and the remaining 6 per cent to industry and universities. Government expenditure therefore continues to be concentrated in its own laboratories.

It has been argued that support through public purchasing was an important factor in the growth of technologically advanced industries, such as computers, in the US (Mansfield [11], [12]); on this basis, a similar role has been proposed for British government-controlled purchases that might benefit the machine tool industry. The bulk of effort in this direction in Britain has been in the development of aircraft and electronics (chiefly computers), and little has been done by government purchasers to encourage the production of more sophisticated machine tools. The current policy emphasises the purchase of British goods whenever available; but this initiative seems unlikely to have any major impact on the machine tool industry. One obstacle the government could help to overcome is the diversity of engineering standards (for example technical and safety specifications) used by government departments. The Warner Report in 1977 [20] suggested that there should be a common set of standards for all public purchasing bodies. An assessment in 1980 [21] noted, however, that there had been very little progress made on these recommendations.

In summary, as part of the more active role seen for government in promoting manufacturing industry, an interest in innovation and technical progress developed in the 1960s, most prominently displayed by the establishment of the Ministry of Technology in 1964. The lack of technological vigour in the machine tool industry had previously been a subject of public concern and it was not surprising that the Ministry of Technology and the IRC took as one of their priorities the creation of schemes to encourage the production of more sophisticated machine tools. The election of a Conservative government in 1970, pledged to non-intervention, temporarily altered these industrial policies, but in 1975, under a Labour government, further schemes were introduced specifically for the encouragement of innovation in the machine tool industry. The philosophy of the current Conservative government has once again swung away from specific intervention.

The Performance of the British Machine Tool Industry
In the period 1966–78 the government spent some £100 million on the machine tool industry including Alfred Herbert (Burchardt [3]), and we shall now attempt an assessment of the effect of this expenditure on the industry's performance. Ideally one would wish

to compare the actual performance of the industry with some estimate of its performance in the absence of assistance. However, it is not possible to know how the industry would have behaved in other circumstances. The machine tool industry did not perform well during the 1970s, but in the absence of government intervention the record might have been even worse. Output as measured by the index of industrial production was 22 per cent lower in 1979 than in 1968 and over a third lower than in the peak year of 1970; this compares with a 10 per cent increase in the output of the German machine tool industry between 1968 and 1979 and a 22 per cent increase in American output between 1968 and 1978. Employment in the British machine tool industry fell from 72,100 in 1968 to 56,000 in 1978, a decline of over 20 per cent. Imports became increasingly important in the domestic market, and in 1979 accounted for 47 per cent of home sales compared with 28 per cent in 1970. The volume of exports fell by 18 per cent, but against a declining total production exports represented a higher proportion in 1979 – 43 per cent as compared with 36 per cent in 1970. In 1978, the most recent year for which we have data, Britain accounted for 6 per cent of world exports of machine tools compared with 13 per cent in 1965. The picture is therefore one of an industry declining in importance on the home and the world markets.

There has been little evidence of any definite rise in innovation.

Table 5.1   Share of NC machine tools in total British production of metal-working machine tools^a (percentages)

1966	2.8	1973	6.5
1967	4.8	1974	6.3
1968	7.8	1975	7.3
1969	8.5	1976	7.2
1970	7.9	1977	8.3
1971	9.6	1978	10.6
1972	6.0^b	1979	11.4

Source: Department of Industry, *Business Monitors*.

^{a}The total includes metal-cutting and metal-forming machine tools, including parts but excluding physico-chemical process machine tools.
^{b}The decline in NC production between 1971 and 1972 may in part reflect a change in the method of data collection by the Business Statistics Office.

The available statistical information on R and D expenditures and employment suggests a peak in 1967, followed by a dramatic decline to about one quarter of the 1967 level in 1972 (possibly, however, due in part to variations in response rate and changes in classification); this was followed by a rise, which left R and D expenditure in the 1970s at probably under half that in the 1960s. There are of course important shortcomings in these figures (created, for example, by the problem of defining R and D activity), and it is perhaps unwise to draw any definite conclusions from them; however they do suggest that, despite the declining output of the industry, over the latter part of the period 1972–8 expenditure on R and D increased. This could well be a reflection of the Department of Industry's MTIS.

As a number of the government-sponsored schemes were aimed at encouraging the development of NC machine tools, another possible indicator of the success of these programmes might be the change in the share of NC machine tools in total production. NC was originally developed in the early 1950s in the US, and Britain was the first country in Europe to adopt NC machine tools. As Table 5.1 shows, the share of NC machine tools in total British production rose rapidly between 1966 and 1971. According to a survey undertaken in 1969 (see Gebhardt and Hatzold [8]), by the end of the 1960s Britain had a relatively high level of diffusion (as measured by the number of NC machine tools per thousand employees); it was below that of America and Sweden but above West Germany, Austria and Italy. However, this early advantage was not maintained during the 1970s, as is shown by the share of NC machine tools in the production of metal-cutting machine tools for a number of countries in 1978 (see Table 5.2). It appears that Britain's NC production has failed to grow at the same rate as that in other countries. British production of NC machine tools declined in relation to total machine tool output after 1971 and it was not until 1978 that the 1971 share was overtaken. Any effect of government policies on the development of NC machine tools, therefore, does not seem to have been sustained. Gebhardt and Hatzold [8] found that government assistance had influenced the decision in favour of NC machine tools in the late 1960s in about two fifths of the British sample of 36 firms, although for the others the influence was negligible. The record suggests that, although there may have been some favourable effect on the introduction of NC machine tools during the period over which the schemes were in

Table 5.2   The share of NC machine tools in the output of metal-cutting machine tools of selected countries, 1978[a] (percentages)

Germany (Federal Republic)	17
Great Britain	16
Japan	29
United States	31

Source: CECIMO/VDW, *International Statistics of Machine Tools 1978*. The data are collected by national machine tool associations.

[a]These shares, based on values in Swiss francs, should only be taken as approximate Italian production figures were unavailable for the whole of the industry, but for the three categories covered – lathes, milling and boring machines, accounting for 44 per cent of production – the share of NC machine tools was 30 per cent.

Table 5.3   Export–import unit value ratios for selected countries' trade in machine tools, 1979[a]

	Average export value	Average import value	Exports/imports value per tonne
	US$/tonne	US$/tonne	
France	7,200	6,900	1.0
Germany	9,100	6,700	1.4
Italy	5,800	4,900	1.2
Japan	5,400	9,300	0.6
Switzerland	15,500	7,400	2.1
United Kingdom	4,700	6,600	0.7
United States	10,100	4,700	1.8[b]

Sources: OECD, *Trade by Commodities* (*Series C*); United Nations, *Yearbook of International Trade Statistics*.

[a]The data are for SITC 715.1, now covered by SITC 736.1, 736.2 and 736.7 under the revised classification.

[b]As US trade statistics relate to the number rather than the tonnage of imports and exports it was necessary to calculate US value per tonne from the trade statistics of other countries. Although it was possible to include 80 per cent of American imports, the coverage of American exports was limited by data availability to 30 per cent and this estimate should therefore be treated with caution. However, the ratio of value per unit for exports and imports from the official US statistics was also 1.8.

operation, this did not continue afterwards.

A third possible indicator of the success of the government schemes in encouraging the development of more sophisticated machine tools can be derived from foreign trade statistics. The Mitchell Committee in 1960 [2] pointed out that Britain's imports consisted of 'high performance and high precision advanced types of special machine tools, whilst United Kingdom exports are mainly standard machine tools' (p. 23), and Saunders [18] found this still true in 1975. Although the statistics on the average values of exports and imports are subject to reservations, the average British export has continued to be worth less than the average import, and its average value per tonne has risen only from 0.6 of that of imports in 1960 to 0.7 by 1979. Table 5.3 gives export–import unit value ratios for the seven major exporters of machine tools in 1977; and, for all other countries apart from Japan, the average value of exports exceeded that of imports. However, the value per tonne of Japanese exports was higher than for Britain, US$5400 compared with US$4700.

The Industry's View of the Government Subsidies
On the basis of publicly available material and interviews with a number of companies of varying size and area of specialisation, we have some information on the industry's assessment of the government schemes. While we would not claim that this constituted a scientifically selected sample, it is of interest to outline some of the views expressed.

The Machine Tool Trades Association argued in its submission to the House of Commons Expenditure Committee investigation into public money in the private sector [9] that, of the government schemes designed during the 1960s, only the pre-production order scheme could be regarded as successful, in that it encouraged users to experiment with new products. On the other hand, it was argued by one of the companies that had been involved as a supplier to the scheme that, as users were not required to justify the profitable use of these machines, they were often not used effectively. The NC trial-period scheme and the stock insurance scheme, as already stated, received little support from the industry, and there was no support for the reintroduction of similar schemes.

The MTIS was favourably regarded by those we interviewed; given the generous nature of the financial assistance offered (a 25–50 per cent subsidy to capital expenditure by machine tool companies) this is perhaps not surprising. The scheme appears to have had some influence on the timing of investment in the industry, particularly as a result of its introduction during a recession. R and D expenditure is often one of the first areas to be cut during a recession and the MTIS encouraged greater expenditure under this head than would otherwise have taken place. However, the approval of those immediately benefiting from the scheme should not be taken as a final judgement of its overall success.

In interviews with the present writer, several companies were also asked to comment on alternative measures that the government might take to encourage innovation. Schemes such as MTIS assume that the inhibiting factor to innovation is insufficient capital available at a cost below the general rate of return on investment. Comments by members of the industry, however, suggest that, although the supply of capital is a constraint in some cases, especially among smaller firms, it is far from being the only barrier to innovation. The high rate of inflation in Britain, the strong pound, and the lack of growing home demand, especially from the motor vehicle industry, were all claimed to be very important. In addition, some firms recognised that they suffered from an inadequate supply of skilled labour both at the craftsman level and among certain types of engineers, for example electronic engineers; it was suggested that improving the conditions and status of engineers, and of manufacturing industry in general, might assist in overcoming this problem (how this might be achieved in practice was, however, generally left unclear).

A further potential area for change was seen in the relationship between business and the civil service; one suggestion was that British civil servants 'needed to go into business'. It was argued on several occasions that British civil servants were not as active as their foreign counterparts in furthering nationalistic objectives, such as gaining foreign orders. As the British civil service tended to follow the letter of the law very closely, British companies did not receive as much support from their government as their competitors. A change in the civil service career structure to encourage a greater flow of people between government and industry might be one step towards developing a civil service which was better able to understand the workings of industry.

Another area where it was suggested that government could initiate change was in public purchasing policy. As the Warner Report [20] concluded, there has been little progress made in creating a uniform set of standards for public purchasers and this continues to create problems for suppliers. A further suggestion was that government could promote 'areas of excellence' within the industries it controlled in order to encourage innovation among its suppliers; but one commentator suggested that there was a danger in encouraging the development of products for which there was as yet no other market demand.

Conclusion

Could the £100 million spent by the government on this industry have been spent more effectively – for example on special grants or loans for engineering students, or on establishing departments within universities to specialise in engineering research for industry? Especially in an industry such as machine tools, technical progress is not confined to the results of laboratory work and highly trained personnel are needed at all levels for a firm to be successful. Perhaps the introduction of vocational training for school leavers or the establishment of nationally recognised standards of apprenticeship training would do more in the long term towards encouraging the development of a more sophisticated and competitive industry than any short-run subsidies.

The decline of the British machine tool industry has been exacerbated by the contraction in demand for British manufactured goods, especially motor vehicles. Given the interdependence of industries, funds directed at innovation in one industry are likely to have little effect unless they are part of an overall programme to improve the competitiveness of British manufacturing in general; and it may therefore be better for government to concern itself first with the general framework within which industry has to operate.

References
[1] Anglo-American Council on Productivity, *Metalworking Machine Tools*, London, British Productivity Council, 1953.
[2] Board of Trade, *The Machine Tool Industry* [Mitchell Report], London, HMSO, 1960.
[3] Burchardt, A., 'The machine tool industry', *The Trade Union Register*, 1973.
[4] Central Policy Review Staff, *A Framework for Government Research and Development* [Rothschild Report], London, HMSO, 1971.
[5] Department of Industry, *Research and Development Requirements Boards. Annual Reports*, 1973–7, London, HMSO.
[6] Floud, R., *The British Machine Tool Industry 1850–1914*, Cambridge University Press, 1975.
[7] Galbraith, J. K., *American Capitalism*, London, Hamish Hamilton, 1952.

[8] Gebhardt, A. and Hatzold, O., 'Numerically controlled machine tools' in L. Nabseth and G. F. Ray (eds.), *The Diffusion of New Industrial Processes: An International Study*, Cambridge University Press, 1974.

[9] House of Commons Expenditure Committee, *Public Money in the Private Sector*, London, HMSO, 1972.

[10] Industrial Reorganisation Corporation, *Annual Reports and Accounts*, 1968–71, London, HMSO.

[11] Mansfield, E., *The Economics of Technological Change*, New York, Norton, 1968.

[12] Mansfield E., Rapoport J., Romeo A., Villani E., Wagner S. and Husic F., *The Production and Application of New Industrial Technology*, New York, Norton, 1977.

[13] Ministry of Education, *Higher Education* [Robbins Report], Cmnd 2154, London, HMSO, 1963.

[14] Ministry of Technology, *The Ministry of Technology*, London, HMSO, 1967.

[15] —, *Report of the Working Party on the Problems Arising from the Cyclical Pattern of Machine Tool Orders*, London, HMSO, 1966.

[16] National Research Development Corporation, *Annual Reports and Accounts* (relevant years), London, HMSO.

[17] Prais, S. J., *Productivity and Industrial Structure*, Cambridge University Press, forthcoming 1981.

[18] Saunders, C., *Engineering in Britain, West Germany and France: some statistical comparisons*, Sussex European Research Centre, 1978.

[19] Secretaries of State for Industry, Scotland and Wales, *Industry Act 1972. Annual Reports*, 1972–8, London, HMSO.

[20] Warner, F., *Standards and Specifications in the Engineering Industries*, London, NEDO, 1977.

[21] —, 'Progress on the Warner Report' (mimeo., NEDC), 1980.

6 Industrial Policy and Innovation in Japan

by G. C. Allen*

A well-known Japanese economist, who takes a jaundiced view of the usefulness of his professional colleagues as advisers on policy, recently asserted that his country owes much of its postwar economic success to the fact that, at the end of the second world war, most of the senior academic economists were Marxists. The postwar government, being Conservative in temper, was naturally not disposed to turn to Marxists for advice. So it perforce fell back on bureaucrats and administrators whose economics had been learnt by experience. Some of these advisers were engineers who had been drawn by the war into the management of public affairs. They were the last people to allow themselves to be guided by the half-light of economic theory. Their instinct was to find a solution for Japan's postwar difficulties on the supply side, in enhanced technical efficiency and innovations in production. They thought in dynamic terms. Their policies were designed to furnish the drive and to raise the finance for an economy that might be created rather than simply to make the best use of the resources it then possessed.

The issue came to a head soon after the war when the government was considering how best to use its exiguous resources for industrial rehabilitation. It was natural that the more orthodox financiers, including the influential Governor of the Bank of Japan, should advocate policies that seemed consistent with Japan's factor-endowment of that time – a huge supply of under-employed labour, an extreme scarcity of capital, and out-of-date technology. The obvious candidates for development were the labour-intensive industries: textiles, clothing, pottery, metal smallwares. It would be folly, so it was argued, to ignore Japan's comparative advantages

* I am much indebted for help in writing this paper to Mr K. Matsuo of the Ministry of International Trade and Industry; Mr K. Narita of the Chunichi Shimbun; Professor Y. Okano of Tokyo University; Professor S. Yamamoto of Kagawa University; and the Anglo-Japanese Economic Institute, London.

in such trades in the pursuit of goals only open to countries well supplied with capital and technical expertise. At first these views had an effect on what was done. The Bank of Japan saw to it that loans were denied (in 1951) for a project for building a new, up-to-date steel works. Sony was obliged to postpone its import of transistor technology because the officials in charge of foreign exchange licensing were doubtful both about the technology and about Sony's ability to make use of it. But, on the whole, the bureaucrats and their advisers at the Ministry of International Trade and Industry (MITI) prevailed. They repudiated the view that Japan should be content with a future as an underdeveloped country with low productivity and income per head. She should bend her energies, in their view, to building up an industrial system based on capital-intensive manufactures. It was true that she was at that time technically backward and short of capital. But there was no obstacle to her importing 'know-how' from the United States, and her large company of well-trained technicians would permit her to assimilate quickly what the West could provide. With a fiscal and financial policy framed to encourage new enterprise and high investment, and by the shrewd use of physical controls, she could ensure that a high proportion of her national income was directed into the creation of the most productive forms of industrial capital. Once the national income started to rise, the effect would be cumulative and a virtuous circle would come into being – rising incomes, increased savings and investment leading to higher productivity and still higher incomes. Close cooperation between government and industry would bring about a concentration of national energies on the chosen purposes, and popular support for the policy would be won by the steady rise in real incomes that would attend the process.

A corollary of Japan's determination to lift her productive capacity to a higher plane of technical and commercial competence was her awareness of the need to adapt her industrial composition to changes in markets and techniques. Structural adaptability was recognised as a condition of the continuous growth in GNP. Moreover, Japan did not simply respond to exogenous forces; she was remarkably successful in anticipating change. In the early 1950s her chief export industries still consisted of labour-intensive trades, where her low wages made her an effective competitor with her western rivals, and her superior management and organisation kept at bay challenges from the developing countries. But, as her policy showed, she fully realised that these advantages were transient, and she soon began to set up a new capacity in several large-scale, capital-intensive trades, notably steel, shipbuilding and chemical fertilisers. By the early 1960s, when these trades were well established, she turned her attention to a number of engineering industries, especially radios, television sets and motor vehicles, as well as to petrochemical products. By the end of the 1960s her motor car, electronics, watch and clock industries ranked with the world's leaders, while her eminence in steel, motor cycles and shipbuilding remained unassailed. The check to her industrial growth after 1973 was followed by a recovery (in 1978) which was associated especially with the further development of her motor, machinery, instrument and electronic manufactures.

In the meantime she had been shedding her older industries. In 1958 she took the critical decision to run down her high-cost coal industry and to base her industrial expansion on imported fuel, especially oil. The pace of the industrial advance, which cheap oil made possible, left her with an economy well equipped to deal with the 'oil shock' in 1973 and its consequences. She accepted also the inevitable decline in her cotton and rayon industries and, recently, in her synthetic fibre industry. Firms in those trades in the last decade have been actively engaged in diversifying their production at home and in the transfer of textile manufacture to other Asian countries, usually in joint ventures with their nationals. The increasing dangers of environmental pollution and the shortage of sites for heavy industries, as well as high fuel costs, persuaded Japan to put a brake on the further growth at home of industries that caused pollution or required large quantities of raw materials and fuel per unit of finished product. She tried to solve the problem of supply by establishing production units abroad, for example, a sintering plant in the Philippines and pig iron capacity in Arabia. She was quick to realise that some newly industrialised countries might soon become serious rivals, even in such industries as motor car manufacture and shipbuilding. So, whereas in the 1950s and 1960s her policy was aimed at creating capacity in the large-scale, capital-intensive trades, she is now directing her efforts towards industries to which her resources of technical skill, scientific expertise and organising capacity can be applied; the 'knowledge-intensive industries' as they are called – computers, micro-chips and instruments of many kinds (MITI [4]). One may conclude that structural adaptability provides a key to Japan's success, a lesson that Britain can surely learn.

Two questions now present themselves. How was the selection of industries for development made? By what process was this done and how was the choice made effective? The selection of the industries was closely related, especially in the early postwar years, to their impact on foreign trade. It was obvious that, until Japan's export trade had been lifted out of the depths to which it had descended, she would be unable to buy the imports required for industrial expansion. Two conditions had to be satisfied before a candidate for growth was acceptable. First, the product must be one for which the income-elasticity of demand in the world as a whole was likely to be high. When choosing among possible candidates, the preference was for those with the highest income-elasticity. The other criterion was that of comparative technical progress. Even if the costs of manufacturing a product were high at the initial stage, it would be preferred to others if there was a probability of exceptionally rapid technical progress which would be reflected in steeply falling costs (Shinohara [11]). At the time when the steel and motor industries were chosen for development, their costs were very high by international standards. In 1954, when I visited a Toyota plant, then in the process of installing the conveyor system of assembly, I found the manager disconsolate because the Japanese steel mills seemed incapable of supplying him with sheets of uniform quality for his car bodies. Twenty years later Japan had become pre-eminent as an exporter of steel and motor cars and she ranked with the world's leaders in the volume of their production.

Japan's success in these and other trades justified the principles of selection referred to, although it is debatable how far those principles were consciously applied *ab initio*, and how far they have subsequently been inferred from the decisions and conduct of the industrialists and the bureaucracy. Her success also refuted the contention of those who held that her industrial strength for many years would be displayed only in the labour-intensive industries. Their arguments were, in fact, too simplistic. To base policy on a dichotomy between labour-intensive and capital-intensive industries was to ignore the contribution that factors other than labour and capital broadly defined could make to production. Factors that were properly to be taken into account in the formulation of policy were the abundant supply of well-trained technicians and applied scientists, the high educational attainments of Japanese workers, the disposition of the people as a whole towards saving, work and organised national effort, the presence of forceful innovators in both industry and government, and the generally high quality of management. It was management that found how to reconcile the ambition to achieve distinction in the capital-intensive, science-based industries with the existence of huge resources of (then) cheap labour. It has been remarked by all observers of the Japanese industrial scene that every large concern operates as the centre of a constellation of subsidiary companies or subcontractors, many of whom operate on a small scale. To them are entrusted processes which the parent firm finds cheaper to give out than to perform itself. These industries thus make the best of both worlds – that of high technology, massive capital equipment and a well-paid, permanent labour force, on one hand, and the world of labour-intensive, small or medium units of production using cheaper labour, on the other hand (Clark [2], p. 49 ff). Skill in organisation has made this consummation possible. How Japan has equipped herself with such competent managers is a matter to be discussed later, along with the question of whether Britain can emulate her in this respect.

Let us now turn to the mechanism of policy-making. By what process were the decisions reached and how were they carried out? We must begin with a consideration of the part played by the state in economic development and especially of the relation between the bureaucracy and private industry. It is paradoxical that the country which, of all advanced countries, has the smallest public sector and the lowest ratio of public expenditure to GNP is yet the country where the state has played a most constructive part in guiding the economy on its path upwards. It may help to solve this puzzle if we point to the contrast between Japan and Britain in the role of the state in the economy and in the relations between the bureaucracy and private industry.

In Britain (and in some other western countries) government intervention in the last century or so usually occurred as part of an effort to redress the deficiencies of the market economy. In general, the interests and purposes of government and of private enterprise were different. Politicians and civil servants occupied different camps from the industrialists. The latter might call on the government at times to defend their interests, but in general they regarded government as a power that curbed and frustrated their activities. In Japan this dichotomy was absent from the beginning of the modern era. Indeed, it was alien to the Confucian tradition inherited from times long past. There were, of course, occasions when businessmen found themselves in opposition to official measures. There were conflicts with the military in the *Junsenji Keizai* (quasi-war economy) period of the 1930s. There have been frequent disagreements about the activities of the Fair Trade Commission. There was effective resistance in some industries to the government's efforts to promote mergers and to oblige firms to adapt to common prices or investment policies in the 1960s. The motor firms in the 1970s tried in vain to persuade the government to abandon measures for controlling exhaust emissions from cars. But, in general, and certainly since the war, policy-making has been regarded as a combined operation in which both government and industry were aiming at the same target – rapid industrial growth.

To suppose that the government coerces industrialists into following policies worked out by politicians and bureaucrats is as false as the notion that big business dictates policy to the politicians of whom they are the paymasters (Tsukuda [12]). The Japanese way is to arrive at decisions by discussions that lead to a consensus. Since the war, when industry and government, with the ready agreement of the people as a whole, have been intent upon a single purpose (the rehabilitation and expansion of the economy), cooperation between the parties has been almost unqualified, disturbed occasionally by differences over means but seldom challenged in principle. This whole-hearted pursuit of a single objective goes far towards explaining Japan's achievements. The chief media for policy-making have been the Industrial Committees of MITI, where civil servants and industrialists meet to decide on future strategies and on the means required for reaching the goals agreed upon. One can easily exaggerate the influence of officials on the behaviour of individual firms. In 1963, soon after the Income-Doubling Plan had been put into operation, I asked the President of one of the chief companies whether his investment policy was being determined by the government's Plan or by his company's own judgement of market conditions. He replied, without hesitation, that it was the latter. (Of course, it may well be that the condition of the market was itself influenced by the impact of the government's Plan.) My conclusion is that the government's most important role has been first to see that finances were available to enable private firms to develop on the lines that they had persuaded the officials to approve, and secondly to provide incentives to investment in the most up-to-date equipment. It had many weapons at its command in ensuring conformity by individual firms to the agreed policies, as well as for the control of the economy in general. On the other hand, it is probable that, whatever the bureaucracy's initial stance, it usually yielded in the end to the importunities of powerful industrialists.

Let us consider in outline the means most commonly employed. Throughout the postwar period (though to a diminishing extent in the 1970s) industrialists have relied on the banks, especially the commercial banks, to supply them with the capital needed for expansion; in general, their equity–loan ratio has been very small. The commercial banks in turn have depended on the Bank of Japan to supply them with funds whenever, as often happened, they found themselves in an 'over-loan' position. The central monetary authorities, through what is called this 'indirect' system of industrial financing, were able to bend the lending policy of the commercial banks to the national purpose. Rates of interest were kept down and manipulated by rigid controls in order to encourage investment. By the so-called 'window' method (that is, qualitative controls over the allocation of loans according to the nature of the client's business), liquid capital was directed into approved destinations. The various official banks, notably the Japan Development Bank and the Export–Import Bank, supported selected projects, especially those related to exports, by granting loans at very low rates of interest. The government did not hesitate to afford the protection of high tariffs or quantitative import controls to industries chosen for development. It provided subsidies to cover costs of investment in new plants.

Firms intent on penetrating into foreign markets received especially favourable treatment. Export bills were discounted at a low rate and cheap long-term credit was given for export-related investments. The taxation system played a leading part in encouraging high investment by industrial concerns. Securities were exempted from capital gains tax; depreciation allowances were lavishly granted; and profits gained from approved projects, especially when connected with exports, were lightly taxed. Through various provisions in regard to special reserves and accelerated depreciation, revenues earned from exports were shielded from tax claims. Likewise, investments designed to bring about improvements in technical methods received tax concessions; for instance, a quarter of any increase in expenditure on R and D during the fiscal year has counted as a tax credit. The provisions for depreciation on plant used for R and D have meant that most of the original cost could be written off in the first year, and in this way the cash flow has been protected in the rapidly growing firms, which were favoured at the expense of the laggards. By its exchange controls, which in the first postwar decade were very elaborate, the government was able to safeguard 'infant' industries from foreign competition in the home market and to stimulate exports. Dumping was encouraged as a means of gaining a foothold in foreign markets.

A process of liberalisation began, under pressure from Japan's trading partners, in the early 1960s, although it was not until the middle 1970s that quantitative controls over imports of manufactures were finally abolished (except for a very few products). The scepticism with which the 'infant industry' argument is commonly greeted is without much justification in Japan's case. When the protected or subsidised industry has become competitive with its foreign rivals (as has usually happened after a few years), support has been withdrawn. As one of the policy-makers himself has stated, 'The policy was: carefully select industries, prevent ruinous competition at the infancy stage, nurse them to competitive stature and then expose them to outside competition.' He added that the principle was to 'phase out all protection' after a period of ten years (Okita [5], p. 97). In other words, the government's policy has been to encourage innovation and structural adaptation, rather than to protect the *status quo*.

By the 1970s industrial subsidies were of little importance and were small indeed compared with those given to British industries. Japanese manufacturers have not regarded protection and state financial assistance as the means to a quiet life. They have responded dynamically to the opportunities that the state has presented to them. In the last few years collaboration has taken a new form. The government has associated itself with private manufacturers and with the *Sogo Shosha* (general trading companies) in transferring certain labour-intensive industries to developing countries. Loans on favourable terms have been extended by the official banks to assist such ventures, as well as for the exploitation of raw material resources overseas (Ozawa [6], *passim*).

The contrast between Japanese and British industrial policy is well illustrated by comparing the experience of the steel industries of the two countries. At the end of the second world war the Japanese industry, besides being small by international standards, was relatively inefficient. Many of the finishing plants had depended on semi-products no longer available, since they had been supplied from Manchuria. MITI, in the early 1950s, drew up the first of several development plans which provided for the establishment, by the now de-nationalised industry, of new, up-to-date capacity located at deep-water sites so that it could handle the overseas fuel and ores brought to it in giant carriers. Assistance, in the form of generous depreciation allowances, various tax exemptions, and cheap loans from the official banks, financed the setting up by private firms of large, new, integrated plants on 'green field' sites. From these the bulk of the steel now comes. In technical efficiency, which depends in part on the economies of scale yielded by the plants, the Japanese steel industry is unmatched (Sato [8], chap. 6). Although the government encouraged the industry to form cartels to control prices and output in periods of recession, these in practice did little to restrain fierce competition among the producers. It was through the flexibility of their pricing during a recession in the early 1960s that Japan gained a footing in the United States, which later became a major customer for steel. The policy resulted in an astonishingly high growth in output – from 5 million tons in 1951 and 22 million tons in 1960 to 112 million tons in 1979.

Contrast this achievement with that of the British steel industry. In 1946 the British Iron and Steel Federation produced its postwar Plan, of which the outstanding features were the 'patching' of existing plants and the 'fair shares' accorded to established firms in its proposals for growth. (I was a member of the Ministry of Supply Committee that reported on the Federation's Plan.) After that the industry was nationalised, then de-nationalised and finally re-nationalised! Even during the period in which it remained in private hands its pricing policy was supervised by the Iron and Steel Board in the interests of 'stability', and it (and the Board) strongly resisted attempts to refer its restrictive practices to the Monopolies Commission. At a time when Japanese prices were flexible and the makers obliged by competition to respond quickly to changes in market conditions, the British steel industry was intent on preserving the *status quo*. When in 1958 it was realised that Britain needed an up-to-date strip mill, the Prime Minister decided, in the interests of regional employment, that the project should be divided so that half the capacity was set up in Scotland and half in South Wales. This decision left Britain with two suboptimal mills! It was not until the later 1960s that Britain had port facilities that enabled her steel makers to make full use of giant ore carriers.

It might have been expected that Japan, in her determination to improve her standing among the advanced nations, would have spent heavily on R and D. In fact, up to recently, the proportion of the national income spent in this way has been quite small by international standards. (Even in 1978 it was only 2.15 per cent, compared with 2.29 per cent for Britain, 2.46 for the US and 2.64 per cent for West Germany: Science and Technology Agency [9], p. 10.) This is partly because of her status as a disarmed country, for a large share of American and British R and D expenditure has been on defence. (In recent years, the proportion of R and D expenditure on defence was 2 per cent for Japan and 45 per cent for Britain and the US.) Another reason is that, for 30 years after the war, Japan was directing her efforts almost entirely to the import and assimilation of western technology. At a time when her problem was to catch up with the West, heavy expenditure on basic research would have been a waste of scarce resources badly needed for new equipment. For the same reason she was under no temptation to squander her substance on 'prestige' products, or those 'on the frontiers of knowledge'. In aircraft she wisely preferred to buy the products of foreign aircraft producers after their governments had spent lavishly on the R and D required before they were marketable. It is consistent with what has been said above that by far the larger part of Japan's total expenditure on R and D has been undertaken by private industry, and that it has been directed towards development work rather than to basic or even applied research. We have seen, however, that the government has assisted the research of private industry by grants and tax concessions. Now that Japan has achieved technological parity with other nations, more money is being spent by the government on basic and applied research both in its own research establishments and by universities and other institutions, often on contract from government departments. Much of this new expenditure is being directed towards work on environmental pollution, atomic energy, data processing and space research (Science and Technology Agency [10]).

The above reference to the small share of R and D that has been taken by defence prompts a further reflection. In the United States and Britain defence has absorbed not only a large proportion of total expenditure on R and D, but also the skill and energy of many brilliant scientists and technologists. Japan, on the other hand, has been able to direct nearly all her resources, human as well as financial, to civil industry and foreign trade.

This brief review of Japan's R and D illustrates the cool realism with which she has appraised her economic problem and the prudence with which she has used her scarce resources. In the early years of postwar development, investment was directed into the equipment most needed to raise productivity quickly, rather than into ancillary services, comforts or amenities. At that time I visited two new steel plants in which advanced equipment had been, or was being, installed. In both, the managers, in apologising for the bad state of the roadways and the mean condition of the offices, explained that they had to concentrate expenditure at that stage on the furnaces and mills themselves. Consider the contrast with the improvident British steel industry, which invested heavily in grand new London offices, while allowing its plants to degenerate into obsolescence.

This discussion has, I hope, thrown some light on the question of why state intervention worked so well in Japan and so unhappily in Britain. But more must be said. In Japan industry and government pursued a common purpose – growth and efficiency; whereas in Britain efficiency in practice occupied a low place in the government's (and perhaps the electorate's) scale of preferences, and there was little sympathy or community of purpose between industrialists and civil servants. Japanese industrialists, moreover, could rely on consistency in policy; the Liberal Democratic Party had been in office for almost the whole of the postwar period. Policies in regard to the economy as a whole and to individual industries did not, as in Britain, chop and change with alterations in the political mood. Private enterprise was given its head and was actively encouraged by the Japanese government, and, being assured of official goodwill, it was usually prepared, when necessary, to subdue its immediate ambitions to the public interest and to work within the guidelines set by common understandings between itself and the bureaucracy. What seems remarkable to a British observer is that this cooperation proved to be compatible with bitter rivalry in the market among individual firms and groups. This rivalry was especially apparent whenever a new product appeared. Then the chief groups fought vigorously with one another for what each of them considered its proper share. British businessmen, as the reports of the Monopolies Commission show, have usually been eager to enter into collusion with one another over prices and market shares. The contrary attitude of Japanese businessmen may be illustrated by the following example. I once described, to a company of Japanese public utility officials and civil servants, the cosy system under which the Post Office in Britain was supplied with telephone cable; whenever it needed supplies, the Post Office entered into agreements with the cable makers' cartel about the prices and quantities and left the cartel to share out the orders among its members. That, I was informed, could never happen in Japan, because the firms would never agree with one another about their respective shares. The allocation would have to be done, if at all, by the government.

The prevalence of this competitive fury in manufacturing industry is not derived from any theory of the merits of a free market. It is a function of the organisation of industry, indeed of society – the divisions into vertical groups in keen rivalry which only the state could qualify or moderate. Fierce competition has been particularly evident among small and medium-sized firms. Among them, whether they are subcontractors or produce directly for the consumer market, price competition is unrestrained. The flexibility in costs and prices (in the manufacturing sector) to which Japan owes much of her capacity to make adjustments to changing economic data can be ascribed in large measure to conditions in this sector.

The source of the dynamism that has distinguished Japanese management is a matter for debate. Toynbee might have found it in the challenge to survival that faced Japan after her defeat and ruin. Some Japanese economists stress the effects of the 'purges' of the leaders in government and industry that occurred in the early days of the American Occupation. The 'purges' swept aside the old-fashioned and over-cautious and opened the way to the young and enterprising. The dissolution of the *Zaibatsu*, for example, contributed considerably to the postwar vitality of the constituents of these groups. (In contrast, the British in the early postwar period were stuck with the leaders left over from the 1930s.)

The quality of the management also owes much to the country's educational system. From early *Meiji* times, or even before, Japan has been keenly aware of the importance of education, including vocational training at all grades, in promoting national prosperity. For many years it has been rare to find among those who adminster large enterprises persons who have not received an education appropriate to the work they have to do. So Japanese management has been in the hands of professionals, although, as the careers of S. Honda and K. Matsushita show, the way to industrial success has not been closed to entrepreneurs of genius, whatever their formal qualifications. Large companies have long been accustomed to recruit the most able graduates from the leading universities

and to give them a systematic training 'in the firm' for the jobs
they have to do.

It is significant that the majority of those who occupy top positions in industry have received a training in science or technology.
A recent inquiry showed that in the chief manufacturing companies
67 per cent of all seats on the boards of directors are occupied by
professional 'engineers' – the term 'engineers' in Japan covers men
trained in some applied science. The advantage of these qualifications in an era of advanced technology is unquestioned, for such
men are equipped to appraise the advice tendered to them by the
technical specialists who serve them. Similarly, a high proportion
of the civil servants in the administrative grades have received a
training in science, including social science. In the Ministry of Science and Technology, one third of the top officials are 'engineers',
and in the Agency for Industrial Science and Technology (a branch
of MITI) only one of the top officials is not an 'engineer'. Thus,
when the Japanese industrialist enters into discussions with officials
he can reasonably expect that the latter have sufficient training to
be able to understand the technical problems involved. Of the 601
universities and colleges in Japan (of very varying grades, it must
be admitted), 342 are concerned primarily with science and technology (Prentice [7]). In 1978 nearly 80,000 students obtained
bachelor's or master's degrees in engineering; the corresponding
figure for Britain (for 1977) was 10,000. In addition, some 15,000
Japanese graduated in engineering at junior colleges and colleges of
technology (Science and Technology Agency [9]). The number of
those engaged in commercial and business studies at different
grades is also very large indeed by British standards, and this has
been true for over half a century. The Japanese business world has
little use for the 'inspired amateur', with a general education but
no training in the disciplines relevant to the work that has to be
done.

In creating their modern educational system based on western
models, the Japanese were fortunate to escape the blight of the
Oxbridge tradition as it developed in the nineteenth century, with
its long neglect of science and technology, its bias in favour of the
professions, politics, public administration and journalism, and its
contempt for industry. In Japan a high proportion of the most
able graduates have for years sought their careers in commerce and
industry. They are encouraged to do so by the acclaim that at-
tends the business leaders as the source of the country's affluence.

The public are invited by newspapers to take part in polls designed to pick out the industrialists who, in the general view, have made the largest contribution to economic growth (Allen [1], p. 27). Thus, Japanese businessmen do their work in an environment of popular approval, whereas in Britain even the names of their counterparts are unknown to the general public. Management in Japan is an honoured profession and attracts some of the brightest spirits.

Much has been heard in the West of *Ringisei*, according to which proposals, initiated at any stage in the managerial hierarchy, are passed to and fro for discussion until a consensus has been reached. The system means that decision-making is prolonged, but once a conclusion has been reached execution is rapid, for everyone concerned is well versed in, and has approved of, the policy. Many proposals originate among the lower managers. It seems odd to outsiders that such a system should prevail in a society that sets great store by rank and order. The system has its blemishes and is not found in all firms; for instance, in some of the most rapidly growing companies since the war, authority has been exercised by the bosses who founded them. But over much of the business world it works well, and it has the merit of ensuring the whole-hearted cooperation of all concerned with management. It may, indeed, contribute to the effectiveness of certain techniques on which the Japanese lay great stress. One of these is quality control. In some businesses quality control is entrusted to units independent of the rest of the management and, where possible, there is in-built inspection of the production line. The result is that final inspection shops in, for instance, motor firms are very small, since errors are corrected *en route*. Japanese firms insist on high standards of performance, not only by their own workforce, but also by their suppliers. The most efficient of them have been able to reduce steeply the amount of capital locked up in stocks because they can rely on hour-to-hour deliveries by their suppliers. Since the Japanese manager has to operate in a fiercely competitive economy, he constantly exerts himself to discover cost-saving methods. A notable result of this obsession with costs occurred in the manufacture of colour television sets, where the number of components per set was halved in a few years and where production reached a scale that made it possible for most of them to be inserted automatically.

One field in which the Japanese are commonly held to be the superiors of the British or the Americans is that of personal relations. This superiority is demonstrated both in the treatment accorded to recruits to management and in the relations between management and the workers. Let us consider each in turn. In the West, when it is a question of filling a managerial post, the job is analysed and specified, and the chosen applicant is he who meets the specifications most exactly. In Japan the job-specification is wider and vaguer. Recruits are chosen for their qualities of character and education, and the job they are set to do is designed to accord with what, as experience shows, best fits these qualities. Moreover, one does not find in Japan the clear-cut distinction between management and the workforce that exists in Britain. The staff does not enjoy privileges withheld from the workpeople. All members of the firm eat in the same canteens and wear the same dress. As a British manager employed by a Japanese firm recently stated: 'In a Japanese firm it is difficult to tell where management begins and ends.'

As to industrial relations, these, according to the President of the Toyota Company, are central to the task of management. The chief features of the Japanese system are well known: 'enterprise unions', a commitment to lifetime employment, wages varying with age and seniority, extensive fringe benefits and a payments system that relates earnings to the prosperity of the firm, especially through the bi-annual bonuses. These arrangements are not universal. The negotiations of the seamen and national railway workers are nationwide in scope. The privileges accorded to 'regular' workers are not enjoyed by 'temporary' workers, of whom there is a significant proportion in most companies. Nor are small firms able to guarantee lifetime employment or to provide lavish fringe benefits. Seniority wages are increasingly qualified by merit payments. So the scene is one of variety, and this is part of Japan's strength as an industrial country and is the source of the flexibility for which she is distinguished. The differential wage system provides the manufacturer with alternative ways of organising production and is a key to the country's competitive efficiency in many lines. Similarly, the lifetime employment and seniority wage systems – where they prevail – along with the absence of inter-union conflict, remove from organised workers any temptation to resist technical change, and keep firms free of jurisdictional or demarcation disputes. Together these constituents of the industrial relations system offer a prescription for industrial harmony that even the long recession of the middle 1970s did not disturb. The seniority wage system, moreover, has exercised a discriminatory effect in favour of growing firms and against those with stagnant trade, for the former employ a higher proportion of young, and therefore relatively cheap, labour than the latter.

The extent to which workers identify their interests with those of the firm is well brought out by Professor R. Dore in his book, *British Factory – Japanese Factory* [3]. If a Japanese worker is asked what his job is, he is likely to reply: 'I work for Hitachi, or Sony, or Nissan.' The British worker's reply to such a question would be to designate his occupation or craft. The Japanese foreman, Professor Dore points out, is the spokesman of a group, not simply the agent of the management for the execution of its orders. The workers' acceptance of a common interest with the management is demonstrated by their practice of forming voluntary groups of shop floor workers, or technicians, with the object of discovering ways of increasing productivity. Such a group at Nippon Steel's Nagoya works was responsible for overcoming the difficulties that attended the introduction of hot direct rolling, by which the costs of reheating the slabs were eliminated. This is just one example of the many improvements in technical or managerial methods that have emerged 'from below' and been readily adopted by firms.

This survey has indicated some of the factors to which Japan's achievements in industrial innovation can be ascribed. To what extent can Britain be persuaded to accept her as a tutor in the areas in which her superiorities have been demonstrated? The reply is sometimes given that the qualities that have fitted Japan for economic success in an era of high technology and large-scale organisation have been inherited from the past, and that the British would have to become Japanese before they could accept Japan as a model. But this objection must be questioned, for many of the qualities and practices that are considered peculiarly Japanese today were not conspicuous until recently. For instance, social and industrial harmony, which many would say are at the root of her achievements, were decidedly lacking before the second world war. Consider the bitter struggles between factions in the Army and Navy, between the military and the *Zaibatsu*, between the tenant farmers and the landlords, to mention only a few. Japan's system of industrial relations, now the admiration of the world, has been a product of the postwar years. The 'enterprise union', for instance, scarcely existed, for trade unions as a whole were oppressed by the authorities and their membership very small. Lifetime employment was not characteristic of an industrial system in which the majority of factory employees were young female textile operators whose working life was two or three years. Public opinion polls show that today about nine tenths of the Japanese people regard themselves as middle class. The results of such inquiries would have been very different forty or fifty years ago, when nearly half the occupied population were impoverished peasants. Since the war one of the chief sources of economic strength has been the priority assigned by policy to industrial efficiency and economic growth. In the 1930s the government, being in the hands of those intent above all else on imperialist expansion, was often at odds with the industrialists. The fact is that the challenge faced by Japan at the end of the war was met by a change of national purpose and the opening up of new paths to its attainment, although, of course, her response was influenced, though not determined, by her historical social endowment. The changes that Britain would have to make in her institutions and system of priorities, if she is to arrest her decline, are scarcely greater than those made by Japan after 1945. Let me then offer suggestions about what might be done:

(1) One of the most glaring contrasts between Japan and Britain is to be found in the quality of leadership in government and industry. For many years past industry has failed to recruit a high proportion of the most able men and its laggardliness in adapting innovations has been one of the results of its administration by the second-rate, and often by the under-trained second-rate at that. The civil service, while it is the preferred career of some of the most able graduates, is largely composed of men who lack the training required to fit them to handle the problems of an age of high technology, and whose education has left them, in the main, without any sympathy with, or understanding of, the business world. (An economic adviser to the Federation of British Industries complained to me, in the days when I was a temporary civil servant, that most of my colleagues in the Board of Trade seemed to regard businessmen as rogues!) Japan's educational system has produced an élite equipped to cope with the technical and economic problems of the modern world. Britain's élite, despite many admirable qualities, is not so well equipped, as the long succession of failures in economic judgement since the war demonstrates. Lately only 7 per cent of the recruits to the administrative class of the civil service have taken their examination in science, and this at the time when the government is responsible for a high proportion of the country's investment, and

when civil servants are called upon to give advice on issues of great scientific and technological complexity.

The government, through its educational policy, and industry, through differential salary scales, can influence strongly the supply of talented men trained in science and technology. The government could fix quotas for the proportion of scientifically trained admissions to the administrative and executive grades. It must be admitted that the quality of engineers in Britain does not compare favourably with that of their counterparts in Japan (and elsewhere), especially as industrial administrators. The education of the Japanese engineer seems to fit him for administrative as well as for technical posts. The criticism is often heard that the training of the British engineer, in its higher reaches, is too narrow to allow him to cultivate commercial aptitudes; to put a financially illiterate engineer in charge of a business is to invite ruin. I suspect, however, that the explanation of the contrast lies in the high proportion of first-class talent that is attracted to the engineering profession in Japan, for their training in management takes place in the firms that employ them. In Britain the low prestige and remuneration of engineers discourage many men of high talent from embarking on that career.

(2) Much of Japan's continued success can be ascribed to her refusal to bolster up failures, and to the incentives given to entrepreneurs for investment in new techniques and product innovations. If Britain's decline is to be halted, efficiency and technical progress must rank as a priority in policy-making (as in Japan), even if this leads immediately to the neglect of other purposes on which she sets store. The fiscal and financial incentives offered to Japan's new industries, *until they have reached maturity*, should be studied and emulated. The British obsession with the conflict of 'Private Enterprise versus the State' should be expunged. It is not the *extent* of government intervention, or the amount of government expenditure on industry, that counts; it is the purpose, nature and quality of the intervention that are crucial. The size of the public sector in Japan is exceptionally small – and its financial record no better than in Britain – but government intervention, directed primarily towards raising productivity, has been extensive and fruitful. This applies to the activities of the local authorities as well as to those of the central government. High and continuous investment in innovations will not be undertaken by industry if the political environment

is not congenial to it – and consistently so. In Japan the bureaucracy, the politicians and the industrialists, have usually worked
together for the same end. In Britain relations among them have
been marred by mutual distrust and by inconstancy in policy.

(3) The harmony in industrial relations enjoyed by the Japanese
since the war has been made possible by deliberately contrived innovations in the wage and employment systems, and in methods of
bargaining. In the factories first-rate men have been put in charge
of industrial relations, and management has encouraged the cooperation of workers of every grade by the uniformity of treatment
accorded to all 'regular' members of the firm. It has also exerted
itself to the utmost to ensure that, when changes are planned,
everyone in the company is fully informed. There is constant inter-
flow of information throughout every establishment, and the management is at pains to ensure that the information is widely ap-
prehended. The Japanese believe that their system of industrial
communication is an essential condition of the avoidance of
disputes through misunderstandings, and the British might with
advantage follow their example.

(4) As long as British trade unions function as a permanent
opposition to the management, one serious barrier to increased
productivity and prosperity will remain. The advantages of the
Japanese system lie in the cooperation of workers and management
in promoting innovations, the avoidance of demarcation disputes,
and the wage differentials which vary both with local conditions
and with the prosperity of the firm. These wage differentials are a
key to Japan's success in organising her industry, for they present
the entrepreneur with a wide choice of technical alternatives. Britain
cannot enjoy these advantages unless she escapes from the institutional impasse in which she finds herself. However, some of the
arrangements for joint bargaining between a firm and the several
unions representing its employees seem to work reasonably well
(e.g. in ICI). If they became more widespread, they might go some
way towards avoiding, at least, inter-union quarrels.

(5) It has been suggested that, in planning investment, the British
firm's perspective is very short (compared with the Japanese coun-
terpart), and that this explains the failure of Britain to introduce
massive innovations and far-reaching structural changes, as the
Japanese have done. The contrast may be explained partly by dif-

ferences in the quality of leadership, but mainly by the less congenial political environment in which the British firm operates; for instance, the inconstancy of economic policy.

(6) The fierce rivalry that exists among industrial groups in Japan has been incompatible with collusive arrangements and has meant that most cartels have had a feeble influence on the price and output policies of individual firms. It is this disposition rather than any theoretical attachment to the virtues of the free market, or the activities of the Fair Trade Commission, to which Japan owes the competitive character of her industrial system, a character that prevails even among oligopolists. Since the British industrialist has shown himself all too ready to enter into collusive arrangements, the British government has a particularly compelling reason for attacking restrictive practices.

(7) Finally, the Japanese can offer one general prescription for material success. Unlike the British, they have shown since the war a laudable disposition to submit political and economic doctrines to the restraints of commonsense.

References
 [1] Allen, G. C., *The British Disease* (2nd edn), London, Institute of Economic Affairs, 1979.
 [2] Clark, R., *The Japanese Company*, Yale University Press, 1979.
 [3] Dore, R. *British Factory–Japanese Factory*, London, Allen and Unwin, 1973.
 [4] Ministry of International Trade and Industry (MITI), *The Vision of MITI Policy in 1980s*, Tokyo, March 1980.
 [5] Okita, S., *The Developing Economies and Japan*, University of Tokyo Press, 1980.
 [6] Ozawa, T., *Multinationalism, Japanese Style*, Princeton University Press, 1979.
 [7] Prentice, H. A. J., *Japan's Technology and Industry*, British Embassy, Tokyo, February 1979.
 [8] Sato, K. (ed.), *Industry and Business in Japan*, London, Croom Helm, 1980.
 [9] Science and Technology Agency, *Indicators of Science and Technology*, Tokyo, 1980.
[10] —, *1978 White Paper on Science and Technology*, Tokyo, October 1979.
[11] Shinohara, M., 'Japanese-type industrial policy' (paper presented to Industrial Policy Symposium, Madrid), OECD, May 1980.
[12] Tsukuda, C., 'Public policy for new industries: Japanese experience' (paper presented to Industrial Policy Symposium, Madrid), OECD, May 1980.

7(I)   Technology in British Industry: a Suitable Case for Improvement

by Keith Pavitt*

Technology, R and D, and Industrial Performance

At the present time British industry's overall performance compared to that of other OECD countries is poor, whether measured in terms of costs, profits, investment or export shares. Much of the policy debate is about short-term instruments influencing wages and other incomes, interest rates and the exchange rate. Yet other OECD countries perform better in spite of much higher levels of wages, and sometimes with high interest rates and steeply rising exchange rates. This is because their industries operate on the whole closer than British industry to international best-practice techniques, which use factors of production more efficiently and therefore allow higher wages at a given level of profitability. If the objective of industrial policy is to reach the levels of industrial employment and real wages prevailing in the richer OECD countries, we must try to understand why Britain lags behind international best practice, and see what can be done to reduce the lag.

Investment and technology

As Salter showed about twenty years ago, the rate of investment determines the vintages of production techniques embodied in the capital stock [42]. In the UK, the rate of industrial investment – per employee and as a proportion of output – has been relatively low [8]. Nabseth and Ray showed in the early 1970s that selected major process innovations diffused more slowly in the UK

* This paper draws on research financed by the Leverhulme Trust on technical innovation and British industrial competitiveness. I am grateful to colleagues at Sussex University for valuable comments and criticisms.

than in many other European countries [29]: see also J. Aylen in [39].

A high and sustained rate of investment is a necessary condition for the reduction of the productivity gap between British industry and that of the major OECD countries. But it is not a sufficient condition. Over the past fifteen years, the so-called 'neo-technology' theories of international trade have offered persuasive explanations of the comparative advantage of high-wage industrialised countries in terms of technological advance (see, for example, Soete [45]). Continuous improvement in technology – defined broadly as knowledge of industrial techniques – is also necessary, as a means both of improving the efficiency of investment, and of creating opportunities for investment.

Studies by Enos [14] and others show that reaching and improving current best-practice productivity with a new piece of equipment takes time, and depends on 'learning'. The capacity to learn from experience depends in part on the technical and organisational skills of management and the labour force. In capital-intensive process industries producing standard bulk materials, important components of these skills are R and D and design activities in the industries and amongst equipment suppliers. The productivity of British industrial investment has on the whole been relatively low (see, for example, NEDO [30]). This could be explained partly by the peculiarities of British labour relations, and by the cumulative effects of inefficiencies resulting from slow growth, but it could also be in part a consequence of low rates of technological improvement.

Not all technical improvements are cost-reducing process innovations. In fact, most are product innovations, a significant proportion of which improve performance rather than reduce costs: increased value-added is sought through greater product utility, as well as through fewer factor inputs. Such product innovation plays a significant role in international industrial competition. M. Posner and A. Steer in [3] concluded that unfavourable price trends could not explain British industry's poor competitive performance between the mid-1960s and mid-1970s. Stout [46] and Saunders [43] have shown that British engineering goods in the 1970s were on the whole cheaper than those from France and Germany, but that they remained relatively uncompetitive. R. Rothwell in [39] and Sciberras [44] have shown that in specific sectors British customers have been willing to pay more for greater technical sophistication in foreign machinery and consumer durables when they believe that the increased purchase price is more than offset by savings over the equipment's lifetime.

Is innovation a consequence of induced investment, or a cause of autonomous investment? Examples can be found along the whole spectrum between these two extremes. In the case of radical innovations in products or processes, many economic historians and other writers in the Schumpeterian tradition argue that investment opportunities are derived from the major and widespread markets opened up. Writers like Mensch [28] have claimed that a slow-down in radical innovation has been one of the major causes of sluggish industrial growth in the 1970s. However, Clarke *et al.* argue that the available empirical evidence does not support such a conclusion [7].

R and D, investment and exports

R and D activities are major sources of technology and technical knowledge, whether radical and major breakthroughs, routine improvements, or the assimilation and learning activities necessary for the effective use of innovations developed elsewhere. Chart 7.1 shows a tendency for countries' civilian R and D to rise as a percentage of GDP as GDP per head approaches the US level. The UK has hardly moved towards the best-practice frontier in terms of either civilian R and D as a percentage of GDP, or GDP per head. Unlike most other major OECD countries, British industry's trend in R and D has not been strongly correlated with its trend in investment [38]. The overall lack of movement by British industry towards the world technical frontier has also begun to show up in the structure of manufactured exports. A number of recent studies have shown that most high-wage countries increased the proportion of their manufactured exports in technology-intensive product groups between the 1960s and the mid-1970s, the increase being particularly marked for Japan [1], [8]. The composition of British manufacturing exports seems to be moving hardly at all in this direction. This writer and Soete have shown in [39] that, in 1974, differences in export shares amongst the industrially advanced countries in technology-intensive product groups (broadly speaking, capital goods, chemicals and durable consumer goods) were closely correlated with national differences in levels of innovative activities. British industry was well behind Germany, Sweden, Switzerland and the Netherlands in relative levels of innovative

Chart 7.1   Civilian R and D as proportion of GDP, and GDP per head relative to the United States, 1963–75

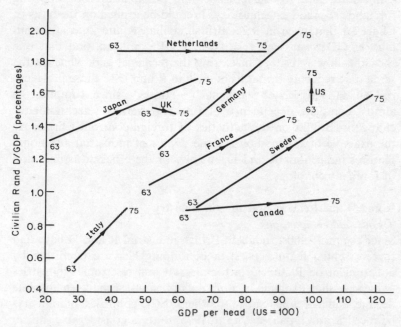

Sources: [33], [35].

activities and export shares in many technology-intensive sectors. In military-related equipment, however, UK performance held up better.

R and D and the objective of industrial policy
Thus, over the past fifteen to twenty years, British industrial R and D has – by comparison with that in most other EEC countries and Japan – stagnated; it has not been closely related to trends in investment, and has not resulted in shifts in the structure of British manufactured exports. The implications of these trends for future policy depend on three sets of assumptions: first, that an efficient manufacturing sector is a necessary condition for a high-wage economy; second, that technological improvements for high-wage manufacturing industry will be equally, if not more important, in future (see OECD [35]). The third set concerns the role of British R and D. Given that many British firms are behind current best-

practice techniques, and that Britain is as a consequence relatively poor, R and D must be severely constrained by what the country can afford, and by the considerable possibilities for importing foreign best-practice technology. It could be argued on the basis of Chart 7.1 that, even in 1975, British civilian R and D as a percentage of GDP was high relative to GDP per head, and that one should follow a strategy of closing the technical gap, whilst at the same time reducing the levels of civilian R and D to those prevalent in Canada. This writer rejects such a strategy, since it implies the almost complete dependence of future patterns of technological change in Britain on the activities of foreign-controlled firms. As the example of Japan shows, some degree of industrial autonomy requires indigenous R and D, if only for the efficient assimilation of foreign technology.

R and D and Related Activities in Industry
Trends and comparisons
Since the mid-1960s, trends in British industrial R and D have had three essential features: first, a continuing heavy expenditure by government on R and D in the aircraft and electronics industries (which we shall examine in more detail below); second, an absolute decline, and a decline relative to other OECD countries, of industry-financed R and D, at least up to 1975; third, a considerable shift in the composition of industrial R and D, with chemicals and perhaps electronics holding up much better than engineering and aerospace. The last two features emerge clearly from Tables 7.1 – 3 (Table 7.3 uses numbers of patents granted in the US as a proxy measure of innovative activities; for a discussion of its strengths and weaknesses see Pavitt and Soete in [39]).

Table 7.1 shows that the absolute decline in British industrial R and D was particularly marked between 1969 and 1975, and that there was an increase between 1975 and 1978. The US share of OECD industrial R and D also went down between 1967 and 1975, mainly reflecting a decline in government-funded R and D, whilst the British decline was mainly in industry-financed R and D (Table 7.2). France, Germany and Japan all increased their shares of OECD industrial R and D between 1967 and 1975 (Table 7.2). The rapid increase in Japan's share of foreign patenting in the US (Table 7.3) probably reflects a shift in emphasis in Japanese R and D away from the assimilation and improvement of foreign-based technology towards indigenous invention and innovation.

Table 7.1 *Trends in British manufacturing R and D expenditure,*[a]
1964–78 (indices at constant prices, 1967 = 100)

	1964	1969	1972	1975	1978
All manufactured products	92	100	93	87	102
(Industry-financed)	(86)	(97)	(86)	(84)	(102)
Chemical, etc. products	91	109	107	114	133
(Industry-financed)	(92)	(109)	(108)	(112)	(136)
Mechanical engineering	74	86	61	67	77
(Industry-financed)	(77)	(89)	(68)	(77)	(89)
Electronics	78	108	106	98	155
(Industry-financed)	(74)	(120)	(104)	(85)	(133)
Other electrical engineering	90	92	74	80	75
(Industry-financed)	(95)	(94)	(66)	(75)	(68)
Motor vehicles	88	99	86	78	79
(Industry-financed)	(89)	(101)	(87)	(79)	(77)
Aerospace	110	99	103	82	80
(Industry-financed)	(70)	(32)	(62)	(59)	(90)
Other manufacturing	96	98	81	78	84
(Industry-financed)	(97)	(100)	(79)	(78)	(92)

Sources: [5], [11], [12].

[a]Deflated using the Department of Industry R and D deflator (see [12]) and with the help of information provided by the Department.

Between 1964 and 1978, UK R and D held up better in the chemical and electronics industries than in aerospace and engineering, the former increasing from 61 to 129 per cent of the latter. The UK chemical industry increased its share of R and D of the OECD industry between 1967 and 1975 (Table 7.2); its performance was particularly striking in agricultural chemicals and drugs, where it sharply increased its share of US foreign patenting between 1963 and 1978 (Table 7.3).

Table 7.2   *Shares in OECD industrial R and D,[a] 1967–75*
(*percentages*)

	Total R and D		Industry-financed	
	1967	1975	1967	1975
United States	62.9	51.4	49.4	45.7
France	6.4	6.9	5.9	6.2
Germany	8.6	11.4	11.6	12.5
Japan	7.3	12.8	11.9	17.3
United Kingdom				
Aerospace	8.9	11.4	..	..
Electronic, electrical	8.7	7.6	9.4	5.4
Chemical	8.5	8.7	..	..
Other transport	8.9	6.4	..	..
Machinery	12.6	7.3	..	..
Metals, metal products	11.3	7.5	..	..
Chemical-linked[b]	16.6	13.5	..	..
Total	*9.7*	*8.7*	*10.7*	*7.6*

Source: [34] (.. = not available).

[a]OECD industrial R and D:
  For totals and chemical 11 countries (Belgium, Canada, France, Germany, Italy, Japan, Netherlands, Sweden, Switzerland, UK, US)
  For chemical-linked 10 countries (as above less Switzerland)
  For all other categories 9 countries (as above less Netherlands).
[b]Food, drink and tobacco; textiles and footwear; rubber and plastics.

Although British aerospace R and D declined steadily in absolute terms between 1964 and 1978 (Table 7.1), its share of the OECD total actually increased between 1967 and 1975 (Table 7.2), mainly because of a more rapid absolute decline in the US. British R and D has also held up strongly in absolute terms in the chemical-linked sectors, mainly because of the long-standing British strength in food processing. The most striking relative decline (Table 7.2) has been in mechanical engineering, metals and other transport. In electronic products, the trend in British R and D is ambiguous. The recent and welcome recovery of R and D must be set against the longer-term decline in the OECD share, and the heavy dependence on the military.

Table 7.3 Shares in foreign patenting in the United States, 1963–78 (percentages)

	1963	1967	1971	1975	1978
France	10	11	10	9	9
Germany	27	26	25	24	24
Japan	5	10	18	25	28
United Kingdom					
Chemicals					
Industrial	17	15	11	11	11
Plastics, etc.	11	15	12	9	8
Agricultural	10	15	10	12	16
Drugs	9	15	10	13	15
Total	*16*	*16*	*11*	*11*	*12*
Machinery					
Engines, etc.	38	30	22	14	10
Farm, garden	17	20	18	12	11
Machine tools	23	18	15	13	9
Office	22	21	17	11	10
Other	22	19	16	12	10
Total	*23*	*20*	*16*	*12*	*10*
Electric equipment					
Transmission, etc.	21	22	18	9	11
Household appliances	15	17	15	9	7
Lighting, wiring	17	21	16	20	14
Total	*22*	*19*	*18*	*12*	*11*
Electronic equipment					
Radio, TV	26	21	14	9	10
Communications	28	22	17	13	12
Total	*28*	*22*	*17*	*13*	*11*
TOTAL UK	21	19	16	12	11

Source: Office of Technology Assessment and Forecasts, *7th Report*, Washington DC, USGPO, 1977; and information supplied to Science Policy Research Unit, Sussex.

In spite of these generally unfavourable trends in British industrial R and D, it is still widely believed that the main reasons for Britain's technological backwardness lie elsewhere, and relate first to shortcomings in other activities necessary for effective innovation (in particular, production engineering and marketing), second to insufficient use of foreign technology, and third to inadequate industrial skills. The (incomplete) evidence suggests that each of these three explanations has partial validity, depending on the industrial sector or the time period considered, but that the level and deployment of British industrial R and D remains an essential part of the problem.

The balance of innovative activities

The belief that the weaknesses in Britain's innovative activities are downstream from R and D grew up in the 1960s, when Williams [50] and others showed that the percentage of GDP spent on R and D was higher than in other Western European countries, although the rate of growth in industrial productivity was lower. He concluded that, given the scarcity of qualified scientists and engineers, the high level of British R and D led to an imbalance between R and D and the downstream functions necessary for successful innovation. With the benefit of hindsight, one can argue that Williams's analysis did not capture the differing trends in non-defence R and D in the developed countries (see [15]). It is certainly difficult to argue today that, outside defence, Britain spends 'too much' on R and D activities.

A related line of argument criticises the present balance of activities within British R and D, claiming that Britain has in fact made a major contribution to radical inventions and innovations, but has been less successful in profiting commercially from them, because of lack of the improvement innovations, and of the engineering and marketing support, necessary to obtain a large market share and to benefit from economies of scale. Evidence in support of this comes from a US study [32] where the 500 innovations in Canada, France, Japan, the UK, the US and Germany, over the period from 1953 to 1973, that were considered by national experts to be most important technologically, economically and socially are identified. Data were collected on just under 400 of these innovations, enabling them to be classified as shown in Table 7.4; the proportion of the British innovations in the category 'radical breakthrough' was much greater than that of any other country, and that in 'improvement of existing technology' much smaller.

However, as with the previous analysis, there remain difficulties of statistical data and interpretation, and of historical perspective. The sample of innovations is small and probably unrepresentative: for example, Germany is allocated half as many innovations as Britain. The distinction between the categories is difficult and

Table 7.4 *Distribution of types of innovation in five countries,*
1953–73 (percentages)

	US	France	Germany	Japan	UK
Improvement of existing technology	41	12	36	38	4
Major technological advance	31	65	50	54	40
Radical breakthrough	27	24	14	8	56
Number of innovations covered	*237*	*17*	*22*	*26*	*45*

Source: [32]

somewhat arbitrary: aircraft innovations, where Britain was strong, may have been classified as more 'radical' than machinery innovations, where Germany was strong. It can also be argued that the period from 1953 to 1973 was transient and historically atypical, especially in the 1950s, when R and D in Britain was relatively much higher than in the rest of Western Europe.

Imports and exports of technology
In the world production of technology, Britain is now a small country. Again it was Williams who pointed out in the 1960s that improvements in British industrial practice depended heavily on imports of best-practice techniques from other countries [50].

One important source of foreign technology is embodied in imports of foreign capital goods. Between 1968 and 1976, British imports as a proportion of home demand increased on average from 20 to 30 per cent in mechanical engineering, 30 to 54 per cent in instrument engineering and 14 to 32 per cent in electrical engineering [49]. This was part of the process, observable in all OECD countries, of intra-industry specialisation, since British exports also grew rapidly as a proportion of output. In addition, however, studies by Rothwell of agricultural and textile machinery in [39] suggest that, in sectors where British imports have grown rapidly, part of the reason may have been the technical inferiority of British capital goods. Rapid growth of import penetration in capital goods may thus reflect in part the purchase of foreign technology to compensate for British deficiencies in design, development and innovation.

There is also a considerable international commerce in technical knowledge, through licensing agreements, and through transfers within multinational firms. Data on monetary receipts and payments for technology collected by national governments, and recently brought together by the Science and Technology Indicators Unit at the OECD, enable us to make some international comparisons. Vickery ([47], [48] and letter to the author, 10 October 1980) warns that these data are not good indicators of the national level of technical practice, since annual payments and receipts reflect agreements reached in previous years for which payments continue, often as a percentage of sales. He suggests, however, that the data can be used as indicators of the international diffusion of technology, provided that a number of imperfections are borne in mind: differing definitions and methods of collection amongst countries; the imperfect pricing of technology in cross-frontier transactions of multinational firms; the international flows of disembodied technology that are not captured by monetary transactions.

If the UK has been importing relatively 'too little' foreign technology, one would expect a low ratio of British expenditures on foreign technology to industrial output or to indigenous R and D, relative to more successful countries. In fact Table 7.5 shows that quite the opposite was the case in 1975, when the UK ratios were higher than those for France, Germany, Japan or the US. However, it also emerges from Table 7.5 that the UK has on the whole a high propensity to export its technology through licensing and direct investment. The ratios of British technological receipts to R and D and to industrial output in 1975 were closer to the US levels than to those of France, Germany and Japan (see also A. D. Morgan in [3]).

This raises intriguing questions in the light of recent work by Krugman [23] on the theory of international trade and industrial production. From a model in which product innovation is the source of the advanced countries' competitive advantage, he concludes that the world pattern of industrial production is determined jointly by the rate of innovation and by the rate of its international diffusion, and that the welfare of an industrially advanced country can be maintained or increased only if its rate of increase of in-

Table 7.5 *Some international comparisons of technological receipts and payments*

	US	France	Germany	Japan	UK
			(US $ millions)		
Payments	473	514	720	697	483
Receipts	4008	192	308	142	491
			(percentages)		
Payments/industry-financed R and D	3.0	21.5	15.4	12.2	25.4
Payments/manufacturing output	0.10	0.54	0.46	0.45	0.59
Receipts/industry-financed R and D	25.4	8.0	6.6	2.5	25.9
Receipts/manufacturing output	0.91	0.20	0.20	0.14	0.60
			(percentages p.a.)		
Growth rate of:					
Receipts[a]	10.9	12.5	15.3	24.4	13.7
Industry-financed R and D[b]	7.6	15.2	15.6	21.0	10.0

Sources: [15], [32], [36], [47].

[a]Over periods 1966–77 (US), 1963–78 (France), 1963–79 (Germany), 1965–77 (Japan), 1962–78 (UK).
[b]Over periods 1966–77 (US), 1962–77 (France and Germany), 1963–77 (Japan), 1962–78 (UK).

novation is equal to, or greater than, its rate of increase of international diffusion of technology.

The last two rows in Table 7.5 show these two rates for five countries, computed on the assumption that the rates of increase in innovation and international diffusion are the same as the rates of increase in industry-financed R and D and in receipts for technology. The figures suggest that the innovation increase is *less* than the diffusion increase for the UK, and also for the US and Japan; the Japanese figures, however, may not be representative of later experience, given the very low initial level of technology exports.

In 1975, 27 foreign-controlled firms were amongst the 100 largest R and D spenders in British industry. R and D expenditures by foreign firms increased from 15 to 17 per cent of the total between 1972 and 1975 [12]. The most striking increase was from 11 to 24 per cent in mechanical engineering, where foreign-controlled firms spent a higher percentage of their sales on R and D. In the upper quartile of firms in the chemical industry, the ratio of R and D to sales was 3.85 per cent for foreign firms, compared with 2.00 per cent for British firms. This reflects the presence in the UK of foreign pharmaceutical companies with strong R and D facilities.

According to a survey of 500 large US firms by Creamer [9], the UK, Canada and Germany are the most important locations for foreign R and D activities by American-controlled firms. Such firms accounted for at least 60 per cent of foreign firms' R and D in the UK in 1975, where it was concentrated in the chemical and transport industries (and not in mechanical engineering as in Germany). Between 1966 and 1975, US firms' R and D in the UK decreased slightly in real terms, and Germany displaced the UK as the most favoured location for US firms' R and D in Europe.

If anything these international comparisons suggest that British firms should be doing more R and D. This could increase the rate of learning and improvement of foreign technology, increase the scale and benefits of foreign firms' R and D in the UK and offset the steady – and inevitable – export of British technology to other countries.

Industrial skills
Accurate quantitative comparisons of industrial skills amongst industries and countries do not yet exist because of the difficulties of collecting data and comparing different qualifications. None the less, many studies show that, until recently, formal education and training have not been a part of British industrial recruitment to the same extent as in many other OECD countries.

Fewer managers and engineers have had formal post-secondary education and training related to their jobs; industrial management and engineering professions have had relatively low status amongst graduates; the intellectual and professional élites have on the whole sought accomplishment in careers other than industry (see A. Albu and N. Swords-Isherwood in [39]). Progress has been made in remedying some of these deficiencies. For example, since the second world war, the number of engineers graduating from British universities has increased considerably and so, as a consequence, has the proportion of practising, professional engineers who are graduates. Some important problems remain, and many have been discussed by the Finniston Committee [13]. Data collected by Marsh *et al.* [27] suggest that the British chemical industry might be closer to its foreign counterparts in its level of professionalism than the British engineering industries.

Until recently much less attention has been given to another British deficiency in skills, namely, the general level of vocational training of the industrial workforce. Statistics are incomplete, and international comparisons can only be rough, but two recent reports [18], [40] both estimated that the proportion of young people entering apprenticeships after the period of compulsory school was between 45 and 50 per cent in Germany, but less than 20 per cent in the UK; and one report estimated that the proportion of the young entering all forms of vocational education in Britain was lower than in all other EEC countries except Ireland.

Policies for R and D
Three conclusions emerge from the above data and analysis. First, many of the difficulties of British industry in improving its technology are complementary and interrelated. There is little point in arguing over whether the biggest obstacle to innovation is inadequate R and D, or inadequate design, or inadequate marketing, or inadequate production engineering, when there are inadequacies in all four. We shall therefore discuss the problems of stimulating R and D in British industry, on the understanding that this cannot and should not be separated from the other features of technological improvement.

Second, the British government plays a significant role in financing R and D, and thereby influencing patterns of technological advance in industry. We shall examine the volume and impact of these measures, where possible making comparisons with other countries.

Third, there are clear differences amongst British industrial sectors in the degree to which they appear able to keep up with the world's pace of technological progress. We shall therefore discuss briefly some of the possibilities and problems of developing sectoral policies for R and D and technical advance.

Encouraging industry-financed R and D and related activities
The absolute and relative decline of British industrial R and D cannot be attributed to the absolute and relative decline of British industrial output, but to the diminishing proportion of output that

many British industrialists have been willing or able to spend on R and D and related activities. As a result of interviews with industrialists, Rubenstein *et al.* [41] concluded that the most important factor influencing the propensity to spend on innovative activities was the general economic climate. Unlike nearly all other major OECD countries, the decline in manufacturing profitability in Britain between 1967 and 1975 was accompanied by a decline in industry-financed R and D (see [21], [37]). If the causality runs from profits to R and D, we can only be pessimistic about the effects of the profit squeeze in 1980 on the recovery in R and D expenditure between 1975 and 1978.

The belief that trends in industrial R and D activities and innovation are sensitive to a variety of market signals is naturally entrenched in the economics profession and amongst policy-makers. It is at the foundation of two radically different views of the way British industry can be made to modernise: the present government's policy of partial industrial disengagement, on the one hand, and the advocacy of across-the-board industrial protection, on the other.

In its simplest form, the present government's policy assumes that disengagement will increase the pace at which efficient firms displace inefficient firms, and at which inefficient firms change themselves into efficient ones. To be successful as a policy for British industrial regeneration, one of two conditions must be met: either that efficient British firms exist to replace the inefficient ones, or that inefficient British firms can be rapidly transformed into efficient ones. Experience suggests, however, that in many sectors neither of these conditions holds.

Cripps and Godley [10] advocate across-the-board tariffs or quotas as a means of increasing the demand for British goods, and consequently raising the expectations, the investment rates and the efficiency of British industry. In a world of rapid responses to shifts in demand, of capital-embodied process innovation, and of rapid learning by doing, such a policy would certainly be successful, but it would not be necessary in the first place. The problem is that British industry responds sluggishly to demand growth, as is shown by international comparisons of manufacturing import and export elasticities with respect to income (Stout in [3]).

Across-the-board tariffs or quotas would also increase the price, or reduce the availability, of foreign capital goods. In an industrial system of growing complexity and specialisation, and where British-designed capital goods are often backward, this would reduce the gains in productivity of British industrial investment still further below world best practice. Finally, we would argue that British industry's present backwardness grows out of the protection afforded by Empire and Commonwealth markets from before the first world war until the 1960s; the same thing would happen in any protectionist regime in the future.

An important part of the problem is the low capacity of British industry to respond to all sorts of signals. This capacity is to some extent a variable independent of the specific economic system of signals, rewards and sanctions. For example, German industry's technological lead over British industry was established in an interventionist state at the beginning of this century, and has been maintained in a liberal system, whilst Britain has moved on the whole from liberalism to intervention.

The British problem can be seen in relation to the length of two time lags. The first is inevitable: namely the time that it often takes to build up the skills and knowledge necessary to develop and commercialise major product and process technologies. The second is not inevitable: namely, the time that often elapses in Britain before lack of industrial skills and knowledge is recognised and remedied. Coping with the first time lag and reducing the second depend above all on the professional competence of management, although criticism of the way in which British industry is financed is voiced by Lorenz [24] and by Carrington and Edwards [4]. They argue that, compared to continental Europe and Japan, the financial criteria against which the performance of British firms are judged are on the whole too short-term; and financial institutions do not have sufficient competence to evaluate medium- and long-term competitive prospects, or to improve management practices.

There is thus a case for properly conceived government initiatives. The NEB appears to have shown that it can think a bit further ahead than private financiers normally can, and the recent initiatives of the NRDC in financing innovative companies in addition to innovative projects is to be welcomed [31].

Government-financed R and D
Table 7.6 shows the pattern of the British government's expenditures on R and D in 1978 compared to other EEC countries,

measured in proportion to GDP. The UK had the highest proportion in defence, although it had been diminishing since 1976, whilst that of France had been increasing over the same period. In only one other category, agriculture, was British government R and D above the EEC average. In the 'general knowledge' category, which is broadly analogous to basic research, the UK was well below the EEC average, and only Ireland and Italy were lower. Using more detailed categories, there were sectors where the UK expenditures were relatively high: nuclear energy within 'energy', civil air transport within 'industry' and both building and water research within 'environment'.

Government funding has had a powerful influence on the pattern of R and D in British industry. As in the US, more than 30 per cent of the R and D performed since the second world war has been financed by government. In 1977, the equivalent percentages for other OECD countries were 20–30 for France and Norway; 10–20 for Canada, Germany, Italy and Sweden; and under 5 in Japan,

Table 7.6   Government expenditures on R and D, 1978
(per 10,000 units of GDP)

	France	Germany	Italy	UK	EEC-9
Earth and atmosphere	3.3	2.2	0.9	1.1	2.0
Environment	4.9	3.4	0.8	2.5	3.3
Health	6.0	6.0	2.3	3.0	5.1
Energy[a]	8.6	14.9	7.8	8.8	10.3
Agriculture[a]	4.4	2.3	1.7	4.2	3.6
Industry	12.0	8.3	4.1	5.3	7.8
Social	1.6	5.0	0.9	1.1	3.1
Space[a]	5.4	4.6	4.7	2.7	4.3
Defence[a]	35.4	13.4	0.6	56.6	22.0
General knowledge	26.5	49.3	19.6	22.2	35.0
Total[b]	108.5	109.4	43.4	108.6	97.0

Sources: [14], [35].

[a]US expenditure under similar categories for 1977 was: energy, 14.7; agriculture, 2.8; space, 16.0; defence, 65.8.
[b]Includes 'not itemised' for France, UK and EEC.

the Netherlands and Switzerland. In the UK, government-funded R and D is heavily concentrated in the aerospace and electronics industries. In aerospace, more than three quarters of R and D performed has consistently been financed by the British government for the development of weapons and for civil air transport. However, the relative importance of aerospace has been going down: in 1964, 68 per cent of government's R and D funds spent in industry went to aerospace and 22 per cent to electronics; in 1978, 42 per cent went to aerospace and 48 per cent to electronics, where more than half of electronics R and D was government-funded.

Defence R and D

Between 1971 and 1977, British government expenditures on defence R and D remained roughly constant in real terms, whilst those on civilian industry-related R and D (comprising civilian technology and other industry and energy sources) were virtually halved. If we were to adhere strictly to the 'Rothschild principle' there need be no discussion of defence R and D in a paper concerned with industrial policy and innovation. According to this principle [6] each department specifies its requirements for R and D and pays for it, and this is all that should be done in the way of a national policy for science and technology.

However, the principle is misleading when considering major national policy options and resource commitments, which inevitably have major opportunity costs, and external costs and benefits. The links between the development, production and sale of weapons, on the one hand, and policies for industrial R and D and innovation, on the other, are inevitably close. Proponents of the present level of commitment to defence R and D stress its positive externalities in the form of arms exports and more jobs. Critics like Maddock [26] stress the longer-term opportunity costs of diverting scarce managerial and technical talent from civilian products and markets. M. Kaldor in [39] goes further and argues that the large-scale British commitment to defence R and D is a long-standing and integral part of Britain's industrial decline. Weapons development has diverted resources from more promising products and markets. It has also created managerial and technical habits that are inappropriate for civilian markets. Concorde, for example, with its emphasis on speed, neglected the overriding importance in airline operations of costs per passenger-seat–mile.

In this perspective, it is appropriate to ask what might be the long-term consequences of the change in emphasis in British defence R and D from aircraft to electronics, and of Britain's successes in selling military electronics equipment. If short-term profit signals are followed, one possible consequence might be the neglect of consumer products and markets. Britain's commitment to consumer electronics R and D has been relatively low over the past ten years or more (see Table 7.3). If one believes that domestic uses of electronics will not go much beyond TV games or video-tapes, then this need not matter. If one believes that the bringing together of television, the computer and telecommunications will lead to wide-ranging applications in information and communication, both in the home and in the office, then any lag behind the world technological frontier should be a cause of national concern.

Civilian high technologies
In 1975, the writer [37] criticised – on the basis of data for 1971 and 1972 – the British government's heavy commitment to civilian aircraft development. By 1977 this commitment had been reduced in real terms to about 14 per cent of the 1971 level. One reason for this considerable change has been the end of the Concorde project, which had weighed heavily on British policy for civil aviation development since the 1960s. It had given credence to the view expressed by Jewkes [22] that many of the justifications for government support for such large-scale R and D projects – in terms of large scale and of strong linkage effects – were spurious, and that the projects were often the vehicle for the technological ambitions of powerful groups in government agencies and industrial companies, rather than carefully worked out commercial ventures.

However, the relatively more successful experiences of government support for the RB 211 family of engines at Rolls-Royce, for the British computer firm ICL, and for the French-led Airbus family of aircraft (in the development of which the UK is now participating) suggest that unbridled technological ambition is not an inevitable outcome of government support for industrial R and D. Furthermore, it is possible to make a case for government support to assist the technical and commercial steps necessary to establish a market position in these high technologies when they may be promising growth sectors for the future, but may not offer immediate prospects for commercial profit.

This is because of the strong disadvantage under which 'following' countries and imitators have had to operate in these industries. In the 1950s and 1960s, US firms had privileged access to the large-scale defence procurement and R and D contracts that were so important in advancing the then nascent technologies. In some sectors (for example nuclear fuels and space communications), legal and political sanction was given to their technological advance. In others, they were able to turn their early advantage in design, development and production into a competitive advantage that created barriers to new entrants through dynamic economies of scale in production (electronic components, aircraft) and through externalities in repair, maintenance and spare parts (aircraft). New firms and countries that wished to enter these industries were therefore constrained to make particular efforts to overcome these barriers and some have succeeded in doing so.

Whilst such arguments can probably justify the present, relatively modest, level of British government R and D support in civilian aircraft, space and electronics, this is less true of the continuing expenditure on nuclear energy R and D. This is now considerably more than government R and D expenditures on aviation, on space, on electronics, or on the whole of the rest of manufacturing technology. Henderson's telling analysis [20] of the costs of the decisions to build Concorde and the Advanced Gas-cooled Reactor appears to have had more influence in the aircraft than in the nuclear sector. Jewkes' observation [22] that high technology is the last refuge of the enthusiastic nationalist may still hold to some extent in nuclear decision-making.

Technological infrastructure
In Britain, as in France, Germany and Italy, general government support to industrial R and D is small outside the high technologies. This reflects in part the ability of industry itself to generate and exploit technological opportunities without great help from outside. It also reflects two characteristics of what we shall call the technological infrastructure: first, the dispersed nature of its constituent parts, whether the laboratories performing research or the industrial users; second, the difficulties of measuring the economic benefits of the infrastructure's R and D, since its results are often used in combination with other information, and are transferred informally to users without any record or monetary transaction. There are the same difficulties in quantifying the economic benefits of university

research, the performers of which can – however – more easily find other justifications for their activities. A pioneering study by Gibbons and Johnston [16] on R and D projects in British industry has shown that universities and government laboratories did produce what the economists describe as a 'public good', since they provided a significant proportion of the inputs of knowledge and information necessary for industrial scientists and engineers working on development activities to solve their practical problems. Government-funded research of a general nature has also been the basis of important inventions which have opened up considerable markets for British companies. The most profitable activities of the NRDC have been the licensing of inventions emerging from British universities and government laboratories; the most successful have been those emerging from sophisticated chemical and biological research [31].

Between 1971 and 1977, government expenditure on R and D related to industries other than the big technologies certainly did not increase, and may even have declined in real terms given the effects of inflation. Britain's expenditures in this category are a noticeably smaller percentage of industry's own R and D expenditure than those of France, Italy and Germany. Over the past ten or more years, the main thrust of government policy has been to increase the responsiveness of the infrastructure to industry's requirements. The amount of contract research undertaken by the research associations has increased markedly, and funding for government laboratories has been transferred to the Research Requirements Boards, which count industrialists amongst their members.

As far as the writer knows, there is no published study which has tried to evaluate the effects of these changes systematically. Even if there is more responsiveness to industrial requirements, a number of problems remain [19], including: (a) the financing of activities for small firms that do not have in-house access to technical competence; (b) the balance between short-term R and D activities that supplement what industry does itself, and the long-term activities that complement industrial activities; (c) dealing with industries and firms that do not have a clear and informed view of their 'requirements'.

University research
Most qualitative and quantitative assessments conclude that, since the second world war, Britain's basic research has on the whole been

amongst the world's best. They also conclude that Britain is better by world standards at science than at technology. Macioti [25] shows that Britain's patenting output per cited scientific paper in 1976 was between a third and a quarter of that of Switzerland, Japan and Germany. On the basis of such evaluations, some analysts advocate the diversion of British resources from science to technology.

This is a mis-specification of the problem. What distinguishes Britain from countries at the technological frontier is not its strong science but its weak technology. In technologically strong countries like Germany and Switzerland, industry has fed very successfully off a strong scientific base, and Japan is now making considerable efforts to promote its own basic research. Data collected by D. Davies of the Department of Industry show that the British chemical industry has been successful in exploiting the results of British basic science, perhaps because it has maintained the level of its R and D activities. Science-based technology – particularly from the chemical and electronics industries – is increasingly pervading the technologies of other industries. A strong basic science will continue to be necessary for countries to remain near the technological frontier. Although it might be tempting and even necessary in the short term to convert scientists into engineers, the longer-term challenge is to get the British intellectual élite – which at present tends to concentrate on science, the humanities and service activities – to shift towards engineering and industrial activities.

In spite of past and present achievements, it will be difficult in future to maintain the quality of British basic science. The UK spends a relatively small proportion of GDP on basic science. Working conditions – in terms of salaries and equipment – are often not as attractive as in other professions and in other countries. Budgets are static and even declining, which makes it difficult to move resources into promising new fields and institutions. This problem is exacerbated by the large proportion of the basic science budget tied up for long periods in fields depending on expensive and large-scale instrumentation (high-energy physics, radio astronomy, space). As a basis for future policy choices, more systematic analysis is needed of the quality of British basic science field by field, of the effectiveness of different methods of funding it, and of the degree to which weak links between British science and technology result from inappropriate science or from inadequate resources spent on improving industrial technology.

Sectoral policies

Within any given set of market signals and constraints, firms will behave differently. To some extent this reflects the rapid rate of change and high level of uncertainty in the industrial environment. Under such circumstances diversity of response can be considered more likely than uniformity to generate economically and socially useful improvements.

However, differences in response can also reflect differences in levels of professional competence, in time horizons and in objectives. For example, in 1967, the profitability of industry in Sweden was as low as in the UK. Whereas British industry-financed R and D subsequently declined until 1975, in Sweden it increased at a rate second only to that in Japan [34]. As Granstrand [17] showed recently, the main Swedish companies decided deliberately to move towards strategies based on technological specialisation and competitive advantage. However, on the basis of past experience, we cannot be sure that, even with high profits, growth and investment, British industry will on the whole invest in the mix of equipment, R and D, skills and the purchase of foreign technology that is appropriate to the objective of a competitive high-wage industry.

Given its recent record, it is likely that the chemical industry will do so, provided that the British government continues to invest in high-quality basic research and education in chemistry and biology. We have also seen that, in nuclear energy, civil aviation and space, barriers to entry may justify an industrial policy involving government subsidies to specific development projects. In electronics, we have argued that the scale of government defence requirements has a major impact on the industrial strategies of electronics firms, and may have led them to neglect promising long-term growth markets.

Three other groups of industries in the UK also need explicit technological and industrial strategies with active government involvement: engineering, iron and steel, and traditional consumer products (excluding food processing). In all cases, the resources devoted to technological improvements have been inadequate by international standards. It could be argued that an active policy in these sectors will, in the long run, be self-defeating, given that – with changing patterns of world demand and industrial location – production in these sectors will now move to industrialising countries. However, this neglects the considerable markets within these sectors that remain sensitive to competitive advantages in skill, design and technology: for example, high-performance machinery in Germany, Sweden and Switzerland; sophisticated, small-scale steel plant in Germany and the US; and industrial textiles in Germany, quality furniture in Sweden, and well-designed pottery in the UK.

Whilst it is relatively easy to define the objectives of a technological policy in these sectors, it is much more difficult to define the policy instruments. In a study of five countries, Allen *et al.* [2] found that, in many industrial sectors, the major impact of government on innovation was not through its direct funding of industrial R and D, but through the transfer of technology from other institutions, or through government regulations. Townsend's study in [39] of the development of British deep coalmining technology showed the importance of the R and D, testing and procurement activities of a large and sophisticated user.

Conclusions and Recommendations

In a modern market economy, nearly all analysts accept that governments should at least help to finance the development of the basic knowledge and skills that industry requires, and create a general economic climate conducive to the activities necessary for technological improvements in industry and elsewhere. Whilst accepting that such governmental functions are necessary, the analysis of this chapter leads to the conclusion that they are not sufficient. Given present trends in the world economy, a competitive high-wage economy requires high levels of skills and technology. Given barriers to entry in certain promising new technologies, and given the short time horizons and lack of professional competence prevalent in certain parts of British industry, investment in such skills and technology may be less than is necessary in Britain. Additional policies related to the funding of R and D, the promotion of skills, the volume and methods of funding of industrial investment and the development of specific sectors will therefore be necessary. Some specific recommendations are as follows:

(1) Policies should be designed to stimulate increases in the general level of British industry-financed R and D activities. As a target, such R and D should reach 10 per cent of the OECD total by 1990, compared to 7.5 per cent in 1975.

(2) There should be a progressive reduction until 1990 in the level

of British defence R and D to the level prevailing in France if Britain retains its nuclear deterrent, or the level in Germany if it does not.

(3) Expenditures on the government's contribution to technological infrastructure (excluding defence and civilian high technology) as a proportion of industry-financed R and D should be increased by 1990 to the level prevailing in Germany. Within this increase, high priority should be given to technical improvements in engineering, iron and steel, and traditional consumer goods (excluding food processing) industries, for which long-term policies of improvement and adaptation should be defined.

(4) Expenditures on the general advancement of knowledge should be increased by 1990 to 0.3 per cent of GDP, compared with 0.22 per cent in 1978. A more deliberate and explicit policy should be developed for allocating resources amongst scientific fields and institutions.

(5) The present level of government funding of R and D should be maintained in civil aviation and space, whilst means should be sought for maintaining or redeploying the British expertise in breeder reactors at less cost. A deliberate policy should be developed to ensure that British industry reaches and remains at the technological frontier in the development of home and office electronics.

(6) Continuing attention should be given to improving engineering skills, and much more attention than at present to the resources and institutions necessary for the widespread improvement of the skills of British industrial workers.

(7) In sectors where British industry is well behind world industrial best practice, the import of foreign technology – through capital goods, licensing or inward foreign investment – should be actively encouraged, and complemented by policies to develop indigenous skills and R and D programmes.

(8) Policies should aim to increase the rate of investment in manufacturing, going beyond the conventional instruments related to demand management, profits, fiscal inventives, exchange rates and interest rates, to include measures to encourage financial institutions to lengthen the time horizon of their investments, and to promote more actively the diffusion of managerial and technical competence in industrial firms.

The problems with supply-side policies are those of sustaining continuity, experience and commitment. Many of the proposed changes would be slow in bearing fruit, and require detailed knowledge of specific industries, specific financial institutions, specific markets and specific technologies. Politicians often want quick results; academics and public officials prefer to deal with the variables with which they are familiar, and which they feel they understand. Unfortunately, technology is often not amongst those variables, which may itself be part of the problem.

References

[1] Aho, C. and Rosen, H., 'Trends in technology-intensive trade with special reference to US competitiveness' (paper given to conference on Science and Technology Indicators, OECD, Paris), 1980.

[2] Allen, T. *et al.* 'Government influence on the process of innovation in Europe and Japan', *Research Policy*, vol. 7, April 1978.

[3] Blackaby, F. T. (ed.), *De-industrialisation*, London, Heinemann, 1979.

[4] Carrington, J. and Edwards, G., *Financing Industrial Investment*, London, Macmillan, 1979.

[5] Central Statistical Office, *Research and Development Expenditure and Employment*, London, HMSO, 1976.

[6] Civil Service Department, *A Framework for Government Research and Development* [Rothschild Report], Cmnd 4814, London, HMSO, 1971.

[7] Clarke, J. *et al.* 'Long waves and technological developments in the twentieth century' (mimeo., Science Policy Research Unit, Sussex University), 1980.

[8] Commission of the European Communities, *Changes in the Industrial Structure in the European Economies since the Oil Crisis, 1973–1978*, Brussels, 1979.

[9] Creamer, D., *Overseas Research and Development by United States Multinationals 1966–1975*, New York, Conference Board, 1976.

[10] Cripps, F. and Godley, W., 'Control of imports as a means to full employment and the expansion of world trade: the UK case', *Cambridge Journal of Economics*, vol. 2, September 1978.

[11] Department of Education and Science/Ministry of Technology, *Statistics of Science and Technology*, London, HMSO, 1970.

[12] Department of Industry, *Business Monitor MO14: Industrial Research and Development Expenditure and Employment*, London, HMSO, 1975.

[13] —, *Engineering Our Future* [Finniston Report], Cmnd 7794, London, HMSO, 1980.

[14] Enos, J., *Petroleum, Progress and Profits: a history of process innovation*, Cambridge Mass., MIT Press, 1962.

[15] Freeman, C. and Young, A., *The Research and Development Effort in Western Europe, North America and the Soviet Union*, Paris, OECD, 1965.

[16] Gibbons, M. and Johnston, R., 'The roles of science in technological innovation', *Research Policy*, vol. 3, November 1974.

[17] Granstrand, O., *Technology Management and Markets*, Gothenberg, Chalmers University, 1979.

[18] Grimond, J. (ed.), *Youth Unemployment and the Bridge from School to Work*, London, Anglo-German Foundation, 1979.

[19] Gummet, P. and Gibbons, M., 'Government research for industry: recent British developments', *Research Policy*, vol. 7, July 1978.

[20] Henderson, P. D., 'Two British errors: their probable size and some possible lessons', *Oxford Economic Papers*, vol. 29, July 1977.

[21] Hill, T., *Profits and Rates of Return*, Paris, OECD, 1979.

[22] Jewkes, J., *Government and High Technology*, London, Institute of Economic Affairs, 1972.

[23] Krugman, P., 'A model of innovation, technology transfer and the world distribution of income', *Journal of Political Economy*, vol. 87, April 1979.

[24] Lorenz, C., *Investing in Success: how to profit from design and innovation*, London, Anglo-German Foundation, 1979.

[25] Macioti, M., 'The power and the glory: a note on patents and scientific authors', *Research Policy*, vol. 9, April 1980.

[26] Maddock, E., 'Science, technology and industry', *Proceedings of the Royal Society of London*, vol. 345, 1975.

[27] Marsh, A. *et al.* 'The training of managers in industrial relations' (unpublished, St Edmund Hall, Oxford), 1976.

[28] Mensch, G., *Stalemate in Technology*, Cambridge Mass., Ballinger, 1979.

[29] Nabseth, L. and Ray, G. F. (eds.), *The Diffusion of New Industrial Processes*, Cambridge University Press, 1974.

[30] NEDO, *British Industrial Performance*, London, 1980.

[31] NRDC, *Annual Report 1979–80*, London, 1980.

[32] National Science Board, *Science Indicators 1974*, and *1976*, Washington DC, 1975 and 1977.

[33] OECD, *National Accounts of OECD Countries 1976*, Paris, 1978.

[34] —, *Trends in Industrial R and D 1967–1975*, Paris, 1979.

[35] —, *Technical Change and Economic Policy*, Paris, 1980.

[36] —, *Science Resources Newsletter*, no. 5, Paris, 1980.

[37] Pavitt, K., 'The choice of targets and instruments for government support of scientific research' in A. Whiting (ed.), *The Economics of Industrial Subsidies*, London, HMSO, 1976.

[38] —, 'Technical innovation and industrial development', *Futures*, vol. 11, no. 6, 1979, and vol. 12, no. 1, 1980.

[39] —, (ed.), *Technical Innovation and British Economic Performance*, London, Macmillan, 1980.

[40] Pike, A., 'Britain's antique apprentice system', *Financial Times*, 2 September 1980.

[41] Rubenstein, A. H. *et al.*, 'Management perceptions of government incentives to technological innovation in England, France, West Germany and Japan,' *Research Policy*, vol. 6, October 1977.

[42] Salter, W. E. G., *Productivity and Technical Change*, Cambridge University Press, 1960.

[43] Saunders, C., *Engineering in Britain, West Germany and France*, Brighton, Sussex European Research Centre, 1978.

[44] Sciberras, E., 'International competitiveness and technical change: a study of the US consumer electronics industry' (mimeo., Science Policy Research Unit, Sussex University), 1979.

[45] Soete, L., 'The impact of technological innovation on international trade pat-

terns: the evidence reconsidered' (paper given to conference on Science and Technology Indicators, OECD, Paris), 1980.

[46] Stout, D. *et al.*, *International Price Competitiveness, Non-Price Factors and Economic Performance*, London, NEDO, 1977.

[47] Vickery, G., *Data Concerning the Balance of Technological Payments in Certain OECD Member Countries: statistical data and methodological analysis*, Paris, OECD, 1977.

[48] —, 'Technological payments in international transactions: a satisfactory measure of the output of R and D and of technological competitivity?' (paper given to conference on Science and Technology Indicators, OECD, Paris), 1980.

[49] Wells, J. D. and Imber, J. C., 'The home and export performance of United Kingdom industries', *Economic Trends*, no. 286, August 1977.

[50] Williams, B., *Technology, Investment and Growth*, London, Chapman Hall, 1967.

7(II)   The Case for Government Support of R and D and Innovation

by D. K. Stout

Diagnosis of UK Industrial Decline

It requires an effort of concentration and imagination to set aside the short-term macroeconomic outlook. The present inhibitions upon investment of all kinds by private industry, and upon serious support of industry by government, are so strong as to obscure the view of what might be gained from a more determined and ambitious technology policy in the 1980s than has been adopted in the 1960s and 1970s. A CBI representative remarked at a recent NEDC meeting that medium and smaller companies had almost given up R and D spending, as if it was a luxury to be enjoyed in better times.

At an earlier Public Policy Conference (Blackaby [1]), we agreed that the relative industrial decline of the UK is a hundred-year story, and this only so far as 1980. It would not take us very far today to concentrate only upon those actions which are politically or financially possible immediately. High interest rates, stubborn inflation and an exchange rate overvalued by perhaps 50 per cent have almost submerged the industrial landscape. The waters will presumably recede, leaving at least some of British manufacturing ground habitable, and a post-diluvian reclamation scheme will then be needed.

I am one of the 'hundred-year' school. This is not the place to re-state the rather untidy diagnosis of past structural failure on which the policy proposals I wish to suggest depend (see Stout [17]). It is untidy because it tries to explain long-term differences between the rate of economic growth of the UK and of competing industrial economies in terms of disequilibrium. It seeks to explain the UK's failure, and their varying degrees of success, in converging more or less rapidly upon (and even overtaking) the moving frontier of highest technology and design set by the most advanced economy.

The processes of decline or advance are both circular and cumulative, and attempts to explain this process for the UK in terms of one dominant feature (unless so general as just to redescribe one of the symptoms of de-industrialisation) have all encountered crippling objections. Most have given ammunition to politicians or relief to bewildered students, but little lasting hope to industry. Protection, export-led growth, indicative planning, the reform of industrial relations, the floating pound, the shock of European competition, industrial democracy, the extension of government intervention, and the reduction of the size and functions of government have had eloquent advocates, persuasive *a priori* arguments, and even a little supporting evidence. Most of us have been more than half-convinced by one or another 'single solution' at one time or another.

To adopt industrial policies designed to encourage industrialists to develop new products and processes, and so speed up convergence, could be to add another nostrum to this already crowded British pharmocopeia. However, the recommendation rests upon two assumptions which Britain's long industrial history and the advance of competing economies appear to justify: namely that improved trading performance in marketable goods and services (especially manufactures) will remain a condition of the growth of our living standards for the foreseeable future; and, left to itself, our *relative* performance will continue to get worse. There is a case for industrial policies which – while they may not reverse industrial decline – will not actually make matters worse, as much of policy (including what passed for industrial policy – 'picking winners' and so on) has done in the past.

Growth depends upon the capacity of an economy to replace old techniques and products with new ones quickly – the process Schumpeter aptly called 'creative destruction' [14]. It rests on a vintage theory of capital (Salter [13]), which can be extended to labour inputs as well. The theory of divergence in growth rates stems from Svennilson (UNECE [19]) and later Lundberg [6]. In the UK the work of Ray [12], Freeman and Pavitt [4], [10] and Gomulka [5] is in this 'disequilibrium' tradition. My own views have moved the same way since 1970, particularly influenced by the large differences in the growth rates of value productivity within the same industry in the UK and other economies starting from the same average level (Stout [16] and [17]). Much of the evidence I have looked at suggests that international market share and economic growth depend upon the speed with which change in products and techniques can be effected. The heterogeneity of labour and the specificity of machines have meant that however confident one might be of the appropriateness of market signals to change the distribution of labour and capital in the right directions, the rate of growth achieved depends upon the *speed* of such responses.

Equally importantly, technical advance is best thought of not as exogenous, but as the rate at which assets are drawn out of an international 'bank' of technical knowledge and applied; and this varies widely. Because advance is embodied in new investment, and because resistance to changes in skill are less when the overall demand for labour is strong, there are well-known virtuous circles in fast-growing economies. But, aside from what can be attributed to differences in the growth rates themselves, there appear to be different degrees of 'viscosity' in different industrial economies established over long periods. If this is so, then the main role of industrial policy will be to speed up the process of continuous re-allocation and redesign. Left to gravitational forces, and with obstacles removed, treacle will flow downhill. But it will remain treacle.

Something of this more dynamic and detailed view of Britain's poor productivity growth can be found in the fresh look that the Brookings Institution, with its increasing consciousness of the causes of the US's own sluggish performance, has taken at the UK (Caves [2]). One economist who has recently put together endogenous technical change, the dynamics of trade advantage (establishing beachheads in new generations of product), and speed of adjustment in the factor market is Cornwall [3]. Such attempted explanations of differences in growth rates have sometimes been called 'structuralist', because they assert that resource reallocations in an open industrial economy determine, to a large extent, its rate of growth. The term is a little unfortunate. It has recently led Peacock [11] to doubt such explanations on the grounds that high growth is compatible with many different patterns of *broad* structural change and that the structural differences between, say, Germany and the UK are more fine-grained than 'structuralists' have in mind. I, for one, do have intra-industry speed of change in mind; and also I do not regard Peacock's first point as constituting an objection to the explanation. What matters, I think, is the evidence of deep-seated differences in the ability of different economies to adapt.

If these differences are, in part, differences in speeds of response to changed market signals, then there is more to public policy than merely ensuring that the market signals are visible. A large technology gap, or design gap, ought, after all, to provide a loud and clear market signal. The problem that industrial economists have to deal with is why in one economy such a gap is filled quickly, while in another only slowly. The work in NEDO on product quality, price inelasticity and export valued-added has suggested that a determined effort has to be made to break out of the trap of possessing established comparative advantage in inferior products, with low income elasticity and generally low opportunities to raise productivity. If the exporter produces what the market expects and demands of him, obedient to *immediate* market signals, the trap may close tighter. It is not for government to try to select and support particular new products, but to establish conditions which make it easier for private industry to do so.

The Acceleration of Technological Change

Slowness to adapt would carry smaller penalties if technology were stationary. There would be a lower relative rate of growth in the sluggish economy as it approached the fixed frontier more slowly, but after the others reached it only the sluggish would still be progressing towards economic bliss.

The situation in the 1980s is quite otherwise. The scope and versatility of digital technology; the vanishing cost and size of the circuits themselves; the new possibility of creating economies of scale without uniformity; the almost endless diversity of possible applications of standard programmes for communication, information and control; and the scope for reliability, safety and energy-saving, put the micro-processor in the first rank of Schumpeterian long waves. Yet other major developments of technique are already overlapping and combining with it – lasers, fibre optics and biotechnology are almost equally 'generic' and rich in potential applications.

The worldwide exploitation of these new technologies seems certain to be very fast, in spite of the probable slow growth of world output over the next few years. The close past relationship between manufacturing output growth, innovation and productivity growth is unlikely now to hold. The technological leaders – the VLSI circuit-makers, for example – are more spread this time between countries, and competition is joined all the more fiercely (and more readily takes product-improvement forms) because world demand for the products that will incorporate these circuits is growing slowly.

Slow world *demand* growth will lengthen the wave but not absorb its momentum. The pace of change in particular *producer* countries may be limited by the increased rate of obsolescence of both physical and human capital, outstripping natural wastage, depreciation and the capacity of our educational and training systems. And combined with slow growth of demand (constrained by energy supplies) some initial reduction in overall employment opportunities will be added to the mis-matching of skills.

The main inhibitors of the speed of diffusion of the new technology within the UK are likely to be fears of redundancy (particularly since unemployment is already so high), and managerial inertia, ignorance and inability to afford to innovate. Since these inhibitions will act less powerfully upon us as *consumers*, in an open economy employment losses would be postponed only for a very short time by refusal to invest in, or to work with, the new technologies. This consideration, and the relationship between R and D and the application of new technology and company success and employment inspired a courageously argued recent TUC report on employment and technology. There have been reports from Belgium and elsewhere that the attempt to reach formal agreements on new technology between management and unions has slowed up its introduction. However, in the UK the failure of the full CBI to give its official endorsement to this document and its proposed guidelines may have destroyed what was a powerful initiative from the TUC towards accelerating technical progress. If so, this will throw a greater weight of responsibility upon the government to lessen the resistance to technical change.

The ubiquity and versatility of the micro-processor in application to both new products and processes means that government encouragement can afford not to try to specify particular products. In Japan the MITI 'Vision' has nominated products where the world income elasticity of demand for exports is likely to be high; those where the prospects for relatively rapid future technical progress are good; and knowledge-intensive industries. The point is that historical patterns of comparative advantage *need not* determine future specialisation: digital technology can remove entry barriers in old preserves, as it has done in the watch industry, for example.

In traditional manufacturing industries – like mechanical engineering – the opportunities for applying new technology depend on further reductions in the cost, not of the chip but of the heavy equipment into which it is fitted, and on the provision of links between the micro-processor and the other functions which it controls – through actuators, sensors and other peripherals.

There are many quite small-scale product innovation opportunities in the peripherals field; but these require R and D investment, which is seriously inadequate in smaller UK companies. The UK has a (diminishing) lead in the preparation of software packages, especially those which are culture-based (like Prestel or Open University teaching programmes). Although many innovations that the integrated circuit makes possible are internationally footloose, those which essentially involve translating a cultural, educational, entertainment or communicated *service* into a mass-marketable *product* ought to be future successes: anything from video-cassettes of the Shakespeare cycle to educational systems or medical diagnostic and treatment centres. Future government budgeting of expenditure on medical and science research, education and the arts ought to try to take these potential economic benefits into account.

But the funding of *development* through to the stage of patentable products and beyond is equally or even more important. Research financed by the Medical Research Council gave British bio-technologists a lead in the field of monoclonal antibodies – a potentially revolutionary development in diagnostics and in versatile commercial preparation of active principles for use in clinical medicine (see, for example, [15]). This lead was enough to establish the academic reputation of the British researchers, but it has not made their fortunes, nor has it established a major new British industry. The early exploitation has largely taken place in the US, making entry difficult for the late-comers.

Industrial Policy Guidelines
There appear to be four broad lessons for government industrial policy:

(1) In many traditionally important export industries – transport equipment, machinery and process plant, for example – low current

profitability, managerial inertia and union resistance to automation will make it difficult for UK producers to reduce costs, and to increase reliability and product quality, so as to keep pace with competitors either in Europe, or, increasingly, in the newly industrialising countries. The option of sufficient compensating devaluation is both unrealistic in the short run and ineffective in the long run. Some of the industries that might follow motor cycles, typewriters, cars and ships have been listed recently by the TUC in its evidence to the House of Commons Trade and Industry Committee. Government policy to encourage a modern competitive nucleus in these industries will have to be directed mainly at reducing the hardship of a much more rapid movement out of existing skills and occupations than natural wastage can cope with.

(2) An unpredictable variety of new products incorporating the new technologies is likely to develop worldwide mass markets, and there will be a far wider range of consumer and small business-user products with more limited but still important markets. In most cases international competitive advantage will go to the country in which the new product is *first* successfully developed. Since there may be fifty or a hundred failures for every success, any country which treats the financing of each of these as a unique investment decision will lose out on most of them. So here public policy should provide development finance on terms which reflect the spreading of actuarial risk rather than unique uncertainty. To avoid 'moral hazard' the risk must still be shared.

(3) There are fields of application of new technology where the government is the main contractor. It is here that the great preponderance of government funding of R and D has gone in the past – into far too short a list of vastly expensive schemes in aerospace, defence and nuclear energy, with fewer external applications to private industry than a broader-based programme would have had. In 1977–8 total central government financing of R and D was £1647 million. Of this, 52.4 per cent was spent on defence projects and only 5.4 per cent on industrial production and technology – hardly more than on agricultural research. Within the government's industrial research budget, electronics and aerospace have been overwhelmingly dominant. Leaving those sectors out, the rest of industry claimed only 8.3 per cent in 1975, including 1.9 per cent for machinery. (The corresponding German figures were 39.5 and 17.4 per cent.) The OECD points out that in most countries 10–15

per cent of government R and D funding was devoted to the promotion of industrial development, but 'the share was much lower in the UK and negligible in the US' [9]. Between 1977 and 1979 funding for 'industrial growth' rose, at constant prices, by 54 per cent in Germany, 46 per cent in Sweden, 13 per cent in the US and 12 per cent in Italy and the Netherlands. It fell by 6 per cent in France and by 15 per cent in the UK (although total public funding for all purposes rose by an internationally comparable 9 per cent).

(4) The strongest case for more government encouragement of industrial innovation is that the social time preference rate must now lie below the marginal cost of funds, after adding an uncertainty premium which the private sector is bound to apply. The high exchange rate, the low current level of domestic activity and the fear of the long duration of the upward pull of future relative increases in the price of oil upon the exchange rate, all militate against risky investment. Only the government can be relied upon to concern itself with the survival of a modern and relevant industrial base when these effects have evaporated. It is not possible to skip a generation of industrial progress and re-enter the technology and the lost markets later.

The Public Good

In spite of all the differences between their political philosophies, there has been little difference in practical terms in what successive British governments have undertaken by way of industrial policy since 1964. All have felt themselves obliged to spend heavily in support of declining industries, and this almost certainly significantly postponed some of the structural changes which were anyway so slow to take place.

Still only about 10 per cent of the total spending of about £2 billion a year in support of industry is designed to assist directly the process of change. The burden of the 90 per cent makes the Secretary of State understandably reluctant to increase the helpful residual. He has, however, often referred to government's role in reinforcing the economy's adaptability, including a limited but continuing place in supporting early state-of-the-art R and D which 'left to himself'· the private investor is unlikely to undertake. In a recent speech he has gone out of his way to encourage companies to make fuller use of such existing aid for R and D as the Product and Process Development Scheme, the Microprocessor Application Project and the Micro-electronic Industries Support Programme. (The sums involved are very small – £26 million a year for the first and about £110 million over several years for the other two together.) The previous Secretary of State spoke in similar terms in favour of what it is now fashionable to call 'positive' adjustment policies. He referred to 'backing, rather than seeking to redirect, the decisions and policies of market-oriented enterprises. What this means in practice is that the government plays a part in sharing the risks attached to some innovative activities . . .' (Varley [18]).

Neither position is very far from the direct reference to government support for R and D as a public good by the NEDC in 1963 '. . . benefits would be obtained from measures to encourage a speedier development of the results of research in industry and commerce and quicker introduction of new techniques, processes and materials . . . important . . . in the van of scientific and technical advance in relation both to new products and . . . new processes . . . support is particularly relevant in cases where the returns to the economy as a whole are greater than the returns to individual firms . . .' [7].

Nothing much is said by Ministers in public about the application of cost–benefit analysis or other techniques to appraise how much should be spent in generating non-excludable benefits (e.g. from training), a growth advantage, a learning-curve effect, a competitive spur, or a post-North-Sea-oil advantage to the tradeables sector; or what social opportunity cost should be attached to the resources employed. Peacock has recently reminded us that discussions at least of proper criteria did take place ([11], chap. 2, p. 4), though the main policy decisions themselves were rather *ad hoc* and politically determined.

In order to be able to justify any particular aid or loan scheme one would need to assess: the elasticity of supply of R and D factors; the additionality of publicly financed R and D; the probable direct commercial benefits; the appropriate social time discount rate; the external dynamic economies; the effects upon competing economies; those transfer payments affecting the use of the resulting innovation; the net benefits recalculated as part of some larger integrated R and D programme, instead of as a piecemeal project; and, most intractable of all, the social opportunity cost of the funds disbursed, bringing into the calculation the whole of macro-economic policy.

There are so many unknowns that all one can be sure of is that, by comparison with an economy like Germany (admittedly richer but not, like us, so backward), we are not devoting nearly enough private plus public resources to the commercial development of new products through to marketing, nor to the pilot applications of new processes.

Learning from Policies Elsewhere in Western Europe

NEDO recently undertook an investigation of those policies currently in operation on the continent which had the intention either of directly increasing the rate of adoption of new technologies, or of increasing the economic and geographical mobility of workers in order to lessen the bottlenecks, the wastes and the hardships from more rapid innovation and the development of high-technology industries (NEDO [8]).

There appeared to be two main reasons why European governments have been adopting such policies. First, it is widely understood by governments of many complexions that energy shortage, new technologies and third world industrialisation are demanding *greater* changes than were required before. Second, at the same time, slower growth and higher unemployment have tended to increase the rigidities of the system.

We looked in detail at over thirty separate schemes. They showed increasing emphasis on policies aimed at promoting the diffusion of new technologies, particularly to small and medium-sized firms. There were several schemes to encourage product and process innovation by assistance ranging from help with R and D costs to help with marketing the new product. For example in France there are innovation grants and refundable loans; in Holland, five-year plans for R and D; and in Germany, R and D support for small and medium-sized firms.

Typical of the thinking behind these measures is the German view that competitiveness now depends crucially upon innovation and quality performance, and that lack of resources should at no point be allowed to hold up a potentially viable innovation. German public spending under its Data Processing Programme and R and D promotion scheme is of the order of £350 million a year, compared with the £90 million or so at present spent (largely through the Research Requirements Boards) in the UK.

There appeared to be a shift *within* sectoral policies specifically towards the application of higher technology to process and product, looking for both rationalisation and diversification, and management restructuring. At the same time, there has been a shift *away* from sectoral policies, towards horizontal policies which promote the diffusion of high technologies, for example, or the occupational and geographical mobility of labour, throughout the economy. Even in the steel industry the emphasis is now more upon redundancy, retraining and regional diversification than on job retention.

There appears also to be increasing emphasis on sets of schemes which reinforce one another. An outstanding example here are the Dutch measures introduced in the last two years relating to investment incentives, sectoral reorganisation and R and D and innovation, all of which are mutually reinforcing. The German package affecting small and medium-sized businesses is another example, and their Data Processing Programme is comprehensive in another sense – it supports projects ranging from pure research to computer education in schools.

In general the emphasis on diffusion means that there is surprisingly little wasteful duplication of effort between countries (except perhaps in *télématiques*). Competition in diffusion can only lead to faster take-up of these new technologies, which in the long run is to everyone's benefit (by increasing productivity and so total resources). The faster the take-up, of course, the greater the competitive edge of our European rivals.

Finally, throughout Europe manpower policies are now seen as an integral part of industrial adjustment. Generous redundancy schemes in France and Luxembourg help to compensate workers caught in the adjustment process and encourage movement from declining sectors, while in Sweden state-subsidised retraining schemes encourage movement into growing sectors. In many of these countries the state accepts extensive responsibilities for training, and both schools and further education institutions are subsidised to ensure that the future workforce has the relevant skills.

Conclusions

I do not think one should harbour any illusions that industrial policy to encourage innovation can, by itself, reverse the industrial decline the UK has been experiencing for so many decades. However, I believe there are policies which will help, and they include the following:

(a) a much *wider* distribution of government R and D funding;

(b) a greater use of the Product and Process Development Scheme and the Market Entry Guarantee Scheme;

(c) the thorough activation of the Research Requirements Boards (which spent only £50 million in 1978);

(d) occasional resuscitation of the Selective Investment Scheme, but used as a means of encouraging scrapping and replacement;

(e) no further cut-backs (in fact an increase) in the long-lead public investment programme for which the government is responsible, especially in relevant education, training and transport;

(f) more constructive use of the SWPs to identify technology gaps and product opportunities;

(g) a tie-in between SWPs and the NEB, and increased NEB funding for the NEB's remaining (innovative) functions;

(h) government support for the TUC initiative for Technology Agreements;

(i) a loan guarantee scheme for small companies on Dutch lines;

(j) the recognition that the government is not responsible for picking 'winner' industries, but for increasing labour mobility, improving long-run employment prospects, and hence reducing the resistance to technical change.

References

[1] Blackaby, F. T. (ed.), *De-industrialisation*, London, Heinemann, 1979.

[2] Caves, R. E., 'Productivity differences among industries' in R. E. Caves and L. B. Krause (ed.), *Britain's Economic Performance*, Washington DC, Brookings Institution, 1980.

[3] Cornwall, J., *Modern Capitalism: its growth and transformation*, London, Martin Robertson, 1977.

[4] Freeman, C. and Pavitt, K., in K. Pavitt (ed.), *Technical Innovation and British Economic Performance*, London, Macmillan, 1980.

[5] Gomulka, S., in W. Beckerman (ed.), *Slow Growth in Britain*, Oxford, Clarendon Press, 1979.

[6] Lundberg, E., 'Productivity and structural change', *Economic Journal*, vol. 82 (supplement), March 1972.

[7] NEDC, *Conditions Favourable to Faster Growth*, London, HMSO, 1963.

[8] NEDO, *Adjustment Policies in Europe*, London, 1980.

[9] OECD, *Science Resources Newsletter*, Summer 1980.

[10] Pavitt, K., 'Technical innovation and industrial development', Part 2, *Futures*, vol. 12, no. 1, 1980.

[11] Peacock, A. T. *et al.*, *Structural Policies in West Germany and the UK*, London, Anglo-German Foundation, 1980.

[12] Ray, G. F., in L. Nabseth and G. F. Ray (ed.), *The Diffusion of New Industrial Processes*, Cambridge University Press, 1974.

[13] Salter, W. E. G., *Productivity and Technical Change*, Cambridge University Press, 1960.

[14] Schumpeter, J. A., *Capitalism, Socialism and Democracy*, New York, Harper, 1942.

[15] *Scientific American*, October 1980.

[16] Stout, D. K., 'Industrial performance in the longer term: technical annex', London, NEDC, 1974.

[17] —, 'De-industrialisation and industrial policy' in Blackaby [1].

[18] Varley, E., 'R and D policy and the Industrial Strategy', London, NEDC, 1979.

[19] UNECE, *Growth and Stagnation in the European Economy* by I. Svennilson, Geneva, 1954.

7(III) Industrial Innovation and the Role of Bodies like the National Enterprise Board

by W. B. Willott*

The purpose of this chapter is to explore the role that a body like the National Enterprise Board can play in stimulating innovation and investment in advanced technology. It considers certain of the main constraints, in particular various forms of risk-aversion; the case for a catalytic government role through a body like the NEB; and some of the practical problems that may occur in such an operation, including those arising from the relationship with government. It will focus less on 'bread and butter' innovation – the steady upgrading of a product, or of production, marketing or service techniques, that marks the well-run company – and more on the exploitation of rapidly moving technologies, or step changes in technology, where the NEB may have a modest but significant role to play.

Factors affecting Innovation
There is no *a priori* way of determining whether the 'right' level of research and innovation is taking place. The only practical way of assessing whether this is likely, and whether there is a case for government intervention, is by considering the main types of market imperfection that can be expected to lead to a misallocation of resources. These generally fall into two main categories: (a) where there is a divergence between social and private rates of return, and (b) where structural causes or attitudes to risk lead to inability to adopt innovations or discoveries effectively.

   Mansfield [4], Arrow [2] and others have examined the problem of the disparity between social and private rates of return. They

* Any views expressed in this chapter are the responsibility of the author and do not represent any formal views of the National Enterprise Board.

noted that it tends to be greater in the case of radical innovations than in relatively minor ones: it is also affected by the degree to which the innovator is subject to competition and the costs of imitating the innovation. A patent system is the normal response to this problem. It enhances the value of such property rights and gives the innovator a temporary degree of monopoly. But, in practice, it may not provide a complete solution. A balance has to be struck between the degree of protection for one innovator and scope for significantly different innovations by competitors. Again, larger firms may be able to secure greater benefits, not merely because they have greater ability and knowledge to exploit the patent system, but because they may have greater financial and managerial strength and access to information to exploit their innovation quickly or to drive a hard bargain with smaller innovators who can only exploit their invention by licensing. Measures to deal with this category of market imperfection are outside the scope of the present paper.

The misallocation of resources resulting from various forms of risk-aversion and from management attitudes and perceptions, on the other hand, are relevant to certain of the operations of the NEB. The evidence of these imperfections tends to be *a priori* and often anecdotal, but is so widespread that the main issue would appear to be not whether they exist but how widespread and important they are. Three main types are set out below.

The size of the risk in relation to the size of the enterprise

If the scale of risks associated with an innovation are such that materialisation of all the down-side risks would threaten the existence of the enterprise as a whole, managers may properly decide that they should not be undertaken. Whether this is the case will depend, in many instances, upon the industrial structure and the nature of the companies in the business area in question. An example, on a large scale, was Rolls-Royce's decision to press ahead with the RB 211. In terms of the project itself this was clearly the right thing to do but, as was evident throughout, the scale of risk was quite outside the company's resources.

The availability of appropriate finance

Traditionally the mature company in the UK has sought to finance R and D and its more risky activities out of retained earnings. However, the Wilson Committee [7] noted that, in most western countries, the ability of companies to generate finance internally has declined since the mid-1960s. This trend has been most marked in the UK, where the decline in companies' internally generated funds and the higher rates of inflation since 1973 have reduced the level of real profitability to a very low figure. Finance for Industry [3] noted that in France, West Germany and Italy there has been a trend towards higher gearing: the banks have become more ready to make longer-term loans at relatively low interest rates and to live with their industrial investments through difficult times. In the UK the banks have, in recent years, become somewhat more flexible, in part due to increased competition from American banks in London. It is hard to discern directly any impact of these trends on the level of industrial innovation, though one would assume that, while a high level of gearing is advantageous in good times, the interest burden is likely to be a severe constraint during stormy periods.

In parallel with this marked decline in real profitability, the UK was the only major OECD country to show a decline in privately funded R and D over the period 1967–75. However, although there may have been some reduction in the finance available to industry, as a result of inflation, and competition from government securities and alternative forms of investment, the bulk of the evidence to the Wilson Committee was that there is little *overall* shortage of funds for industry at the price levels obtaining. Where gaps occur these are for particular types of industrial investment – such as very high-risk innovative projects – or in the terms on which the finance is available, which may not meet the perceived needs of the borrower.

The decline in internally generated funds has been paralleled by the growth in the power and importance of the investing institutions. With total assets of over £80 billion at end-1978, of which getting on for half is in company securities, their aggregate importance is large. But they tend to focus their attention on the top 100 or so quoted companies and exert a powerful influence on these. On the other hand, their individual stake in each company tends to be relatively small, reflecting both a desire to spread risks and a recognition that a substantial shareholding effectively locks in the shareholder. All this results in a degree of fragmentation that makes it difficult for a company to build up a special relationship with a limited number of shareholders or for the shareholders to sort out any problems with management at an early stage. Moreover, the performance tests to which these institutions submit themselves in general lead to financial, essentially short-term, yardsticks for judging success and this has its influence on companies in which they invest.

The debate on this subject has brought about some changes in attitudes, but the NEB experience is that, with some distinguished exceptions, the majority of investing institutions still judge that their fiduciary duties require them to favour industrial investments which offer a running, and preferably growing, yield. However, innovation or development on any scale requires a continued commitment with no immediate financial return over a period of several years. It is therefore likely to be difficult to find many institutions willing to finance start-ups, new-technology-based companies with green field activities, or those where high risks and investments are needed relative to the size of the company.

An underlying aspect of this is the personal relationship between the financial investor and the innovator. W. Kingston has suggested in [1] that, because of the uncertainty involved in any innovation, every decision to invest involves an emotional element (empathy between the investor and the innovator, or an innovation that fires the investor's imagination). He draws the conclusion that individual investors are capable of investing in only a limited range of projects; and that to ensure that an adequate number of investments are brought forward to commercialisation it is necessary to have a large number of potential decision-makers. The trend towards greater concentration of funds in financial institutions, Kingston argues, has reduced the number of such decision-points and, correspondingly, the number of decisions to invest in new business.

This thesis is difficult to prove or disprove. However, the Advisory Council for Applied Research and Development (ACARD) [1]) records that American studies of large firms have suggested that the existence of a 'product champion', or in-house entrepreneur, within the firm has been a significant factor in a company taking up new ideas quickly and efficiently; and it seems reasonable to assume that this will hold as true for financial institutions as for large companies.

As well as the centralisation of decision-taking, the concentration of financial investment decisions in the hands of investment managers rather than individual entrepreneurs may also contribute to increased risk-aversion. Where managers are essentially salary earners, the personal up-side benefits of a successful gamble are small, while the down-side risks of a disaster are severe. In the US, especially the west coast, a major source of finance for new high-technology activities has come from venture capitalists who pull together their own money and the capital of other rich individuals to back entrepreneurs. For a variety of reasons, including taxation levels, social attitudes and the relative absence of a wealthy technologically-oriented middle class, nothing on a similar scale has yet developed in the UK.

The behaviour of innovating companies
Several imperfections are immediately apparent:

(1) The existence of monopoly or oligopoly, unless there is effective exposure to world competition, is likely to have its impact on the rate of innovation (though monopolistic profits from one activity can provide the cash to fund innovation in other areas).

(2) In the UK 100 firms control some 70 per cent of manufacturing output (and the pattern is not dissimilar elsewhere). If one assumes that in each firm key decisions are made by, at most, three or four people, most of the major decisions about innovation in the UK are made by 300–400 people. In such circumstances their personal experiences and prejudices, and relations with each other, are likely to be important, and the process of decision-taking far from that of a free market. Mansfield [4] has argued that innovation is better handled the fewer the decision-makers involved, and indeed decisions by a few individuals are likely to be better than decision by committee. But since, in any sector, there is a limited number of companies, a number of opportunities are likely to be missed.

(3) Another important constraint is the 'culture' of each company. Any well-established company contains a corpus of received wisdom, based on experience, which is ignored at peril. This has a number of effects. Firstly, such organisations find internal inhibitions against radical changes in direction. Unless he is absolutely sure of his ground – and where uncertainties and risks are high this is by definition not the case – an executive will be hesitant, in his career interests, about challenging the received wisdom since, in general, his private expectations of reward in the event of success are unlikely to match the down-side risks. Moreover, the sheer effort of attempting this, and mustering the necessary support for a radical innovation, can be daunting.

(4) The management style of a company is obviously important.

Some structures are better adapted to particular priorities. A highly centralised organisation may stifle individual initiative. A company that grows essentially as a financial conglomerate may not encourage or facilitate the flow of resources into innovative areas; it may be too concerned with short-term profitability, because this is the correct thing to manage in such a conglomerate where central management can have little real feel for the longer-term aspects of a diverse set of activities.

(5) The structure of the companies in a particular business area may also be a constraint. The particular range of skills may not be found in one firm and personalities may inhibit cooperation or restructuring for a time. While market forces should, in the end, lead to suitable adjustments, this will be too late if, in the meantime, overseas companies whose structures are better adapted or more flexible secure a dominant market share and competitive advantage.

(6) Other practical constraints are the problem of entry against competitive products from older technologies which may be well down their learning curve; reluctance to write off prematurely major investment in existing technology; the mere organisational effort needed to find and to focus the necessary human and financial resources.

Clearly some of these factors apply particularly to larger companies and less so to smaller entrepreneurial firms. However, the evidence about the relative propensity of large and small companies to innovate is far from conclusive. Small firms will tend to have an advantage in having closer linkages between the various functions within the company, and more flexible management structures. Large companies, on the other hand, are better able to obtain and exploit information, are less vulnerable to budgeting changes and constraints, better able to afford the 'entry fee' to new technologies and, from their in-house strengths and knowledge of the particular industry, will be better able to assess the market potential of a new product or process. Mansfield [4] and Scherer [6] have concluded that, in general, large firms are not proportionately more innovative than small, save where the introduction of products and processes requires greater resources; and, in the case of certain industries, for example, size may even have a moderately stultifying effect on innovation.

Another reason for inadequate innovation is differences in time-scales. Major innovation is a long-term process, both technically and in the development of the market. The balance of risks and benefits can be abruptly changed in mid-stream by governments for shorter-term political reasons without regard for the industrial implications. The different time-scale of financial institutions has already been mentioned. Firms themselves may be operating under financial constraints or other pressures which shorten time horizons. For all these reasons the pace of innovation may be sub-optimal.

The Case for Government Involvement
Do these imperfections in the operation of the market matter? Is the misallocation of resources sufficiently significant to warrant government intervention? It is certainly arguable that the operation of competitive forces and of the financial markets provide an effective mechanism for transferring resources from the non-competitive to the competitive companies; that there is evidence that governments cannot reliably make commercial judgements better than the private sector; and that if other governments seek to misallocate resources that is no reason for us to – indeed it is sensible to sit back and take the benefit of their efforts. It is of particularly doubtful value for a number of governments to concentrate funds on the same fashionable high-technology sector, like aerospace, in pursuit of a market of limited size.

Clearly, it is true that governments should play a major part in ensuring that the various markets – for labour, capital and the exchange of ideas – operate as efficiently and smoothly as possible. That said, there are a number of factors, some general, some particular to the UK, which complicate this picture.

(1) The worldwide competitive situation in many manufactured goods is shifting rapidly, reflecting to a considerable extent the loss of western political control of the third world. Because of low wage costs in developing countries and the ease of transfer of mature technologies, price competition in basic manufactured products is keen. The developed countries are, therefore, in general, retreating from such areas and moving into higher-technology, higher value-added products which can command a premium on price. Government adjustment policies are designed to ease the pain of the former and encourage the latter.

(2) Indeed Utterback has argued [8] that the US and Europe should be seen as the main source of product innovation; that Japan's competitive strength is process innovation – developing ways of producing these products more efficiently; and that the third world should be the major area of low-cost large-volume production. On this scenario it becomes even more vital for a country like the UK to be constantly innovating.

(3) While there is plenty of scope for market segmentation and specialisation, western countries are bound to be aiming at similar markets and product areas, currently away from material- and energy-intensive areas and into 'knowledge-intensive' areas. Modest government support, *effectively* applied, can make a major difference to relative competitive positions. For example, the French government has brought it about that six of the top ten computer software companies in Europe are French, while the Japanese have, over a period, brought a succession of industries to world dominance by close cooperation between government and industry.

(4) Some of these product areas may prove to be of strategic importance. Certain technologies tend to be basic to many industries: the transistor, the computer and micro-chips are cases where preservation of a substantial technological lead may exert a pervasive effect on competitiveness throughout many sectors of industry.

(5) While technology may be readily transferred, there will be a permanent time lag. In a dynamic environment with a continual process of innovation, the receiving country will always be at a disadvantage unless it can either produce goods with an extremely marked productive efficiency (as has been the case for many years in Japan), or it can pick up and accelerate the pace of its own development of the innovation.

(6) This is particularly apparent where there are discontinuities, such as step changes in technology; where the entry fee is very large in relation to the size of the companies concerned; or where the product is large and indivisible, like a nuclear power station or modern process plant.

(7) The time-scales of innovation are often crucial. It is only possible, in some cases, to keep together a capability in an industry if the level of demand is above a certain minimum. If it falls below this the skills may be dissipated and it may not prove possible to rebuild that capability in less than five to ten years.

(8) Moreover, the innovating firm will tend to try, as a matter of conscious policy, to limit the rate of diffusion of its technology. Most overseas plants of American semi-conductor companies, for example, do only limited design and development work, this being reserved for headquarters.

Government Intervention

Whether governments *should* intervene must depend upon an assessment that the benefits (including spin-offs) outweigh the costs. This is difficult to do rigorously, and whether other governments are also intervening must be a factor in the equation. Whatever the theoretical answer, the fact is that all governments support R and D in industry to a greater or lesser degree, whether or not they pursue other interventionist industrial policies. The crude OECD figures (Table 7.7) show the proportions of business R and D expenditure in the main OECD countries funded by the public and private sectors in 1975.

Table 7.7   *Sources of funds for business R and D, 1975*
(*percentages*)

	Private	Abroad[a]	Government
United States	64.4	—	35.6
France	69.2	5.4	25.4
Germany	78.9	3.2	17.9
Italy	90.6	2.9	6.5
Japan	98.2	0.1	1.7
Netherlands	90.0	6.4	3.6
United Kingdom	62.8	6.3	30.9

Source: OECD [5].

[a]Inward investment.

These aggregate figures reveal little about the proportion of government funding for its own purposes (for example, defence) and that going for general economic purposes. And, given the difficulties of reconciling different definitions of R and D, the figures cannot be taken too literally. But individual study of different countries shows that they all use some forms of assistance, such as tax relief, awareness programmes, tariff or non-tariff barriers, public purchasing, loans and grants.

The UK is no exception. The instruments of government policy range from a 100 per cent tax allowance for R and D expenditure to the provision of risk finance (cost-sharing contracts and pre-production orders) or subsidies (grants) under a variety of sectoral schemes, the Product and Process Development Scheme and the Requirements Boards. The NRDC licenses intellectual property funded by the public sector and provides finance for the earlier stages of development in return for royalties. The NEB also plays a role, to be considered shortly.

Where public finance is involved, questions of resource allocation and selectivity immediately arise. Different countries have adopted different solutions. In France it is possible for the government directly to back, by various means, chosen companies in selected sectors. In Germany support for industrial R and D has been focused much more sharply than in the UK on a limited number of key sectors, including basic engineering, and has been administered largely on a delegated basis by the various independent institutes: but independent panels of businessmen play an important part in choosing the sectors and approving individual cases for support.

A similar pattern has been followed in the UK. As soon as selectivity is introduced, implying decisions by government to channel support in the most cost-effective way in individual cases, judgements have to be made about the likelihood of commercial success and of profitability. Businessmen have, therefore, been drafted in, both to bring to bear their knowledge and commercial judgement, and to deflect some of the possible charges of arbitrariness. The Requirements Boards and Advisory Committees for the sectoral schemes are all composed of businessmen. General assistance under the 1972 Industry Act is handled by businessmen seconded to the Department of Industry and subject to the approval of an independent Industrial Development Advisory Board. The NRDC is staffed by people with a commercial or scientific background, and the NEB is run as a commercial organisation. It is interesting that a number of state holding companies with activities similar to those of the NEB exist in seven or eight OECD countries.

The National Enterprise Board
The NEB is therefore only one instrument of government policy to

encourage innovation in the UK. It is a relatively young organisation but, in the five years of its existence, has undergone some
radical changes. Conceived in 1973–4 on the model of such overseas
agencies as the Swedish *Statsforetag*, and envisaged as a major
agent for social change and the redistribution of ownership in UK
manufacturing, the NEB has, under both Labour and Conservative
governments become much more finely focused in its activities. It
now effectively has four roles: a management role for companies
that may be passed to it by the government and for its existing
investments; industrial investment in the regions; the provision of
loans to small firms; and as a catalyst in the field of advanced
technologies. It is in this last role that the NEB has a part to play in
promoting innovation. The remaining sections of this paper describe in more detail this role of the NEB, the rationale for how the
NEB actually operates, some of the problems inherent in the
operation of such a body and how these might be minimised.

The present Guidelines, laid down by the government for the
NEB for its high-technology activities, are essentially as follows:

(a) it should seek to avoid duplicating what the private sector is
doing or is planning to do;
(b) it should, wherever possible, invest in conjunction with the
private sector;
(c) its role should be catalytic, aiming to encourage new activities
by the private sector, and an essential part of this is that the
NEB's investments should be turned over and disposed of to
the private sector as soon as commercially practicable;
(d) the NEB is, in doing all this, required at all times to act in a
commercial manner unless directed otherwise by the Secretary
of State.

It would be possible to operate in a variety of ways to meet this
remit. For example, given that the essence of the role is that the
NEB is prepared to take on higher risks and/or wait for a longer
time for its return, it might be possible to develop an underwriting
approach. But, in practice, given the limited number of investments
involved, the need for a reasonably conventional financial structure
for its ventures if private sector participation or disposal to the
private sector is to be possible, and the need to be able to make
substantial profits on successful investments to offset the failures,
equity financing has been the norm.

In the high-technology area NEB investments have tended to be of three kinds. First, there are the major initiatives, like Inmos (manufacturing standard micro-electronic memories or micro-computers), Nexos (electronic office systems), and, most recently, Celltech (applying genetic engineering). Secondly, there are a variety of smaller ventures, in fields like medical electronics and software applications, which may have resulted from an NEB initiative or from an approach to the NEB. Finally, there have been companies rescued by the government or the NEB when they were in financial difficulty, like Cambridge Instruments, Ferranti and ICL. The importance of high-technology investments can be seen from the Table 7.8, which shows the largest current NEB investments.

Table 7.8   Main NEB investments, 1980 (£ million)

Aregon (viewdata systems)	4.5
British Underwater Engineering (underwater engineering equipment)	7.0
Cambridge Instruments (scientific and medical instruments)	15.0
Data Recording Instrument Company (peripherals)	15.0
Inmos (micro-electronic components)	21.0[a]
Insac Products Ltd (computer software)	4.0
Monotype (printing machinery)	3.5
Nexos (electronic office systems)	16.0
Q1 Europe (micro-computer office systems)	2.0
United Medical Enterprises (medical equipment exporter)	6.0
Wholesale Vehicle Finance (motor distributor finance)	11.0

[a] £50 million committed.

The NEB currently envisages a carefully planned and worked out programme to bring forward a succession of initiatives, similar to Nexos or Celltech. It also expects to continue to pick up a number of approaches from entrepreneurs or small companies with ideas worth exploiting, when the risks and finance needed rule out conventional financial support. To carry out its functions effectively the NEB has been reorganised to correspond to its three main functions: new initiatives, management of investments, and divestment.

How does this general scheme fit in with the gaps which we have identified in the operation of the market? Given the requirement that the NEB should operate in a commercial manner, without subsidy, there is no way in which it can close the gap between the social and private rates of return on a project. Its role is to fill some of the gaps left by the various kinds of risk-aversion identified earlier which are particularly inherent in high-technology projects.

First, like any substantial institution, it can help to finance or underwrite an investment that, because of its size, is too risky for the resources of the individuals or company concerned. In other words, the NEB will finance start-ups or development projects that the private venture-capital organisations are unwilling to finance at present. In doing so, the NEB has to be clear in each case why private sector finance is not forthcoming: where the proposition appears viable, this is usually a question of the general policy or lack of flexibility of the companies concerned, lack of strategic appreciation of the situation, or the attitudes of the individual managers concerned.

Secondly, many NEB investments have been made because the received wisdom or inherited commitments (like massive investment in plant or in a market rental base) prevent existing companies from moving fast enough. Inmos is an example where, prior to its launch, the agreed view in the industry was that it was not worthwhile for UK manufacturers to make standard chips. While it is too soon to say whether Inmos will succeed, that received wisdom has now been challenged: indeed GEC subsequently announced plans for a joint venture with Fairchild to manufacture standard chips, though Fairchild have now withdrawn. Again, although the UK office machinery industry, as early as 1976–7, expressed great concern about its ability to move fast enough into modern electronic systems, it proved difficult to make any rapid, significant moves, largely because of the structure of the industry and of the companies concerned. Nexos appears to have a substantial lead in the UK in the integration of text and voice that is generally believed to be the future course of management and office systems.

The same is true about the gap in the provision of finance. Until very recently, few of the major financial institutions have shown themselves comfortable investing in new technologies and high risks. The North Sea is generally held out as the exception that disproves the rule, but it is arguable that it became fashionable; that the strength and reputation of the Seven Sisters and the ability to perform a full risk analysis reduced uncertainty; that people taking decisions involving risks tend to seek comfort by 'chatting around' and, once an activity becomes fashionable, its acceptability becomes mutually reinforcing. Financial institutions also argue that they mobilise large funds for property investments (but a ten- or twenty-year view would hardly suggest a high degree of risk!). The debate in the Wilson Committee that led to divided views about the case for a North Sea oil fund to support industrial investment reflects the concern about the financial gap. But one of the aims of the NEB, in its catalytic role, is both to encourage the institutions to become more 'comfortable' with high-technology investments and to stimulate more of a venture-capital approach to funding.

The sceptic is entitled to ask why, given the imperfections of human nature, the NEB can succeed where others fail. Part of the answer is that the NEB is an organisation whose objectives are specifically to identify, appraise and seize opportunities for the UK. The attitudes of the staff and the culture of the whole organisation are, therefore, geared to making things happen that would not otherwise happen. In other words, its function is to question the received wisdom in British industry and financial institutions and to act as catalyst for change. The obverse of the coin, of course, is that the NEB lacks the accumulated experience and knowledge of any good, established firm about the industry, its customers and the behaviour patterns of the other competitors. Experience can lead a company automatically round the most obvious open man-hole covers. The NEB has, in a sense, to work harder and more analytically. It also needs to compensate for in-house experience by finding ways of drawing on outside experience, and it has developed the practice of seeking a range of outside advisers, in addition to Board members, to participate in and criticise projects as they develop. The lack of experience is also one of the fundamental reasons why the NEB itself seeks private sector participation from the outset, to provide an independent cross-check on the merits of an investment, on the way it is set up and the people selected to run it (and, ultimately, to facilitate divestment).

A related problem arises in the management of investments. Here the lack of established management and long experience of a particular industry is an obvious handicap. But, like other private sector venture-capital organisations or holding companies, the NEB seeks to overcome this by ensuring that the new ventures have a strong board and management and that the performance of the company and of the management are tightly monitored. Here again, there are great advantages in having a small number of strong private sector partners, who can each bring their own viewpoints and expertise to bear and ensure that the management is effective.

How does the NEB identify opportunities for major initiatives? There is, in fact, a broad consensus on the key technologies for the future. The recent succession of ACARD reports is as convenient a list as any. The Japanese are quite open about their priorities and this, too, is a pretty good guide. In setting up a new initiative, its success and the NEB's ability to attract private sector partners depends upon the thoroughness of the groundwork in establishing the gap and the right approach to filling it. The NEB has also been successful in establishing good links with leading scientists in research and academic institutions; one of the features of the academic culture in this country is that such people often find it difficult to work satisfactorily with private sector commercial companies, but find it easier to cooperate with a publicly owned body. The recent setting up of Celltech is a good example, where the skills and enthusiasm of the distinguished scientists at the MRC Laboratory of Molecular Biology at Cambridge and in other leading academic institutions will be linked to the exploitation in the UK of their discoveries; and but for the initiative of the NEB this would not have happened in the foreseeable future.

The essence of the NEB is that it can accept greater risks and take a longer view than a private sector organisation of its size. In principle, therefore, it can combine the advantages of small size and speed of movement, with the resources and credit rating of a much larger organisation, namely the government. There is an inherent dilemma here. The Board, of commercial people, are having, in effect, to apply their commercial judgements of risk and reward in the knowledge that the NEB cannot go bust. This is not an issue of principle but one of degree. In principle the larger financial institutions could carry similar risks (and with examples like the setting up of Prutech there is evidence of greater willingness to do so). But it does mean that the Board must guard against the risk of becoming a source of soft money. If an organisation like the NEB is to recruit able and motivated staff they are bound to become enthusiastic about their projects. Over a period of time, too, a Board becomes committed to its past decisions. It is in no way unique in this and the only protection is the professionalism and ability of the eminent Board members, the interplay with the other shareholders, and the commitment of the Board and its staff to a commercial approach to investments.

A further dimension of the NEB's role comes from its relationship with government. In particular:

(1) The impact of politics: while this is more apparent in some of the other functions of the NEB (such as its 'hospital' cases, the concern about regional employment and, most recently, the interest in small firms), nevertheless, politics and the conflicts between different government objectives can affect the NEB. An example is Inmos where the decision of the NEB to back the company's wish to site their first UK manufacturing facility at Bristol, rather than in an assisted area, ran straight into the regional policy problem. The result was a very substantial delay, which ultimately reversed the balance of advantage in favour of South Wales, given the availability of regional grants; but it had an impact on the shape and commercial prospects of the company.

(2) Because the Secretary of State for Industry is responsible for the NEB to Parliament, appropriate arrangements have to be made for financing and monitoring: and certain decisions by the Board (investments over a particular size, and all disposals) require approval by the Secretary of State. There is an inherent tension between public accountability for decisions and the basic purpose of the NEB, which is to be an instrument able to do some of the things that government cannot, that is to behave in a commercial manner. There is therefore a potential risk of second-guessing the commercial judgement of the Board (and the present government, in seeking to reduce the level of delegated authority, has increased the proportion of NEB decisions which require its consent).

(3) There is, at present, something of an internal contradiction in the NEB's Guidelines, which require it to behave commercially at all times, and yet to dispose of assets as soon as is commercially practicable without regard to its financial duty.

(4) The interplay between NEB and government and the requirement to seek statutory approvals can delay decision-making. Normally that can be planned for, but in a fluid and fast-moving situation it can complicate and make more difficult a proper commercial approach.

(5) This extra dimension can make it more difficult to recruit staff

from the private sector who are unused to political pressures and the government decision-making process.

(6) The need to liaise with government and to cope with Parliamentary and press interest requires the NEB to carry more staff, and hence higher overheads, than a comparable private sector organisation.

Conclusions

(1) There is room to improve the UK's performance in adopting and exploiting innovations.

(2) The government is inevitably intervening in a whole variety of ways which affect industry and industrial innovation and which constitute its industrial policy.

(3) The NEB is one relatively modest instrument of that industrial policy.

(4) Whether the NEB will be successful it is too early to say: the proof of the pudding will be in the eating. But if it does prove successful it will be an extremely cost-effective instrument of policy.

(5) The NEB criteria and approaches are far from unique and have their counterparts elsewhere as other countries fight to help their industries to gain a competitive edge internationally.

References

[1] ACARD, *Industrial Innovation*, London, HMSO, 1979.
[2] Arrow, K., 'Economic welfare and the allocation of resources for invention' in National Bureau of Economic Research, *The Rate and Direction of Inventive Activity*, Princeton University Press, 1962.
[3] Finance for Industry, in Treasury, *Evidence to the Committee to Review the Functioning of Financial Institutions*, vol. 4, London, HMSO, 1978.
[4] Mansfield, E. *et al.*, *The Production and Application of New Industrial Technology*, New York, Norton, 1977.
[5] OECD, *Trends in Industrial R and D in Selected OECD Member Countries, 1967–1975*, Paris, 1979.
[6] Scherer, F. M., *Industrial Market Structure and Economic Performance*, Chicago, Rand McNally, 1970.
[7] Treasury, *Report of the Committee to Review the Functioning of Financial Institutions* [Wilson Committee], London, HMSO, 1980.
[8] Utterback, J. M., private communication, 1980.

7(IV)　Catching up with Our Competitors: the Role of Industrial Policy

by D. T. Jones*

On present trends most of Britain's industrial competitors will probably have caught up with the US in terms of labour productivity within this decade: Germany, France, Benelux, Scandinavia and Switzerland in the mid-1980s, and Japan somewhat later. Britain on the other hand will have only half that level of productivity, and presumably also that living standard. The reversal of this relative decline in economic, and particularly industrial, performance, the origins of which go back at least a hundred years, is the major challenge for any industrial policy pursued by the government.

This chapter attempts to outline some of the steps that might be taken to develop an Industrial Strategy, particularly in the light of the experience of other Western European countries. First we outline some important factors to be considered in drawing up such a strategy. Our definition of industrial policy is broader than in conventional studies, and discriminatory policies seeking to influence strategic decision-making in oligopolistic sectors are not seen as incompatible with horizontal policies towards innovation, education and training, small firms, etc.; these are discussed in turn.

The story of Britain's poor industrial performance throughout the century is summarised in [14]); important recent contributions include Blackaby [6], Pavitt [15], Caves and Krause [7] and Prais [16]. Pavitt also summarises the disturbing evidence on Britain's record in developing new innovations in Chapter 7(I), noting that in

* This paper was written in the context of a research project at the Sussex European Research Centre into government intervention and structural adjustment in European industry, funded by the Volkswagen Foundation and the Anglo-German Foundation. It draws heavily on ideas developed in the project, though the author alone is responsible for the views expressed in this chapter.

any discussion of British industrial performance chemicals and military-related equipment stand out as exceptions. This raises the question whether industrial policy in future will be more appropriately directed towards promoting the development of new innovations or towards the imitation and adoption of technologies developed elsewhere.

In addition to increasing import penetration in many product areas and growing differences between the unit values of British engineering exports and those of her European competitors, the Maldague Report [10] noted a perverse pattern of specialisation in British trade: in the 1970s it was becoming more concentrated on products with a lower skill content and decreasingly involved in more sophisticated goods with a higher skill content (the Italians were in the same position). There is, however, a particularly wide spread between the best and the worst firms within individual sectors in Britain, whether measured in terms of productivity or of wage levels, with the best firms often well abreast of international competition. What is disturbing is the survival of a rather large tail of poor performers which have neither been squeezed out of existence nor forced to adopt best-practice techniques.

One of the clearest implications of increasing economic divergence between Britain and the rest of the EEC is the growing incompatibility between the operation of the EEC in its existing form and continued British membership. It will become even more difficult to meet domestic expectations of rising living standards and the temptation to opt out of the world trading system will inevitably grow. The serious consequences of accepting this outcome, both for domestic industry and living standards, and for the continued functioning of the world trading system, itself under considerable pressure, have not been fully appreciated to date. On the other hand it is difficult to envisage a positive strategy aimed at turning round British industrial performance that does not involve at least some recognition and accommodation by Britain's trading partners.

The context in which such a strategy has to be devised is also far more difficult than a decade or so ago. Quite apart from the prolonged worldwide recession, Britain is caught between the rapid pace of technological change being set by the leading nations, such as Japan, in the downstream applications of electronics technology on the one hand, and the emergence of competition in less sophisticated goods from the newly industrialised countries on the other.

Simply to maintain the British position demands more rapid structural change than hitherto and, unlike the circumstances in which the US achieved technological leadership in the postwar period, technological change is not now being driven by large military programmes. Another new factor is the growing part played by governments in technological competition, to the extent – as in the case of France – of staking their whole future on ensuring that they are represented in the potential growth industries of the future. Irrespective of whether they succeed or not, the pressures on countries some way from the technological frontier are intensified.

Although there might have been room for some optimism in the 1960s, there can be no doubt now that Britain needs to catch up. Different policies and economic philosophies are appropriate for countries in different relative positions, and there is a critical time lag between an important change in that position and the related change in perception of the appropriate policy stance and economic outlook. The time lag is greatest in government, which represents the lowest common denominator of what is possible politically. Hard though it is to accept, the free market is not the best ideological framework for conducting industrial policy when falling behind, as is Britain. A more eclectic approach to policy-making is required, although the market mechanism should still be seen as important for signalling the optimum allocation of resources.

Improving the overall performance of the supply side of the economy, and beginning the process of catching up, necessitate a whole panoply of different policies; there are no easy answers. The recognition by all recent commentators that Britain's problems lie essentially on the supply side, and that these problems have persisted through quite different macroeconomic policies, indicates that such a strategy should not only be a central feature of government policy, but also be seen as a complement to whatever macroeconomic policies are pursued on the demand side. The more recent monetarist orientation of French macroeconomic policy is not seen as incompatible with an extensive programme of highly discriminatory policies pursued by the Ministry of Industry. The whole thrust of government policy-making in France was initially geared to overtaking Britain, and thereafter towards catching up with Germany, while it now quite consciously seeks to emulate many features of the Japanese economy. Policy-makers such as Stoffaes [17], the work of CEPII [8] and the report of the Industry Commission on the Eighth Plan [9] all see this in terms of a struggle involving mobilisation of 'the entire nation'.

The Nature of Industrial Policy

From what has been said it is clear that our definition of the nature and objectives of industrial policy is somewhat wider than conventional studies that focus on the instruments used and their effectiveness. It essentially includes all actions which, consciously or unconsciously, seek to modify the structure and workings of the industrial sector of the economy. One important dimension is government involvement in the decision-making framework of industry, particularly oligopolistic industry – the form of organisation in many sectors. In some countries, such as France, the state plays an important role in this process, but less obviously so in others such as Germany.

Oligopoly, with high entry barriers, economies of scale, large capital requirements, long lead times, relatively homogeneous products and often a degree of public (monopsonistic) procurement, involves taking a much longer view than is normal in a competitive market. This is true in industries at the forefront of technical progress where, once the direction of technical change has been established by a multitude of small innovative firms, larger firms are better able to raise sufficient capital, undertake the substantial risk and internalise the benefits of innovation over time. It also applies to other aspects of strategic decision-making in sectors where a limited number of firms dominate the domestic industry. Survival in such industries involves staying in the market, and mistaken or short-sighted decisions may result in elimination with little chance of re-entry. The consequences of mistaken investment decisions only become evident much later, by which time the situation may have compounded itself. At this point governments are faced with the difficult decision whether, given a temporary breathing space through government support, the firm can be returned to viability.

A close and continuous dialogue between the main actors within this framework greatly facilitates such choices, thereby reducing the element of uncertainty, and may forestall or more quickly reverse potentially disastrous strategies. A system where this dialogue is an in-built feature of relationships between banks, firms, industry associations and government, and between firms themselves, such as in Germany, or where these relationships are internalised in big industrial groups, such as the Japanese *Zaibatsu*, is an important advantage in industrial and technological competitiveness. Such a framework places greater emphasis on non-price factors – quality and reliability – in technological change, and is accompanied by a well developed and highly competitive small-firms sector. The traditional arms-length relationships between firms, trade unions, banks, government and small firms seem therefore to be important impediments to innovation and competitiveness in Britain. The role of the state in this context is, on the one hand, to represent the interests of the nation where these differ from those of the companies themselves, by intervening selectively or mobilising a consensus in a particular direction and, on the other, to reinforce weak links in the private planning framework. French industrial policy in the last two decades has been concerned in both these directions.

Industrial Policy and Strategic Decision-Making

As indicated earlier, a fundamental change of attitudes towards improving productivity and the technological competence of British industry is a pre-requisite for the success of any set of industrial policies. Such a drive to catch up with our competitors involves re-examining the roles of, and the relationships between, the major participants in the decision-making framework. Although the trade unions have a major influence on Labour Party policy, the link between the Conservative Party and industry is not nearly so strong; few members of Parliament or the Cabinet come from a business rather than a professional background. A large part of the initiative for such a re-examination will therefore have to come from industry itself, and the recent CBI declaration that they would pursue such an exercise and argue the case of business more vigorously is a welcome development. Although perhaps unable to take the initiative, the government can respond by developing appropriate industrial policies.

In this exercise and in defining the role of government, a great deal can be learnt from other countries. This is not to argue for the wholesale transplantation of foreign practices into this country, but it can indicate the direction in which to seek UK solutions. For instance, we do not have an industrial banking tradition as in Germany, whereby via their own and proxy shareholdings, and by representation on the boards of large companies, the banks play an active supporting role in long-term strategies. Their extensive experience of the strategies of other companies within their portfolio, and their interest in maximising the success of all these companies greatly facilitate cooperation in developing new technology. These close links between companies have been extremely important in the engineering industry (for instance), where frequent contacts on a continuing basis focus the technical efforts of a firm on the emerging requirements of a customer firm. British companies, on the other hand, often pride themselves on buying from the cheapest supplier, with no continuing obligation. The industrial associations, such as the VDMA, which have no direct equivalent in Britain, are also important as filtering mechanisms in technical change and in developing a consensus on the future direction of an industry.

Simply to concentrate on the inadequate provision of long-term funds in this country, for instance, misses the point that it is also the German banks' ability to assess long-term strategies independently that is important. This can help greatly to reduce uncertainty when taking decisions and should not be regarded as an unwarranted and unnecessary intrusion on the proper functions of management. Likewise institutional investors, who are increasingly important sources of funds for British industry, and who claim they do not want any involvement in decision-making, act as a positive disadvantage in this process. Apart from the question of whether they could really dispose of their shares in a major company that got into trouble, the uncertainty over their intentions increases the risks involved.

One answer to these weaknesses in the British environment is for the state itself to provide the funds, or at least the guarantees, as the French government does through the nationalised banks or via the Ministry of Industry. The question then becomes one of whether the state can also assess independently the long-term strategies proposed by the companies. An alternative, fully private solution involves the banks developing an industrial capability and altering their role in relation to industry. Such a dramatic change is unlikely in the short-run in this country, even though this is the direction in which the argument is leading. A mix between a public and private solution is then required.

It is increasingly recognised that the state has a legitimate interest in the long-run performance of major companies, particularly in high-technology sectors and in firms that are in severe trouble. Whether a strong presence in a new product area is achieved often depends crucially on the strategy and strength of leading firms; the difficulties of influencing the behaviour of such firms in France is described by Dosi in relation to semi-conductors (Chapter 8). With firms in trouble, the implications for the balance of payments and the whole network of suppliers of letting such a firm go under are often unacceptable to the government; a mechanism whereby mistaken strategies are identified before they become critical is therefore needed. Both of these situations require that suitable institutions and internal capabilities be devised involving the government, and a whole range of instruments mobilised to support the strategy.

The next question is what kind of competence is needed within the government. In France and Japan the industry ministry is integrated into the general business environment, in part through the common background and experience of officials and colleagues in private business. These ministries have also become very influential in the overall government framework, enabling them to attract some of the best candidates. In France the ministry recruits from the same sources as leading firms and indeed is seen as an important route to senior management positions in industry; promotion within the ministry is quick, and after extensive exposure to the problems of particular industries at national level civil servants leave for jobs in industry. Their average age is exceptionally low compared with the rest of the French civil service, and the part of their career when they are full of new ideas is spent in the ministry seeking to influence decision-makers in industry. The situation is somewhat like that of a high-flier in a company who is able to challenge the decisions of his boss on even terms and without prejudice to his career. Although final decisions are thus influenced by the state, they rest ultimately with private management (Dosi, Chapter 8). The end-result is not only that government officials and industrialists are talking the same language, but that the officials' opinions are considered and respected.

Although there has been some attempt in recent years to improve the industrial experience of civil servants in this country, it by no means bridges the gap between government and industry. The French example cannot be dismissed by saying it would be impossible to implement in this country. Given the central importance of industrial policy in regenerating British industry, the case for creating a separate industrial civil service, with its own recruitment and career structure, and regular interchanges of personnel with industry, should be seriously considered.

Another feature of the British environment is the uncertainty and diversion created by the alternating two-Party system. Much civil service time in the first two years or so of any new administration is spent in educating the new industry Minister to the realities of government–business relationships and away from ill-conceived schemes or ideologies inherited from the period of opposition. Any industrial policy requires a certain degree of continuity, so that it might be appropriate for the institutions operating the kinds of policy considered here to have some independence from the day-to-day decisions of the Department of Industry.

The view of the evolution of a particular technology implicit in the above analysis, inspired by Dosi (see references in Chapter 8) and Hill and Utterback [13], enables us to identify the roles of different public institutions in the decision-making framework. Initial evaluation of new ideas and embryonic technologies is quite properly the role of ACARD, which has produced an excellent series of reports in recent years (see for instance [1], [2]). To an extent this evaluation is undertaken also by BIPE, a semi-governmental technical research organisation, in France, though in addition it is making detailed assessments of the state of the technology in different countries in connection with a major initiative to support new strategic technologies coordinated by the CODIS Committee. The initial exploration of the different directions a particular technology might take is best performed by a diversity of, often small, innovative companies. Support for this kind of activity, by backing ventures that might not otherwise go ahead, and disposing of the investments back to the private sector as soon as they become profitable, is the prime role of the NEB, now that it is no longer a holding company for lame ducks.

So far there seems to be no appropriate institution in Britain to back individual firms in products where the direction of technology is clearly established, not only to exploit the inherent growth potential or the externalities of a generic technology, but to secure a place in the resulting world oligopoly. Quite clearly MITI in Japan and the CODIS strategy in France seek to do this in carefully selected areas in the context of national priorities. Nor is any systematic attempt made in this country to assess structural trends in the world economy and identify areas where Britain's future specialisation in the international division of labour might lie. CEPII, a research arm of the *Commissariat du Plan* in France, also performs this function: see their reports (e.g. [8]). This is not an independent crystal-gazing or picking-winners exercise, but an attempt to mobilise and influence the French business community.

The absence of institutions capable of performing these two roles suggests the creation of an Industrial Structure Commission, with a semi-independent status similar to the NEB. Whereas the NEB draws on the financial community for staff with experience in the venture-capital field, such a Commission would be staffed with people experienced in running a business and drawing up long-range strategies, both technological and marketing. Two further roles might also be performed by such a Commission. The first is regular public monitoring of large companies which, because of their importance in the economy as a whole, experience a degree of implied protection in that governments would find it hard to accept their demise. Essentially this would be an independent check on their efficiency, not simply in terms of short-run profitability but taking account of the Schumpeterian trade-off between static and dynamic progressivity, which is quite different from an investigation by the Monopolies Commission into whether they are abusing their dominant position in a particular product market. This function is related to the second: that of providing an early warning of firms facing difficulties that could lead to the government rescuing them if not corrected. The emphasis on intervention in particular firms suggests this is not a role for NEDO, which is concerned with whole sectors. Although these ideas may be thought controversial, they are offered here to stimulate thinking about the future of industrial policy in this country and clearly need to be worked out in more detail.

Horizontal Industrial Policies
In addition to the discriminatory policies outlined above, a set of non-discriminatory industrial policies is also necessary, either where the infrastructure is concerned, or where the firms are too numerous for individual government attention. These policies are dealt with more fully elsewhere in this volume and so they receive less attention here, though they are at least as important as the policies discussed so far. One of the most important needs in the longer term is to rectify the under-investment in human capital that has been a permanent feature of British industry throughout this century. The main deficiencies, in terms of both quality and quantity, in the facilities for training in industrial skills, from those for skilled engineers through skilled craftsmen to non-skilled employees, are now well documented (Albu [3], Barnett [4], [5], Daly and Jones [11]). Progress in this area is disappointingly slow, and it is a national scandal that almost no systematic national provision has been made for training school leavers who do not go on to some form of higher education or training. Many opportunities to intro-

duce such a scheme, such as those existing in most continental countries for most of this century, have been passed over.

A complete structure for industrial training at each level, found in countries like Germany, is unlikely to be adopted in the current economic climate in Britain. A more realistic approach would be to experiment with as many schemes and courses as possible. For instance, instead of trying to create a national system of vocational training for 16- to 18-year olds (which would remain the ultimate objective), the government should encourage local experiments directly involving local industry or particular firms, the trade unions and the local technical college or polytechnic, as in Germany. Similarly, experiments such as the GEC-sponsored course in engineering at Bath University should be encouraged; not only are they a direct response to company needs, but they do not challenge vested interests in the educational and professional establishment, the strength of which can be seen from the rearguard action against the proposals of the Finniston Report [12]. Such policies are the only way of guaranteeing the longer-term competitiveness of British industry.

Pavitt (Chaper 7(I)) has dealt with government support for R and D, and other contributors have described the role of the NEB and the record of schemes to promote technical change in the machine tool industry. We would only add that much could be learnt from the whole range of policies to support R and D, particularly in small and medium-sized companies, introduced in recent years in Germany. These include midwifery support for new companies, with tax holidays for the first few years and blanket tax allowances for R and D expenditure, including its employment costs. They were in part introduced explicitly to counter a bias in the R and D support programme towards large companies.

Although support for small business has become fashionable in the last few years, this has so far resulted in little action. It is, of course, important to continue to investigate ways in which small firms can have access to capital, either through the existing institutions or by creating local, secondary capital markets. It is also important to create particularly favourable conditions for small firms undertaking the risky search for the direction in which a new technology might develop. (Dosi notes the importance of spin-off companies in the US electronics industry in this role.) If one accepts that new forms of organisation involving greater employee participation may be a way out of the stalemate over industrial relations in Britain, then small firms are important in this process also. A thorough review of the legal impediments, including employment legislation, to such organisational experiments must accompany any measures to reduce the financial constraints on such firms.

None of the industrial policies discussed in this chapter, even if seen as part of a comprehensive industrial policy, will transform the performance of British industry overnight. What is quite clear is that without such a medium-term programme no macroeconomic strategies of the government, whether monetarist, Keynesian or protectionist, are going to succeed in reversing Britain's long-run relative decline. The present critical situation offers the opportunity to rethink the direction of industrial policy. However, if this opportunity is not seized, the bitterness between the social partners may become too great for the development of the necessary consensus on which to build such an Industrial Strategy.

References
[1] ACARD, *Joining and Assembly: the impact of robots and automation*, London, HMSO, 1979.
[2] —, *Computer Aided Design and Manufacture*, London, HMSO, 1980.
[3] Albu, A., 'British attitudes to engineering education' in Pavitt [15].
[4] Barnett, C., *The Collapse of British Power*, London, Eyre Methuen, 1972.
[5] —, 'The hundred years sickness', *Industrial and Commercial Training*, June 1977.
[6] Blackaby, F. T. (ed.), *De-industrialisation*, London, Heinemann, 1979.
[7] Caves, R. E. and Krause, L. B., *Britain's Economic Performance*, Washington DC, Brookings Institution, 1980.
[8] CEPII, 'Specialisation et adaptation face à la crise', *Economic Prospective Internationale*, no. 1, January 1980.
[9] Commissariat Général du Plan, *Preparation du Huitième Plan 1981–1985— Rapport de la Commission Industrie*, Paris, La Documentation Française, 1980.
[10] Commission of the European Communities, *Changes in the Industrial Structure in the European Economies since the Oil Crisis, 1973–1978* [Maldague Report], Brussels, 1979.
[11] Daly, A. and Jones, D. T., 'The machine tool industry in Britain, Germany and the United States', *National Institute Economic Review*, no. 92, May 1980.
[12] Department of Industry, *Engineering Our Future* [Finniston Report], Cmnd 7794, London, HMSO, 1980.
[13] Hill, C. T. and Utterback, J. M. (eds.), *Technological Innovation for a Dynamic Economy*, New York, Pergamon, 1979.
[14] Jones, D. T., 'Industrial development and economic divergence' in M. Hodges and W. Wallace (eds.), *Economic Divergence in the European Community*, London, Allen and Unwin, forthcoming 1981.
[15] Pavitt, K. (ed.), *Technical Change and British Economic Performance*, London, Macmillan, 1980.
[16] Prais, S. J., *Productivity and Industrial Structure*, Cambridge University Press, forthcoming 1981.
[17] Stoffaes, C., *La Grande Menace Industrielle*, Paris, Calmann–Levy, 1978.

7(V) The Adoption and Transfer of Technology and the Role of Government

by G. M. White

This paper considers the role of government in encouraging innovation and its diffusion. More specifically, it discusses the influence of government on the demand for technology and its transfer throughout the industrial structure. In such a role the government may complement or compete with market forces, so that theoretical and practical problems will arise from this activity.

Some Background Considerations

Certain general themes may be identified from the literature on innovation and the legitimacy of a government role:

(1) The prima facie case for government involvement derives from the argument that market mechanisms will tend to under-invest in technology because of market imperfections in confronting risks and the existence of externalities which cause social and private rates of return to diverge.

(2) The role of technology in growth and international competitiveness has provided governments with additional justification for involvement. This was particularly so during the 1970s, when technology-gap theories of international trade were widespread and world competitive conditions (particularly the advent of developing country competition) encouraged the view that comparative advantage required industrialised countries to adjust their structure to medium- or high-technology products.

(3) However, the conditions in which under-investment in technology obtains are so imprecisely known that no specific guidance

is available on the appropriate level and nature of government involvement. There is a danger that the general proposition of externalities and risk-aversion will be interpreted in practice so that government involvement will be found necessary wherever it is politically expedient (Eads [5]).

(4) The form of government involvement must take note of the evidence that successful innovation and diffusion tend to be characterised by close interaction between the innovation source, the production process and market requirements. The importance of awareness of market potential, and unimpeded flows of information between R and D, production and marketing activities, and user needs has been stressed by Mansfield *et al.* [8], Braun and Bessant [4] and Pavitt and Walker [9]. Governments may be expected to have problems in managing this balance of activities, particularly as successful innovation seems also to be characterised by certain flexible organisational structures not often to be found in government bureaucracies.

(5) Some prescriptions for the appropriate government role advocate that it should not extend to the later development stages, where market awareness is so important, but be restricted to basic and applied research. However, this begs difficult questions concerning the whole justification for government investment in particular research activities: how assessment of market potential can be brought to bear on the investment decision; when the umbilical cord between government and the private sector should be formed and cut; and how R and D results can successfully be developed and disseminated in the market.

Reviews of the performance of government R and D activities are not as extensive nor as detailed as one might expect. During the 1970s they revealed a number of common preoccupations, concluding that: there were weaknesses in the dissemination of government research work; government research activities were not informed by market needs; research was science- rather than technology-based; research was biased towards very high technologies; small firms had been neglected; and government projects tended to develop their own momentum and vested interests with little regard to economic viability. At the same time there was an increasing awareness, probably derived in large part from Japanese experience, that technology could influence competitiveness by being observed and absorbed from abroad. It was inferred that the mechanisms by which technology from all sources could become known and transferred rapidly into the production system were important. No one country needed to cover all technological areas, but it must have the information on which to judge where technological effort was best allocated to produce competitive products and an economy which could respond flexibly and rapidly to technological advances from any source. These conclusions on government policy towards innovation have been shared by a number of countries and have generated a common response (see ACARD [2], Abernathy and Chakravarthy [1], Anglo-German Foundation [3], Royal Swedish Academy of Engineering Sciences [11], Horwitz [7]).

Governments' desires to become involved in the innovation process have been reinforced, but the ardour with which they seem prepared to embrace major technology projects and carry them all the way to commercial development in the market has cooled. The emphasis which may now be found in many governments' official publications on their role in technology transfer and diffusion is not without theoretical and practical difficulties. Improvements in the flow of information may involve selectivity in deciding what information and for whom. Moreover, there may be explicit or implicit subsidies involved. Public versus market choice is likely to be a central issue. It is the intention of this chapter to explore these difficulties with reference to various countries' practices.

The Role for Government

Mansfield *et al.* [8] have provided evidence of a substantial divergence between social and private rates of return on innovation which corroborates that less than optimal investment in innovation will be likely under market conditions. In such circumstances the government may seek to improve the conditions favourable to innovation, to enhance the entrepreneur's ability to appropriate gains (e.g. through patents) and ultimately to compensate for the lack of incentive to innovate by subsidising R and D.

There may also be corporate and financial risk-aversion which may result in less than optimal innovative activity. The vulnerability of smaller firms and their lack of resources for experiment, portfolio management, etc. may make them particularly risk-averse. However, risk-aversion may be a more general phenomenon which causes projects to be rejected which have acceptable expected rates of return from the most likely outcome because the down-side risks, if they all materialised, would jeopardise the innovator's viability. In these circumstances the government may seek to increase the innovator's willingness and ability to assess the benefits of innovation. It may also seek ways to reduce the risk associated with innovation, not by subsidisation which might not discriminate adequately between economic and non-economic projects, but by risk-sharing schemes jointly arranged with the innovator and/or the financial institutions.

In its efforts to absorb externalities and reduce risk-aversion the government needs also to strike the balance between increasing the private innovator's ability to appropriate the gains from his activity and avoiding the welfare losses to other producers and consumers which might arise from conferring monopoly rights on the innovator.

Of course, the government is bound to be involved in the technology market place. It accepts responsibility at least in part for education, defence, health, the environment, energy and growth. Its involvement in these areas requires it to act as a supplier, disseminator and consumer of scientific and technical knowledge, products and services, and to negotiate directly with the private sector in the development, diffusion and provision of enhanced goods and services. However, the government's involvement in the innovation aspects of these activities is probably still best guided and assessed according to the principles of externalities and risk-insurance.

Government Incentives for Diffusion

Government policies for the encouragement of innovation and diffusion are many and varied. Here we consider government activity through collaborative research centres and advisory services, financial assistance to civilian R and D, and public purchasing.

Collaborative research centres

Nearly all industrialised countries have networks of collaborative research agencies which straddle the various interests involved in the innovation process. Collective research has been on the increase in most countries because of the growing awareness of its value in creating an infrastructure of knowledge which may be more readily available to a large number of users in the private and public sectors, and in drawing together research activity and user needs. Governments have recognised the possible value of collective research and to varying degrees have harnessed it to their innovation and industrial policies (e.g. particularly, in Japan).

In their different ways countries are striving to strike the difficult balance between providing the necessary impetus for long-term and high-risk research, while ensuring that it is ultimately directed to industry's perception of market needs. Put another way, this balance can be seen between modes of behaviour which at their extremes may be characterised as *introspective* research and *responsive* reactions to expressions of current need. There is evidence that, in resolving these two modes of behaviour, collective research is developing a complementary third mode which might be called *provocative*. The increasing experience of research centres with the areas of failure in the innovation process has inclined them to more selective and provocative action. Thus, it would seem that only 5–10 per cent of firms in a sector will be active innovative contributors to the research associations, and that it will be the 25–40 per cent who have innovative potential, but who will tend to be small firms and whose needs will be poorly articulated, who should be the main target of collective research endeavour.

Moreover, research centres seem increasingly to recognise that the heaviest burden of costs and risks in the innovation process tends to fall in the non-technical factors. They have been paying closer attention to the services they can provide in easing the production engineering problems of installing new techniques into an old system, the quality control and training problems, and the difficulties for management and marketing in bringing new products into production and to the market place. Such changes in the operational mode of research centres require changes in resource requirements which need to be recognised by governments in their funding and monitoring. This seems to be happening to some extent, for example, in the emphasis in the UK on technology transfer, and the recognition that different policies may be appropriate in technologies such as micro-electronics which have a relatively low threshold size and may have applications across a large number of sectors.

Technical or market information and advisory services
Whilst research centres provide the main mechanism in most countries for technology transfer, their activities have increasingly been supplemented by government initiatives. These have been directed at ensuring mutual exchanges of information and collaboration

between research agencies, and encouraging the demand for technology, particularly from small and medium-sized companies. The objective is to organise a market for technologies. Like the research associations, government efforts in technology transfer have become more provocative, in recognition that transfer requires more than simply the passive dissemination of information and that efforts need to be focused. Companies have to be positively encouraged to review the potential benefits of technological change and this requires transfers of knowledge and people between industry and the research agencies (particularly the universities).

Most countries have industrial liaison officers at universities. The National Science Foundation in the US has established innovation centres at some universities. In Sweden particularly strenuous efforts are made to link the universities with the research associations (an area in which the UK is not particularly strong). In the UK there is an experiment with a Teaching Company Scheme, in which higher engineering degrees are organised jointly between a company and a university. Innovation fairs, exhibitions and competitions are now being organised in a number of countries. Most countries are developing integrated information networks bringing together patent and other technology information (overseas as well as domestic), and in Sweden there is an attempt to knit this network together with data on technology gaps and requirements in Swedish industry. Innovation advisory services are springing up, often organised on a regional basis to tap local expertise and experience.

The more active policies for technology transfer are represented most notably in Germany by the activities of the *Fraunhofer* Society and the work of the VDI Technology Centre. The latter appears to operate in a particularly provocative mode, which is justified on the grounds that risk-aversion stems from ossified financial and technical attitudes towards new technology. The VDI sets out with a small number of staff but a lot of expertise (including non-technical) to challenge conventional wisdom, and it does so in a sectoral and company-specific way. It combines this activity with the more usual responsive routine of most of the technology institutes.

It could be argued that all this activity to promote technology transfer, as it increases the better assessment of risk and the absorption of technical change, might also inhibit the incentive to invest in innovation by increasing the difficulty for an innovator in appropriating all the gains. But, as with the patent system, it is necessary to strike a balance between the increased incentive to innovate derived from greater gains and the benefits to general economic welfare from the rapid diffusion of technological change. The current flurry of activity in most countries in technology transfer policies reflects a welcome swing of the pendulum away from government preoccupation with increasing private gains by means of patent rights too rigidly implemented and subsidies given (in the main) to large companies.

Financial assistance

In most developed countries there has been a pronounced tendency for large companies to absorb the lion's share of government R and D aid to industry. Thus, in 1975 in the US 80 per cent went to firms employing more than 25,000; in France 90 per cent went to the twenty largest firms; in Germany 65 per cent went to firms employing more than 25,000; and in the UK 80 per cent went to the ten largest companies in terms of their R and D spending. This occurs for a number of reasons: emphasis on high technology such as aerospace with high entry costs; the greater likelihood that larger companies will know of government schemes; and the requirement that larger companies bear part of the R and D expenditure themselves, which means that the distribution of government promotional funds according to the size of companies will be correlated with the distribution of industry's own R and D expenditure. Relative to the sort of government–large company financial linkages implied by these figures, government activity for technology transfer and aid to small companies is very small beer indeed.

The precise nature of the financial linkages between government and the large companies is difficult to ascertain, particularly in some of the advanced technologies where the government may also be the purchaser of the final product. It is often not possible to determine whether the conditions in the corporate sector warrant government subsidy or risk-sharing. Most countries, including France, Germany and Japan, appear to favour subsidies. In Germany the *Bundesministerium für Forschung und Technologie* funds R and D projects by means of grants. According to one report [10], 50 per cent of BMFT promotion funds during 1974–7 was allocated to projects which were fully funded by the BMFT (70 per cent of funds was for projects funded by grants of 50 per cent or more from the BMFT), chiefly on the major technological development lines and prototype and demonstration facilities. In Germany the use of grants has been extended to the small and medium-sized companies, which can claim grants to cover 30 per cent of the value of contracts placed with the *Fraunhofer* network of research institutes. Grants are also available to contribute to the costs of depreciable assets purchased for R and D purposes, intangible assets (such as patents) and R and D personnel. All this suggests that the main justification for government involvement is sought in the externalities rather than the risk argument. Even the Venture Capital Company, established in Germany in 1975 specifically to absorb the risks associated with development, has 75 per cent of potential losses covered by the Federal government.

In Japan the government's involvement in major research projects reflects the same preoccupation with externalities – the 50 per cent grant for MITI projects, tax relief for R and D expenditure, and special depreciation allowances for fixed assets for R and D. The various financial institutions in Japan designed to provide support for small and medium-sized companies, and to cover the development and commercialisation phases of innovation, tend to operate on a risk-sharing basis, but are relatively minor in government support to R and D.

The UK has a stronger tradition of risk-sharing arrangements, particularly for the later stages of innovation such as launching aid (see Gardner [6]). In civil aeronautics and space it is recognised that a mixture of basic research funding (by subsidy) and development assistance (by risk-sharing through launching aid) is appropriate. The Requirements Boards and the Product and Process Development Scheme both offer support on the basis of a 25 per cent grant or a 50 per cent contribution to costs, with provision for recovery by means of a levy on sales. The NRDC has a statutory requirement to balance its revenues against outgoings and yet has written into its charter the recognition that potential external benefits from innovation could justify a predisposition to give innovation projects the benefits of any financial doubt. Thus, running through British practice is an explicit acceptance that risk-sharing or subsidies will be appropriate in differerent circumstances.

There have been problems in defining the specific circumstances under which one form of support should be preferred to another. The greater emphasis in the UK on risk-aversion as a justification for government involvement may have led to apparently greater preoccupation with the funding of commercial development projects. Such ventures may not have been attended by a particularly high success rate. However, as Gardner points out, this need not be for reasons inherent in the risk-sharing concept, but in the choice of circumstances in which it is employed. There may be some occasions on which government can establish risk-sharing schemes with the financial institutions (rather than with the innovating company alone), enhancing their risk-bearing capability and tapping their resources and expertise in project management.

Risk-sharing ventures have a major advantage in that their very nature makes assessment of failure and success more transparent. Government grants to the private sector are less easy to assess because their monitoring and control require estimates of both expected and realised external benefits. The German and Japanese reliance upon grants is accompanied by close liaison between the companies and the sponsoring ministries. The BMFT screens individual projects by a committee comprising government, company and labour representatives, and independent consultants. It is difficult to believe that the BMFT does not consider commercial development projects, but it is less easy than in the UK to ascertain the extent to which this occurs and the returns on BMFT expenditure for this purpose.

Finally it should be noted that the apparent bias towards large companies may also be due to the bureaucratic nature of government schemes and a lack of familiarity with them amongst smaller companies. Watkins and Rubenstein [12] discuss this more fully from a UK point of view. They conclude that there was low awareness of government schemes and, indeed, that interest was not particularly high among the companies canvassed. Recommended ingredients of government schemes were continuity, publicity, market orientation at the earliest possible phase, concern for manufacturing facility design, up-dating of project specification, and managerial quality. They report that companies felt public purchasing was likely to have a greater impact (for better or worse) on innovation and its commercial exploitation than government schemes designed to promote innovation directly.

Public purchasing and regulation
Government purchasing and regulation can be important influences on the market potential for innovation in particular product areas. This has been increasingly recognised by governments, most of whom are now consciously experimenting with their purchasing and regulation policies to take cognizance of both positive and negative effects on innovation. More work is needed to appreciate the effects

of regulation. The effects and problems of widening the objectives of public purchasing to include the promotion of the technical capability and international competitiveness of industry have also not been discussed in the literature to any great extent. The following discussion does not do justice to the complications of the subject, but offers some thoughts on what should be a central consideration.

The role of public purchasing will be different depending on how far demand specification is possible and on the market structures characteristic of suppliers and purchasers. Most procurement activities are thought of in terms of a competitive model, where the product is standardised, there are a large number of suppliers, there are no entry restrictions, the government market share is small, and buyer choice and supplier rivalry can be restricted to price. No other incentive to efficiency and innovation is then thought necessary beyond competitive tendering on the basis of lowest price. However, this straightforward competitive model may not be particularly widely applicable. Very often the highly fragmented nature of public demand (for example by the autonomous local authorities) may cause widespread differences in demand specifications and as a consequence fragmented supply. Under these conditions the lowest-price tender may still be higher, and the quality of product lower, than if public demand had been aggregated, common specifications used and cost-savings achieved through longer production runs and plant economies of scale, with product quality enhanced through incremental innovation. Market aggregation to remedy this situation has been a major theme in the discussions of procurement policy. However, the implication that greater centralisation of purchasing should be preferred cannot be advanced as a general proposition. Oligopsony and oligopoly have their own disadvantages and can create difficulties between public sector purchasers and private sector suppliers.

These difficulties are apparent from the considerable – and sometimes costly – experience of governments in dealing with oligopolies or monopolies for the provision of new products, particularly for defence. The lessons that have emerged are relevant to the way in which governments should exercise their market power in evaluating the performance of new products and reducing market and technical uncertainty.

Apart from the benefits which derive from the use of performance rather than design specifications, and of lifetime costing, the major lessons relate to the government–private sector linkage. Governments have created problems (for efficiency in the private sector and for their own public accountability) when they have proclaimed commitment and certainty where there can be none. Thus, quite often planned programmes of public purchasing, on which companies base investment and other decisions, are not announced and organised with due regard to their inherent uncertainties.

The purchase of new high-technology products, in which uncertainty characterises public sector demand and its specifications, has to be seen as a choice not from a set of specific end-products, but between actions initially consistent with a wide range of such alternatives and a process of narrowing the choice as development proceeds. The latter describes what Williamson [13] has called task partitioning and others have termed incremental review and evaluation. It suggests that there are discrete stages in innovative projects which deserve separate specification of objectives and risks, and which may be allocated to different suppliers by different means. The advantages are seen in reduced uncertainty as objectives are refined and evaluation occurs as the project proceeds. Task partitioning is also likely to increase the number of smaller contracts and thus to reduce entry barriers, increase competition, soften the harsh cyclical effect arising from the birth and death of large projects, and tap the innovative potential of smaller companies. Current practice tends to favour contracting entire projects to the large companies (usually on the grounds of high capital cost, scale economies and administrative convenience). There are grounds for thinking that different phases of a purchasing project can be specified so as to secure the appropriate advantages presented by different supply conditions. The benevolent use of public monopsony power is about how supply conditions can best be used and developed.

Conclusion

The experience and study of innovation suggest that it is a complicated, if not messy, process. The government as supplier, distributor and user of technical know-how, goods and services is present in the technology market place. Yet neither the character of the innovation process nor the theoretical justification for government involvement are ever likely to be sufficiently precisely known to enable a clear and self-contained role for government to be defined. Certainly it is too limiting to circumscribe the government's role by reference to the theory of externalities and subsidisation alone. The government may respond to corporate and financial risk-aversion and manage its own policies in public purchasing, information provision and education in ways which may encourage innovation but need not involve subsidy.

Governments would be advised to adopt a diversity of approaches to the promotion of innovation. The interaction between a multitude of factors which is a hall-mark of the innovation process should also characterise and enhance government involvement. Thus, direct support of R and D by subsidies will undoubtedly remain a feature of government policy, but it needs to be complemented by other measures. Government support for commercial development requires closer attention to objectives, the nature and extent of risks, managerial qualities and market potential than perhaps has been the case in the past. Risk-sharing rather than subsidy schemes should be given first consideration under these circumstances and should be contemplated with financial institutions as well as innovating companies.

Governments may influence the environment in which innovation occurs by increasing the private sector's ability and desire to innovate and by encouraging the diffusion and transfer of technology. This aspect of government activity has received little emphasis in the past and current developments to emphasise it more should be encouraged. Governments may influence the environment for innovation:

(a) indirectly by means of tax provisions and incentives, by increasing the flow of information and personal contacts between research agencies and the industrial sector, by ensuring full access to patent protection at the same time as limiting the abuse of such protection, by educational and training policies, and by increasing the supply of information about technological developments overseas;

(b) directly through public purchasing specifications, ordering programmes, procedures and organisation, and the provision of advisory services on non-technical as well as technical matters – which would probably have to be selective to some degree in terms of sectors, companies and technologies.

Finally, the institutional and administrative arrangements by which governments conduct their innovation policies are an important ingredient in their success. They need to be a careful blend of central coordination and decentralised operations. They need to breed close liaison with all the parties in the innovation process and to have sufficient flexibility to allow for some degree of experiment.

References

[1] Abernathy, W. J. and Chakravarthy, B. S., 'Government intervention and innovation in industry: a policy framework', *Sloan Management Review*, Spring 1979.

[2] ACARD, *Industrial Innovation*, London, HMSO, 1978.

[3] Anglo-German Foundation, *Integrated Policy Concept of the German Federal Government for Research and Technology in Relation to Small and Medium-sized Companies*, London, 1978.

[4] Braun, E. and Bessant, J., 'Influential factors in manufacturing innovation' submission to Department of Industry, May 1980, to be published shortly.

[5] Eads, G., 'US government support for civilian technology: economic theory versus political practice', *Research Policy*, vol. 3, April 1974.

[6] Gardner, N. K. A., 'Economics of launching aid' in A. Whiting (ed.), *The Economics of Industrial Subsidies*, London, HMSO, 1976.

[7] Horwitz, P., 'Direct government funding of research and development: intended and unintended effects on industrial innovation' in C. T. Hill and J. M. Utterback (eds.), *Technological Innovation for a Dynamic Economy*, New York, Pergamon, 1979.

[8] Mansfield, E., *et al.*, *The Production and Application of New Industrial Technology*, New York, Norton, 1977.

[9] Pavitt, K. and Walker, W., 'Government policies towards industrial innovation', *Research Policy*, vol. 5, March 1976.

[10] Rembser, J., 'Promotion of technology transfer for small and medium-sized industrial enterprises in the Federal Republic of Germany' (paper given at the International Licensing Conference, Sydney) March 1979.

[11] Royal Swedish Academy of Engineering Sciences, *Technical Capability and Industrial Competence*, Stockholm, 1979.

[12] Watkins, D. S. and Rubenstein, A. H., 'Decision-makers' responses to industrial innovation incentives' in M. J. Baker (ed.), *Industrial Innovation*, London, Macmillan, 1979.

[13] Williamson, O. E., 'Economics of defence contracting' in R. N. McKean (ed.), *Issues in Defence Economics*, New York, National Bureau of Economic Research, 1967.

Comment on Chapter 7

(I) by P. D. Henderson

Of the five papers comprising this chapter, two are by civil servants and the other three by economists in university posts. As it happens, this occupational division corresponds with a marked difference in the tone and content of the papers, and an element of 'role reversal' can be discerned. On the one hand, both the papers by officials are imbued with a strong measure of what is often thought of as distinctively academic caution. By contrast, all three academics hold more decided and confident views about what needs to be done. All of them favour the adoption by British governments of a much more active and purposive strategy in relation to industrial innovation, and are optimistic about the gains which might accrue from such a strategy.

My sympathies in this matter lie with the officials. In this comment, I shall concentrate almost entirely on the reasons why I find it hard to accept either the analysis or the prescriptions which are set out by Pavitt, Stout and Jones, treating certain broad lines of argument which are common to all three papers while drawing on them individually for illustrative purposes. Although most of the argument that follows has therefore a strongly negative character, I shall conclude by trying to sketch in barest outline a possible alternative approach to the choice of industrial policies.

All three academic authors place high hopes on what Stout refers to as 'a more determined and ambitious technology policy'. Pavitt thinks of it as a means to influencing not only the growth rate of potential output – the 'underlying' rate of growth – but also the level of employment, and hence the extent to which a given productive potential can be realised. Both Stout and Jones accept the view that the relatively poor performance of the British economy is a secular phenomenon, which goes back a century or more. Each of them looks to Industrial Strategy as a means of escaping from this situation of relative inferiority. To quote Jones's formulation: 'The reversal of this relative decline in economic, and particularly industrial, performance . . . is the major challenge for any industrial policy pursued by the government.'

The idea that the industrial policies outlined in these papers could possibly bring such spectacular gains to the British economy strikes me as far-fetched. Considering first the relatively recent phenomenon of high unemployment rates, for some 25 years after the second world war average unemployment moved between 1 and 3 per cent, whereas the economy now seems to have entered a range of possibly 5 to 8 or even 10 per cent. The reasons for this extremely disturbing change are neither clear nor agreed. However, there appear to be no grounds for thinking that a major part of the explanation is to be found in the supposedly unenterprising character of the industrial policies which successive governments have pursued – the more so since these policies have shown a very large measure of continuity over the years, and have tended to become more 'interventionist' with time.

As to the more fundamental long-term problem of economic performance, I find it hard to take seriously the notion that more than a century of apparently chronic inferiority, which the most discerning commentators in our profession from Alfred Marshall to Henry Phelps Brown have ascribed to a complex of related phenomena which have deep roots in British history and institutions, could be brought to an end, even over a substantial period, by changes of the kind which are here proposed. Is it possible to believe that such a transformation will be set in train by such measures as restoring the Selective Investment Scheme (Stout); raising the share in GDP of expenditures on the 'general advancement of knowledge' from 0.22 per cent in 1978 to 0.3 per cent in 1990 (Pavitt); creating 'a separate industrial civil service' (Jones): 'more constructive use of the SWPs to identify technology gaps and product opportunities' (Stout); or a further extension of the existing generous measures designed to stimulate investment in manufacturing industry (Pavitt)? Even if one considers the whole range of proposals made by each and all of the authors, there is in my view a lack of proportion between the ends envisaged and the means which are here outlined, as is indeed recognised by Stout in the first sentence of his conclusions.

This general impression is strengthened by two more specific considerations. First, the connections between R and D expenditure and innovation, and between innovation as here defined and better economic performance, are in each case uncertain and problematical. One cannot simply increase the flow of R and D expenditure within the system, and expect that this will automatically be reflected in greater competitiveness and a higher rate of growth of productivity: the fruitfulness of these expenditures will depend on the channels into which they are directed, and still more on the way in which their results are used. This in turn depends on the competence, vision and organising capacity of managerial and technical cadres, and on the extent to which the environment in which they operate is favourable to change. It may well be, as Carter argues in Chapter 3, that the capacity of British industry to handle the process of innovation is chiefly limited by 'standards, habits and attitudes' that form part of the British managerial culture. In so far as the failure to innovate successfully is attributable to these and related factors, it is unhelpful to place so much emphasis on greater spending by governments on R and D, or for that matter on higher investment as such. This basic point is insufficiently acknowledged in two of the three papers I am concerned with. Pavitt accepts it explicitly, but consoles himself with the reflection that the level of R and D remains 'an essential part of the problem'. Nothing in his paper persuades me that he is right about this.

A second reason for scepticism about the effects of the measures proposed is that most of them are far from novel. With the partial exception of Pavitt, the three authors make remarkably little reference to the past and its lessons. One would not gather from what is said here that industrial policies, science policy, and the volume and direction of R and D support had been virtually continuous subjects of concern to British governments over the past thirty years or so; nor is there any consideration of the conscious efforts made to accelerate economic growth through the medium of government support for science and technology. We hear nothing about the 'white-hot technical revolution', nor of the spirit and programmes that were associated with the now-forgotten MinTech. Yet the experience of these policies, and the fact that they have made no discernible difference to the British predicament, are surely of some relevance to judging the potential usefulness of a further though more ambitious experiment of a very similar kind. Reading these papers, I was reminded of a phrase used by Diaz-Alejandro in a very different context, where he refers to those for whom 'the history that can be forgotten begins yesterday or perhaps even today' [4]; and as a person who was himself involved in some of the arguments and policies of the 1960s, I experienced a disheartening sense of futility and *déja vu*.

So far I have considered only what seems to me a lack of proportion in the unrealistic expectations that are held out of salvation through Industrial Strategy. If this were all, one could perhaps think of the arguments and recommendations of these papers as fairly harmless, even though far from convincing. I believe, however, that some of the ideas and proposals are positively misguided, and that they are associated with forms of reasoning which have exercised a damaging influence on British economic policies and performance ever since the end of the last war. Two aspects in particular strike me as unfortunate. One is what might be termed the 'soap opera' approach to the choice of industries and projects for support, while the second is the lack of concern with history and accountability.

On the question of choice, all three authors convey the impression that it is both possible and useful to identify at a high level industries or activities which are somehow intrinsically worthy of support; this indeed is a principal element in the 'Strategy'. It is true that both Stout and Jones explicitly disavow the doctrine of 'picking winners', but the rest of what they say is not consistent with this welcome disclaimer. Probably what they have in mind is 'winning' firms; but they have no inhibitions about the idea of picking winning (and losing) industries or products. Thus Stout describes a class of 'inferior products' which is to be avoided, and refers with apparent approval to the MITI 'Vision'; while Jones is impressed with a suggestion that British trade may have acquired 'a perverse pattern of specialisation', through an increasing reliance on industries with a low skill content.

Such an approach to questions of assessment and choice seems to me to resemble the script of a soap opera, both in its level of subtlety and in the extent of its concern with the complexities of real life. The idea of designating heroes and villains within the Standard Industrial Classification is misconceived, for three related reasons. First, it pays too little regard to the principle of comparative advantage. Thus it is entirely possible that because of certain long-established features of the British scene, such as are referred to by Carter and Allen (Chapters 3 and 6), British-based firms *in general* (for one should not expect uniformity here) will be at an increasing relative disadvantage in many skill-intensive and technology-intensive lines. In so far as this is the case, there will be positive benefits from remaining in what Pavitt refers to disparagingly as the 'second division'; and any large sums of money that are spent simply for the sake of changing the output-mix towards supposedly more 'advanced' industries are likely to yield low social rates of return. Second, the approach takes too little account of the pervasive uncertainty that surrounds the future: the way in which comparative advantage will actually work out cannot be determined *ex ante*, even by high-powered committees such as ACARD. Third, this whole way of posing the problems of choice gives far too much initiative and authority to the centre, and to high levels of decision-making. There is no reason to suppose that centralised 'strategic' choices are likely to produce better results than a more modest approach, in which a greater measure of responsibility for the way in which funds are used rests with those who are close to the processes and markets concerned.

The fact is that one cannot sensibly decide the allocation of resources, in R and D or in anything else, with reference to generalised notions of a country's manifest industrial destiny. All three authors have in my opinion become tainted with what Wiles, in an excellent discussion of this and related themes, has termed 'structure snobbery'. Two pertinent observations by Wiles are worth quoting here. As to the British trade dependence on older and less sophisticated products he remarks that: '. . . the way out, of course, is not to force nor even to subsidize exports of the new goods . . . The solution is to improve the [factor] endowment; i.e., to push technology forward in a general way, and see what happens' ([6], pp. 202–3). As to the question of which trade structure is best for the growth of an economy, he suggests that the appropriate answer is 'whatever appears *ex post* to have suited'. As change takes place and techniques become more sophisticated within the system, the 'optimal' product-mix will likewise change; 'but toward what products, only the then constellation of world trade and techniques can tell us' (ibid, p. 209).

The second worrying aspect of the approach in these three papers is that so little reference is made to the need in officially sponsored schemes to monitor developments; to be constantly prepared to reassess the evidence and to modify ideas and programmes accordingly; and to introduce and maintain in expenditure programmes an adequate measure of accountability. As Peck observed in 1968, 'projects should be initiated experimentally and reevaluated frequently, using both technical and economic criteria of success' ([5], p. 483). A strategy which fails to provide for this is unlikely to do much good.

The particular weaknesses noted above are four: the belief in manifest destiny, the neglect of uncertainty, the bias towards centralised decisions, and the lack of concern for results, assessment and accountability. In British ways of thinking – though not in the papers before us – these are all too often associated with other mistaken beliefs. On the technical side, the most worrying symptom is the state of mind which I have termed 'bipartisan technological chauvinism', in which deep convictions of manifest destiny are combined with insularity, xenophobia and an excessive faith in British technical capability. On the economic side, one enters the luxuriant jungle of do-it-yourself instant economics, in which perhaps the most consistently flourishing growth takes the form of a belief that any country stands to gain from resort to every conceivable mercantilist practice that can be adopted without giving rise to retaliation. In cases where the whole range of these misconceptions has held sway, and where the characteristic weaknesses of British administrative conventions – undue concern with procedures, over-centralisation, obsessive secrecy, and lack of personal accountability – have likewise been in evidence, the results have been appalling. Possibly the clearest instance of this is to be found in the nuclear power programme, which by good fortune has been the subject of scholarly inquiry in Williams's recent survey [7], and in the two penetrating studies by Burn [2], [3].

Some time ago I suggested that the British public sector had been associated with two of the three worst investment decisions in the history of mankind, and that this was no mere coincidence. I believe that the attitudes of mind which made this possible are still both widespread and influential. While both Pavitt and Stout are well aware of past mistakes, and rightly concerned that the aerospace and nuclear industries may still be absorbing too large a share of R and D expenditures, I think they take too little account of the possibility that any 'strategy for innovation' in this country is likely to be coloured, if not dominated, by the perceptions of the world which I have tried to summarise above. It is admittedly unfair to criticise ideas for the company they may keep; but in all these papers I would have welcomed a more explicit awareness of the risks that may be associated with British aspirations to 'first division' status.

In a somewhat more positive spirit, and taking account of a wider range of issues and policies that bear on innovation, I would make the following summary points:

(1) In actual R and D support, the main emphasis should be on helping markets to work better. As White points out, there are various ways of attempting this, and not too much is known about their effectiveness and prospective social rates of return at the margin. Hence the approach should be experimental, with an emphasis on accountability, evaluation, and learning from experience. It is important not to lose sight of the point that R and D expenditures are a means not an end, an input rather than an output. While it is advisable to keep a close eye on what other countries are doing, their policies in this area are not necessarily to be emulated: foreigners also may be subject to various forms of structure snobbery and more or less naive mercantilism, and it is better not to follow them down this road.

(2) As several other chapters in this book argue, the main potential contribution of governments to better innovative performance may be indirect, through policies designed to improve the quality of British managerial and technical personnel.

(3) Likewise, government policies can affect indirectly the incentive to innovate and to improve industrial performance. Possibly the main single line of approach here is competition policies, on which Allen lays a good deal of emphasis.

(4) Within the public sector, I would myself attach importance to ending protectionist practices, both open and covert, in relation to procurement, not only by government departments and nationalised industries but by private firms which become vulnerable to official suasion, such as those now operating in the North Sea. This would further sharpen the edge of competition for British firms, and I believe that if consistently pursued it would lead to a reduction in defence R and D expenditures, which like Pavitt I think may well be too high in absolute terms.

(5) With respect to industrial policies in general, I would lay more emphasis than Silberston on the extraordinary variety of the measures that are now in operation, and the extent to which these discriminate, in ways for which there is no firm justification, between areas of the country, industries or activities, and forms of expenditure. I believe that there is a case for reviewing the more general policies relating to investment incentives and location, while at the same time trying to establish a more consistent approach to treating the specific cases – the lame ducks, high-flyers, ewe lambs,

sacred cows, dark horses and white elephants. My own preference would be for a greater emphasis on general and non-discriminatory measures, at the expense of those which are selective and discretionary. Contrary to a widespread impression, the present government has not moved in this direction.

(6) An area of policy which is equally relevant, though not covered elsewhere in this volume, is that of trade policies. These will clearly affect the extent to which British firms face competition, and hence the incentive to innovate.

(7) A further relevant aspect, which is rightly mentioned by Stout, is that of adjustment policies – that is to say, measures which are designed to make economic changes, including those which arise from innovations, more acceptable. Nearly a century and a half ago John Stuart Mill, probably inspired by the fate of the handloom weavers, asserted the principle that 'there cannot be a more legitimate object of the legislator's care than the interests of those who are thus sacrificed to the gains of their fellow citizens and posterity'. I am not sure how much progress has since been made in translating this principle into a set of workable and consistent rules for application.

Finally, it should be noted that a programme such as that which I have just sketched does not by any means imply an inert or passive role for governments. Here as elsewhere, the task of devising measures which serve the threefold purpose of supplementing markets, making them work better, and trying to ensure that attitudes and institutions are adapted to a rapidly changing world places very considerable demands on the centre. It would be quite misleading to suggest that in the subject matter of this book there is a stark and inescapable choice between 'Industrial Strategy' and *laissez-faire*.

In one of several extraordinarily perceptive articles on the British predicament, Phelps Brown has summarised his argument by referring to the need to 'change our culture'; and he suggests that this may involve a general overhaul of traditional institutions, such as took place during the period from 1830 to 1860. His concluding words are that 'by now we stand in need of a new Age of Reform' ([1], p. 29). Although historical parallels have their dangers, I think it is worth recalling that there were two main ingredients in the set of reforms that he refers to. On the one hand, there was the freeing of markets, most notably through the gradual establishment of free trade. On the other hand, there was a whole series of changes that were designed both to improve the environment in which market forces operated, and to extend the responsibilities of the state in areas where market provision could not be relied on exclusively. In common with several other contributors to this book, I believe that British government policies towards innovation need to be directed in large part towards improving the climate in which it takes place, by influencing in various ways the underlying culture. At the same time, I believe that this approach should be combined with measures which would enable more effective use to be made of market opportunities. It seems to me that the now widely prevalent notions of an Industrial Strategy for Britain pay too little attention to the former aspect of the problem, while in their belief in centralised, protectionist and discretionary modes of operation they represent a step in precisely the wrong direction.

References
[1] Brown, Sir Henry Phelps, 'What is the British predicament?', *Three Banks Review*, December 1977.
[2] Burn, Duncan, *The Political Economy of Nuclear Energy*, London, Institute of Economic Affairs, 1967.
[3] —, *Nuclear Power and the Energy Crisis*, London, Macmillan, 1978.
[4] Diaz-Alejandro, Carlos, 'Delinking North and South' in Albert Fishlow *et al.*, *Rich and Poor Nations in the World Economy*, New York, McGraw Hill, 1978.
[5] Peck, Merton U., 'Science and technology' in R. E. Caves and Associates, *Britain's Economic Prospects*, London, Allen and Unwin, 1968.
[6] Wiles, Peter, *Communist International Economics*, Oxford, Blackwell, 1968.
[7] Williams, Roger, *The Nuclear Power Decisions*, London, Croom Helm, 1980.

Comment on Chapter 7

(II) by R. W. Archer

This comment is based on three of the five papers on possible government strategies – those by Pavitt, Willott and White. The other two papers were not available at the time of writing this note. I have also taken account of the sections of Chapters 2 and 6 which bear on this theme.

There is substantial common ground between the three papers in Chapter 7. All are agreed on the case for government intervention to modify the pure operation of the private enterprise system. There is no advocate for even a modified version of *laissez-faire*. Willott and White argue the theoretical case in very similar terms: the tendency for the social rate of return on innovation to exceed the private rate of return; risk-aversion, corporate and financial, leading to the undue discouragement of longer-term projects; and imperfections in company behaviour. The problem of how to translate this approach into recommendations for action is neatly and rather plaintively summarised by White. 'Neither the character of the innovation process nor the theoretical justification for government involvement are ever likely to be sufficiently precisely known to enable a clear and self-contained role for government to be defined.'

Pavitt approaches the issue differently by identifying one dominant weakness in UK industry: the weakness of technology arising from poor industrial skills and knowledge which, in turn, arise from a poor general level of vocational training and lack of technical strength in management. This weakness in technology is reflected and reinforced by low industrial R and D expenditure and a low capacity in industry to respond to signals. This approach leads logically to the general recommendation of more government action to improve industrial skills and knowledge, and special support to improve the effective deployment of skills and knowledge throughout industry.

When it comes to specific recommendations, Pavitt and White, despite their different approaches, recommend broadly similar action: for example, a diversity of often unglamorous policies, joint government–industry projects on R and D at the technological frontiers, the use of public procurement policies to encourage innovation. White stresses the desirability of risk-sharing, not only between government and industry, but also between government and financial institutions. Pavitt supports properly considered government initiatives on longer-term projects, for example through the NEB. This links with the second half of Willott's paper, which presents a convincing case for the industrial logic of NEB policies, whilst recognising their limitations. He stresses, in particular, that whilst NEB projects can counter risk-aversion, they cannot close the gap between social and private rates of return because of the requirement that the Board acts in a commercial manner.

My main criticism of these three papers is that, whilst the analysis is well argued, thorough and generally convincing, the specific recommendations tend to be brief and not developed to a point where clashes with the policies of the present government or its predecessor are clearly apparent. One feels that they could be read by a wide spectrum of policy-makers, who could each find in them the intellectual justification for their own particular line of policy.

Shonfield's Chapter 2 bears on many of the same themes, but in a harder hitting and more controversial vein. He starts from the same premise as Willott and White – the gap between the social and private rates of return on innovation. He reinforces it by stressing the additional disincentives to longer-term investment from the increased uncertainties of the 1980s and the need arising from the energy crisis for a major adaptation of productive equipment to the change in relative costs. He recognises the waste inherent in the use of public funds to support industrial R and D expenditure, but nevertheless recommends a generous allocation of funds for this purpose.

It is Allen's Chapter 6, however, which in my view puts the cat amongst the pigeons. He attributes the Japanese success story to six main factors:

(a) the quality of government intervention, based on widespread understanding of technical matters by government, officials and industry alike;
(b) the selectivity of government intervention – concentrating on limited areas selected on logical criteria and then backing them

to the hilt, both financially through the commercial banks and
by protection of infant industries until they mature;

(c) the quality and status of industrial management based on a
more technically oriented educational system;

(d) the determination of all concerned to back restructuring of
industry and to resist the political temptation to support
outdated technology;

(e) the combination of 'consensus' on the achievement of growth
and efficiency (covering not only industrial management and
the labour force, but also government, officials, banks and the
general public) with intense competition between the leading
firms in each industry;

(f) substantial buying in of know-how from abroad with the emphasis of domestic expenditure on development rather than research.

He concludes with some far-reaching recommendations, for example, quotas for scientifically trained recruits to the higher reaches
of the civil service, encouragement of structural change by selective
incentives for new technology, emphasis on quality not quantity of
intervention.

It appears to me that the analysis of Japanese success is much
more fruitful as a basis for specific recommendations than either *a
priori* reasoning or picking over the bones of UK failures. It is
striking that most of the issues which proved crucial to Japan's
success find little if any place in the other four UK-based papers
(with the major exception of Pavitt's stress on our poor industrial
skill and knowledge). The reason perhaps is that so many of the
Japanese factors are qualitative and do not fit easily into the quantitative or political terms in which we tend to conduct our domestic
controversies.

The emphasis on the quality of intervention in Japan seems to
me the most fundamental point of all and yet the most difficult to
follow. It is easy to create new institutions. Within a few years it
may also be easier than it appears today to provide public funds.
But qualitative improvement is altogether less amenable to instant
action and I feel that the longer-term measures which could contribute to this end should be explored in some depth.

8 Institutions and Markets in High Technology: Government Support for Micro-electronics in Europe

by Giovanni Dosi*

Fast technical change in semi-conductors is mainly responsible for what is often called the 'micro-electronics revolution'. This paper discusses the relative role of institutions and market mechanisms in the process of innovation and imitation in the semi-conductor industries of Western Europe. It is important to distinguish between policies appropriate in those countries where the objective is to reduce imitative lags, and to preserve some domestic industry; and policies appropriate in countries already on the technological frontier. Further, some policies may be very much in line with what companies themselves want. Others may involve national objectives, which can be independent from, or even in conflict with, the immediate interests of the companies concerned.

The analysis of industrial policies of the various European governments needs to be set against some hypotheses about the nature of the innovation process, the international structure and trends in the industry, and the European place within it. The first section of this chapter briefly outlines these hypotheses; the second section summarises the history of policies towards semi-conductors

* This paper is largely based on Dosi [1] and [2], forthcoming publications which arose out of a study undertaken at the Sussex European Research Centre on structural adjustment and government intervention in European industry. I would like to thank Professors Tibor Barna, François Duchêne and Chris Freeman, and Daniel Jones, Geoffrey Shepherd, Jürgen Müller, Keith Pavitt, Ed Scibberras and Mick MacLean, who contributed with comments, criticisms, information to the research on which this paper is based, and Professor Michele Salvati without whom the research would not have been possible.

in Germany, France, Italy and the UK; the third section discusses the similarities and differences in approach between these countries; the fourth section draws together some general conclusions on the role of public institutions and industrial policies, both in the innovation process and in the imitative process in countries which lag behind.

Technical Change and the Structure of the Semi-conductor Industry
Technical change in this industry has been extremely rapid throughout its history, with a high rate of substitution between 'new' products and 'old'. It can be argued that 'technology', defined in the broader sense as a set of items of knowledge, procedures, experiences of successes and failures, physical devices and equipment, etc., presents several conceptual and methodological similarities to those that modern epistemologists attribute to 'science'. More precisely, as scientific paradigms [6] or scientific research programmes [7] determine the fields of inquiry, the problems, the procedures and the tasks, so does technology. Looking, so to speak, 'downward' along the stream of science–technology–production, economic forces, together with more institutional factors, operate as *selective mechanisms* within the greater set of scientific and technological possibilities. Furthermore, once a path – a 'technological paradigm' – has been selected and established, it shows a momentum of its own, which contributes to defining the directions in which the problem-solving activity moves; they are defined by Nelson and Winter [8] as the *natural trajectories* of technical change.

In the first two decades of the industry, particularly in the US, the pattern of technical change in semi-conductors appears to originate from a rather complex interplay between institutional factors and strictly economic mechanisms. Among the former are the technical requirements, research policies and procurement policies of public agencies, primarily the military, and the directions of inquiry of the major electrical companies undertaking research in the field. Among the latter, the nature of the American market as characterised by the emergence of several new 'Schumpeterian' companies (generally spin-offs from established firms) which rapidly diffused the innovations and undertook the risk-taking task of exploring, by trial and error, different possibilities of technical change, is well documented. If one defines the technological frontier as the highest level of experience, scientific and technological knowledge, and manufacturing capabilities reached upon a technological trajectory, the economic and technological history of semi-conductors is also the history of the establishment of the American lead on that technological frontier. It also appears that the innovative process in semi-conductors has some cumulative features, so that the likelihood of future advances depends also on the position that one occupies *vis-à-vis* the existing technological frontier.

There are two kinds of entry barrier in this industry; a *dynamic* barrier, arising from the differential advantages in unit costs accruing to the first-comers – learning-curve effects; and in the late 1970s *static* economies of scale increased in importance, due to increasing capital requirements and minimum thresholds for R and D.

Micro-electronic technology is affecting an increasing number of industrial sectors. The process of diffusion does not appear to depend entirely on market forces, such as changes in relative prices, relative profitability, licensing policies, etc. It depends also on such 'externalities' as information flows, technological and manufacturing knowledge not embodied in physical devices or patents, synergetic effects between different technological areas, and the like. Linkages and interdependencies between semi-conductors and downstream sectors are becoming crucial; hence the tendency towards vertical integration, both downward from semi-conductors to users and in the other direction.

These aspects of the process of technical change and its diffusion provide some of the strongest arguments for government intervention. One of the basic driving forces for industrial policies in electronics has been a national perception of the strategic importance of the industry. The development of a strong electronics industry has been seen as a form of long-run insurance for a country (a) to reach (or to remain at) the upper end of the international division of labour; (b) to exploit the growth potential of high-technology industries; and (c) to maximise the technological fall-out upon interrelated industrial sectors.

American dominance of the world semi-conductor industry has only recently been challenged by the Japanese. This dominance is illustrated by the innovation–imitation time lags, and by the share of American-controlled production as compared to the size of the American market. Europe accounted for 27 per cent of world semi-conductor consumption in 1976 but only 17 per cent of world production, of which only 13 per cent was European-controlled. For integrated circuits alone, European production was 11 per cent, of which 9 per cent was European-controlled. The situation in 1978 was broadly similar. European technological lags in some fields are sometimes as long as three or four years. European labour productivity in this industry is roughly estimated at between less than one third and half of the Japanese level, which is somewhat higher than in the US.

The pattern of international specialisation and trade follows the technological capabilities of the various countries. Semi-conductors show a 'truncated product cycle': new products are substituted for old products before countries not at the technological frontier have succeeded in entering the market with the older products. European companies have followed imitative strategies throughout the history of the industry. During the 1950s and early 1960s they specialised in those discrete semi-conductors which suited their traditional fields of specialisation, in consumer and industrial electronics, and in France and the UK, to a lesser extent in military electronics. The emergence in the 1960s of integrated circuits and later, in the 1970s, of micro-processors, strengthened the American advantage over Europe. Moreover, direct American investment in Europe in the late 1960s and early 1970s made the survival of European companies more difficult.

When the American companies, in the middle of a slump in demand, established a world price during the so-called 'price war' of 1970–1, all the European producers were forced out of the high-volume standard market with only five exceptions: Philips (Holland–Germany–UK–France), Siemens (Germany), SGS (Italy), SESCOSEM (France), which then concentrated only on analogue integrated circuits and discrete devices, and AEG-Telefunken (Germany), which mainly produced semi-conductors for consumer electronics. Even then, these five companies made heavy losses for a long time. After a decade only Philips is believed to be making profits on its semi-conductor operations; some estimates suggest that Siemens broke even at the turn of the decade, 1979–80; while the other three are still in the red.

Only financially strong and/or government-supported companies could remain in the semi-conductor business. Large companies like Philips and Siemens could adopt far-sighted strategies because, due to their size and degree of vertical integration, they could internalise the advantages of a strong (and expensive) effort to improve their capability in this fast-developing technology. For most of the other European companies the only realistic target has been to survive in the markets where they were already operating, or in more protected niches like custom-designed and military semi-conductors. This has been the strategy of British, and to a large extent French, companies.

The History of Public Policies
The history of public intervention in the European industry can be divided into three phases. The first phase is one of limited intervention in military-related areas in France and the UK, lasting from 1950 to the mid-1960s. This phase occurred precisely during the period when the technological trajectories of the industry were established in the US. The European industry, broadly speaking, followed an imitative pattern. However, in France and the UK military-related R and D support and procurement policies were on a very small scale compared to the huge innovative effort fostered by the military in the United States. The French and British military policies did not have much effect outside the strictly military field – although in the UK they did perhaps enable some companies to remain in the industry and encouraged the maintenance of R and D activities in the most advanced technological fields. During this period public support in Italy and Germany was negligible.

The second phase, between the late 1960s and mid-1970s, saw the establishment of computer-related policies in France, Germany and the UK. With the creation of the Ministry of Technology in 1964, the UK started an 'Advanced Computer Technology Project' to share the cost of applied research in computers and computer-related technology with the companies; a small part of this went to semi-conductor research. All through the 1960s, most of the publicly funded research in the UK came from the military. In France, the 'Plan Calcul' of 1967 provided FF91.6 million between 1967 and 1970 to the component industry, mainly to the semi-conductor company SESCOSEM, which belonged to the Thomson group. This was constituted in 1968 through a merger, fostered by the French government, between SESCO (from Thomson) and COSEM (from CSF). Later the two parent companies themselves merged. Germany, with the first Data Processing Programme of 1967 provided some minor R and D support to the semi-conductor industry. Italy in the 1960s had no specific plan for electronics; the only public provision was the Technological Evolution Fund of 1968, which provided long-term low-interest loans and R and D subsidies to the entire manufacturing industry. The semi-conductor industry recieved as little as L3.6 billion between 1968 and 1978, comprising L3 billion as a 5 per cent interest loan and L600 million of subsidies. In the 1960s, public policies do not explain much of the differences in innovative capabilities between European countries. These differences arose more from the technological strength of the companies involved in the sector, their interest in the new technology (for both commercial and in-house use), and their autonomous research efforts.

The third phase, from the mid-1970s onwards saw the establishment of specific policies for semi-conductors and their application in all four countries. Public institutions began to focus on the relation of semi-conductors to the rest of the electronics industry and on their strategic role in advanced user sectors.

In Germany, with the second Data Processing Programme of 1969, the scope of intervention covered the major areas of high technology in the electronics field – semi-conductors, computer hardware, peripherals, software and computer applications. The scope of industrial policies in electronics covered basic research, applied industrial research, applications of both computers and semi-conductor components, education and training. In 1974, the provisions for semi-conductor components were made into a specific plan, lasting until 1978. BMFT support continued thereafter, although not through a formal plan. German support to the electronics industry in general and the semi-conductor industry in particular was larger than in other countries (Table 8.1).

In the UK, a specific semi-conductor programme was introduced in 1973, to support R and D projects in nationally owned semi-conductor firms. The nature of the UK programme is described by Willott in Chapter 9.

France did not have a specific programme related to semi-conductor components until 1977. Before then, policy was primarily concerned with the subsidisation of semi-conductor activities in the Thompson group. The 1977 plan was specifically aimed at the development of integrated circuit technologies and production, and gave finance for R and D activities in both French companies and joint ventures with American firms. In addition to the plan 'Informatisation de la Société', devoted to electronic applications in end-using sectors (FF 400 million, net of the amount allocated to semi-conductors), the 'Plan Circuits Intégrés' involves a total of FF 660 million over four years. Within the plan 'Informatisation de la Société' there are also provisions costing FF 10–15

Table 8.1   Government support for the semi-conductor industry in UK, France, Germany and Italy,[a] 1964–82

	Period	Amount
		(US $ m)
United Kingdom		
1. Micro-electronic Support Scheme	1973–9	21
2. Component Industry Scheme[b]	1977–	10
3. Micro-electronic Support Programme[cd]	1978–	111
4. Inmos	1978–82	101
5. Microprocessor Application Project[cd]	1978–82	111
6. Support for micro-electronics under Product and Process Development Scheme[d]	1979	54
7. Other (annual average)[e]	1964–77	2–4 p.a.
8. Military (annual average) (estimated)	1970–9	4–6 p.a.
9. Non-business institutions and universities (annual average) (estimated)	1966–78	4–6 p.a.
Germany[f]		
1. BMFT support	1969–72	23
2. BMFT Electronic Component Programme	1973–8	118
	1979–82	74
3. 2nd Data Processing Programme	1969–76	32
4. 3rd Data Processing Programme	1977–8	..
5. Synchroton Radiation Project	1981–2	26
6. Military and space	1964–8	..
	1969–76	33
	1977–82	..
7. German Research Association	1964–76	22
France		
1. 1st *Plan Calcul*[g]	1967–70	36
2. 2nd *Plan Calcul*[g]	1971–5	33
3. *Plan Circuits Intégrés*	1977–80	132
4. Non-business institutions and government laboratories (annual average) (estimated)	1964–75	10 p.a.
	1976–82	..
5. Military	1964–82	..
Italy		
1. Technological Evolution Fund		
(a) grants	1968–78	1
(b) loans	1968–78	4

Table 8.1 (cont.)

	Period	Amount
		(US $ m)
2. Electronics Plan (Law 675)[h]		
(a) grants	1980–2	96
(b) loans	1980–2	60
3. Military	1964 82	..
4. National Research Council project on solid state physics.	1964–82	..

Sources: see Dosi [1] (. . = not available).

[a]Figures cover grants, subsidies and transfers on capital account unless otherwise stated. Regional incentives are excluded, also low-interest loans except in Italy.

[b]Total scheme involves $40 million, of which amount shown in the table went to semi-conductors.

[c]Amounts are estimates of what the Conservative government might retain from schemes introduced by their predecessors.

[d]There may be some overlapping in these items.

[e]Includes funds from the Advanced Computer Technology Project of 1964.

[f]Figures include R and D performed by industry and by other institutions.

[g]Includes expenditure on other electronic components, but the bulk of the sums shown are believed to be attributed to semi-conductors.

[h]Grants, subsidies and other transfers to the business sector only. It should be noted that these figures refer to proposed and approved amounts, which differ from the actual cash available at the time of writing.

million for micro-processor application development grants. As far as financial support is concerned, one should add also the long-term low-interest loans from the Credit National.

In Italy there was no substantial intervention in the electronics sector until 1978, but it was one of the sectors affected by the 'Industrial Restructuring, Rationalisation and Development Law' (Law 675/77), which was intended to provide guidelines and financial support to a dozen industrial sectors, either because they were 'technologically strategic' or because they were facing strong adjustment pressures. In the 'Electronics Plan' one sub-sector considered is electronic components, of which semi-conductors are the most important part. The financial assistance was supposed to be distributed over the four years 1978 to 1982. Up to the time of writing, November 1980, nothing had been paid out. The other parts of the

Electronics Plan, concerning computers and office equipment, telecommunications, consumer electronics, automation and industrial electronics, as well as to some extent the machine tools plan, may be considered as special provision for micro-electronic applications.

Policy Instruments

We now turn to a brief cross-country survey of policy instruments. The first set of policies comprises R and D support through subsidies, research contracts and low-interest loans. This has been by far the most important instrument of intervention in all European countries. In addition, some research activities have been undertaken directly by public institutions and government agencies. This was especially important during the 1950s and 1960s in the UK (military research establishments) and France (military research, *Centre National d'Etudes des Télécommunications* and the *Commissariat à l'Energie Atomique*). In the 1970s the *Commissariat* itself set up a manufacturing activity (EFCIS) with the participation of the Thomson group. In Germany, a significant amount of research (pure and applied, generally non-military) is undertaken by the *Fraunhofer* institutes. The Association of German Engineers (VDI) has recently established a 'Technology Centre' in Berlin, operating mainly as an advisory–consultancy body for small and medium-sized firms. A similar role is performed by the Technology Advisory Services of the Chambers of Commerce and by the RKW. In Italy some research projects have been undertaken by the National Research Council (CNR), either autonomously or in collaboration with private firms.

The second area is procurement policies, mainly in the military and telecommunications fields. Military procurement was relatively important in the UK and France, but much less so in Germany and Italy. As a percentage of total demand, however, it was generally declining. Telecommunications procurement usually follows a 'buy national whenever possible' policy in all the major European countries. The telecommunications market is growing rapidly. Total public procurement (military, aerospace and telecommunications) in Europe as a whole may be estimated at around 20 per cent of the market.

There are also policies concerning investment grants, subsidies and transfers on capital account. These are not exclusively for semi-conductors but more general, often part of regional policies. For the semi-conductor industry they seem to play a substantial role in the UK, especially with regard to location in Scotland. Recent semi-conductor investments in France, both nationally owned and joint ventures, are believed to have been financed on preferential terms and to have been granted regional incentives. Italian electronics (as well as other manufacturing) investments in the South generally receive – on a fairly automatic basis – the investment grants and low-interest loans provided by *Cassa del Mezzogiorno*. Regional (*Länder*) provisions are also significant in Germany, although it is difficult to assess the degree to which the electronics industry (and in particular semi-conductors) have benefited from them.

The fourth set of policy instruments is tariff and non-tariff protection. All EEC countries apply a 17 per cent *ad valorem* tariff to semi-conductor imports, which is the highest among the industrialised countries. The EEC did not agree to any reduction of that tariff at the recent Tokyo Round of GATT. The tariff does not appear to reduce imports significantly. Even for devices produced in Europe, it is well below the cost differentials between the Japanese and American industries on the one hand and European industry on the other. A high protection in components decreases the degree of effective protection for electronic goods. A form of non-tariff protection is the existence of national technical standards, especially for telecommunications and military components. At present a set of European technical standards is on the way to being approved by EEC members. In addition some American and Japanese producers claim that import licensing in France and Italy represents a protective barrier (USITC [14], p. 63).

The fifth form of government involvement is through promoting structural change – mergers, the constitution of new firms, nation-alisation, the planning of the areas of activity of individual firms, etc. In France, public institutions have always favoured mergers and this lead to the formation of SESCOSEM in 1968, and finally in 1978 to the concentration in the Thompson group of almost all French-owned semi-conductor production. Furthermore, the state had an active role, first in authorising and then in financing and negotiating terms for the joint ventures between St Gobain and National Semiconductors, and between Matra and Harris, both in 1978. Under both agreements the French partner has a 51 per cent share and the American partner 49 per cent. It is believed that the American companies provide the technology and the French part-ners and the government the financial backing. Continuing public support is conditional on the achievement by the new companies of the targets agreed in advance with the DIELI (*Direction des*

Industries Electroniques et de l'Informatique) in terms of the transfer of technology and levels of production. St Gobain and Matra are not electronics companies but diversified groups willing to expand into the most promising areas of electronics. St Gobain recently purchased a share in CII-Honeywell Bull and in Olivetti. Finally, the last 'IC Plan' provides for a pattern of specialisation among French firms, joint ventures and the Philips subsidiary (RTC) (see [1]).

In semi-conductors, the British government followed no explicit structural policy until the constitution of Inmos by the NEB. In the 1960s it favoured the merger between the semi-conductor divisions of Eliott and Marconi in Marconi Eliott Microelectronics. The attention of the British government has been, however, focused on computers for a long time: there it had a direct or indirect role in the series of mergers that led to the constitution of ICL, in which the government itself kept a share until 1979. In Germany, there was no significant 'structural' policy; there did not appear to be any need for one.

In Italy, although any kind of conscious 'supply-side' policy has been absent for a long time, the most important action has been the purchase by STET (the telecommunication and electronic holding company of IRI) of SGS, after Fairchild left the joint venture with Olivetti and Telettra (Fiat). In the same period STET acquired other electronics companies, either from other holdings of the same IRI group or from third owners. It could be argued that in these acquisitions STET was acting like any other private company. It is doubtful, however, whether any other Italian company would have intervened in SGS (and covered its persistent losses) were it not part of a large and financially solid (at the time) holding. In the Italian electronics field, only the state-owned telecommunications company seemed to be in this position.

Policy Differences and Effectiveness
We now turn to an assessment of the degree of similarity or difference between the actual – rather than the stated – 'philosophies' underlying the policies: specifically, the relationship between policies and the objectives of the firms.

It is widely believed that the electronics sector confirms a general pattern, differentiating Germany's more market-related policies from French and British ones which are more interventionist and discretionary (Grant and Shaw [4]). The hypothesis proposed here, in a somewhat provocative way, is that beneath the differences, there are significant similarities.

The actual 'philosophy' that appears to be common to the European policies examined here seems based on two assumptions. The first could be summarised as 'you cannot tell the firms what to do', and the second, related to the first, assumes that the strategies of the firms are generally consistent with public objectives.

As far as semi-conductors are concerned, there appears to be a lot of correspondence between the strategies of domestic companies and the provisions of policy actions, which have to some extent been reinforcing these 'neutral' trends. In the French case, the actual policies can be represented as the result of a stalemate between the 'national' objectives of the *Délégation à l'Informatique*, and the objectives of the companies themselves. In this stalemate the *Délégation* seldom had the power to implement political decisions, and often the final result was a compromise between conflicting private interests, for example, CGE and Thomson, the two major electronics groups. When national targets were indeed provisionally set, as in the case of the establishment of CII in computers, the latter was considered by CGE and Thomson (which retained the formal ownership, although an overwhelming percentage of the funding came from the state) an unwanted child, to be sent to the orphanage as soon as possible. The stalemate was not only between the private sector and the *Délégation*, but inside the private sector itself; many times each of the two companies has been more concerned to prevent the other from expanding in electronics than to expand itself. In semi-conductors the story is similar: SESCOSEM is at least partly a child of the *Délégation*, as Thomson had been going to sell SESCO to General Electric; since then it has been kept alive mainly with public funding. CGE had already, in 1968, sold its semi-conductor division to Philips. A deeper commitment by the Thomson company to semi-conductors is fairly recent.

French electronics is sometimes taken as an example of the failure of industrial planning if it conflicts with the working of the market mechanism (Zysman [15], [16]). In my view it represents, on the contrary, the failure to pursue coherent planning if it conflicts with the strategies of each company. Whenever a conflict has occurred between private and social (real or supposed) returns, public institutions have shown themselves incapable of making the latter predominate. Incidentally the *Délégation*, which for a long time has been known as the 'representative of national interests', was strongly in favour of a European solution in computers (and eventually in components); private industry in France was more in favour of an American solution – which was seen as less risky and with bigger prospects of short-run profitability.

In other countries this conflict does not seem to arise because the aims of industrial policies are, more or less, made to coincide with the already existing structure and strategies of the companies operating in the field. Considering the options open to policy-makers: (a) leaving the semi-conductor sector altogether and concentrating on applications; (b) maintaining a design and custom manufacturing capability; (c) improving and/or developing technological and manufacturing capability in the standard American-dominated market; one can notice a fairly close correspondence between the chosen policies and the original structure and features of the industry itself (Sciberras [12]). It may well be that these are the only options available – other more 'offensive' strategies are either impractical or very difficult. The likely consequence, however, seems to be the maintenance of the relative differences between the American and European industries and also among European countries themselves.

There is little homogeneity among European companies, and they can be subdivided between those operating in the standard market and those operating in the custom market. For most of them, the only reasonable strategy is very defensive – survival by maintaining the 'relative distance' between them and their American competitors, and following a more or less 'imitative' pattern. Broadly speaking, this has also been the objective of public industrial policies.

In spite of these similarities in the 'philosophy' of public intervention, the differences in execution are considerable. They concern mainly *comprehensiveness*, *timing*, the initial *structural conditions* industrial policies have to deal with, and the *magnitude* of the intervention.

Germany
With respect to all four indicators, Germany seems to come out best. First, German support programmes for data processing, components, applications and software are comprehensive. This is important, given the strong interactive mechanisms between users and producers. German policies for semi-conductor components (primarily R and D support) have been implemented in an environment in which the specialisation of the biggest German manufacturers is clearly established, and some companies (primarily Siemens and Valvo-Philips, but also AEG) due to their size and vertical integra-

tion can internalise the advantages of improvements in semi-conductor technologies. Second, support for R and D in semi-conductors, initiated around 1969, has since 1972 been substantial enough
to finance several projects in products, production technologies and
applications. Third, the companies themselves were keen to remain
and develop products in this sector. In Germany, the companies
themselves appear to finance some 60–80 per cent of their R and D
in this field. Some estimates for France suggest a comparable figure
there of 20–30 per cent. (Possibly preferential government loans are
included as government finance in the French calculations, but not
in the German; however, this would still leave a wide gap between
the two figures.) The German strategy has not been one of 'leap-
frogging' (like the Japanese), but rather one of a quicker 'imitative
pattern' over a wide range of products and technologies, the speeding-up of the rate of diffusion in applications, and advancement in
'basic research' and in new and promising technologies such as
opto-electronics, solid state solar cells, etc.

German policies have had some success. Probably on average
the 'imitative lag' of German industry is somewhat shorter; one
firm (Siemens) has reached the breakeven point and the 'coverage
ratio' (domestic German-controlled production as a share of national consumption) in integrated circuits has considerably increased. However, the technological lag is still there.

United Kingdom

In Britain the bulk of intervention until the mid-1970s was concentrated on computers: British semi-conductors had only a secondary
place (Grant and Shaw [4]). Given the British situation on the supply
side, it is doubtful whether much more could have been done, particularly after 1970–1 when GEC practically left semi-conductors
and Plessey and Ferranti gave up any intention of moving into the
standard high-volume market. The limited Micro-electronic Support Scheme, started in 1973 with a funding of £10 million, took
six years to be used. Before the constitution of Inmos, any more
ambitious policy would have required some structural change such
as a merger or the constitution of a new company. Some believe
that the Inmos experiment is 'too little, too late' (Grant and Shaw
[4], p. 4). In computers a merger policy proved to be fairly successful with ICL, although, as the French semi-conductor case shows,
such a policy might be a necessary but not a sufficient condition if
there is a complete lack of commitment on the private side; in

those cases direct public intervention (either in the form of NEB–Inmos or with actual nationalisation of the IRI–SGS type) is likely to be much more effective.

In Britain, after British companies had withdrawn from the big markets, the limited policies followed until recently probably just enabled the domestic producers to remain where they were, while military and telecommunications procurement protected two of the main areas of activity of British-owned semi-conductor firms. The recent constitution of Inmos is a large, ambitious attempt to leapfrog into VLSI (very large scale integration). The risk is high, but, given the remarkable staff of technicians recruited on both sides of the Atlantic, the bet appears worthwhile.

France
The French case (page 193) is an example of the conflict between national objectives and private strategies. Policies certainly helped the French industry to survive, but did little more than this. Given the general reluctance of the private companies, the determination to 'safeguard the appearance of a purely private solution' (memorandum of the *Délégation*, quoted in [5]) prevented any more ambitious or more efficient industrial policy.

There are signs that the situation is changing. First, the Thomson group seems much more committed than before to the 'semi-conductor game'. Second, the massive programme of developing the telecommunications network has provided a push towards technical improvements and has opened up a profitable market, guaranteed through the procurement policy. Third, big diversified companies – such as St Gobain and Matra – are now entering the field. Fourth, there is renewed government interest with the 'Plan Circuits Intégrés' of 1977 and the institution of the coordinating and monitoring 'Mission pour les Circuits Intégrés'.

Italy
Italian industrial measures may not be 'too little' but are certainly 'too late'. Italian planning is more in the nature of self-planning by the industry itself. The STET group in general and SGS in particular, together with other private electronics firms, have been asking for some kind of industrial policy since the beginning of the 1970s, supported by the trade unions and the Parties of the left. These policies were finally approved in the 'Restructuring' law of 1978, but it is open to doubt whether any such policy will

ever be implemented. The central task in semi-conductors seems to be the strengthening of the technological and manufacturing capabilities of SGS-Ates over the entire spectrum of integrated circuits, and especially in MOS (metal-oxide–silicon) memories and micro-processors, where the Italian company has been relatively weak.

The Italian plan in semi-conductors aims at objectives similar to the German ones; both are focused on domestically owned producers. This is facilitated by the company structure which exists. In other sub-sectors, like consumer electronics and electronic instruments, the lack of any supply-side policy will probably make the plan largely in-effectual. Further, this compares German policies which have already been implemented with Italian unfulfilled intentions. Italian policies may perhaps succeed in some reinforcement of the technological and manufacturing capability of SGS, which – by European standards – is already fairly good. Actually two crucial questions have still to be solved. First is the strategy of the state-owned STET group (to which SGS, together with Italtel, manufacturers of telecommunication equipment, and SIP, the telecommunication utility company, belong); the question is whether it starts behaving like an integrated company with clear nationally oriented manufacturing strategies, or will continue in a mediocre form of survival, subsidised by the utility itself. Second, there is the possibility of collaboration between the manufacturing companies of STET and Olivetti.

Policies towards Foreign Firms

In some countries, especially the UK and to a lesser extent France, there is a kind of policy schizophrenia between stated objectives – strongly nationally oriented – and actual policies, which are fairly keen to subsidise foreign investment. This may be because Euro-pean firms themselves have recently begun to put pressure on public authorities to encourage joint ventures. In some countries this 'second best' alternative might be the only practical one. However, this is an area where governments might find themselves subsidising developments which would have taken place anyway.

This was almost certainly the case with the joint ventures of GEC–Fairchild (now in doubt); St Gobain–NS and Matra–Harris. In an interview, a manager stated that in some cases, through vari-ous support schemes, public funds can reach up to 60 per cent of the *total* cost of investments. This net zero sum game is mainly played between the UK, France and Ireland. There is a difference however. France is prepared to give special subsidies to joint ventures after a complex bargain on technology transfers and production targets. The other two seem ready to finance any electronic investments. It is possible that Ireland may have gained from these policies, since – apart from differential labour costs – it does not appear to have other locational advantages. Neither Germany nor Italy seems to be in the race at all. For the UK, on the contrary, it simply appears to be a case of subsidising investment.

The main policy instruments in Europe have been R and D subsidies to projects more or less defined by the firms themselves. The role of these subsidies has been the topic of considerable discussion in the literature (Pavitt and Walker [10]). In relation to the European semiconductor industry, the problem is whether it represents an appropriate tool of industrial policy. Although the subsidies are intended to reduce technological lags, they may, in fact, simply support the R and D projects autonomously defined by firms which have much less ambitious targets in mind. Second, R and D subsidies risk being a substitute for private financing, without adding substantially to what a firm would have otherwise undertaken. The very limited evidence on the subject is somewhat contradictory. In the French case, subsidies may have been partly substitutive. It could be argued, however, that without these public funds the French industry might have been sold to foreign firms. In Germany subsidies may have had a positive net effect, although it could be argued that large companies like Siemens have the financial strength to do what they did without government support. In Italy – if implemented – the plan would probably produce a net increase in the R and D efforts of Italian industry.

Conclusions

A distinction may be fruitfully made in the history of an industry between the periods of 'emergence' and 'maturity'. The 'emergent' phase is the initial stage when technological trajectories have not been clearly established, and the search for them is a process of trial and error. This phase needs institutions which produce and direct the accumulation of knowledge, experience, etc.; it also needs a multiplicity of 'Schumpeterian' risk-taking actors, ready to try different technical and commercial solutions. In the second phase of 'oligopolistic maturity', technological trajectories are much more defined, technical progress proceeds to a much greater extent *juxta propria principia*, the structure of supply is more stable, and the process of diffusion of technical change in related sectors is linked to a process of vertical integration from and into the sector which originated the 'dominant' technical change. The semi-conductor industry could be placed in the first stage until the 1970s, and is now heading towards the second stage. This does not necessarily imply a slowing down of the rate of technical progress, but simply a rather more defined direction of change.

Throughout the first stage European companies generally followed imitative strategies. Public policies to a great extent recognised and accepted these strategies, and were designed to make the process of imitation quicker and/or financially less onerous. European policies did not, however, generally intervene to alter the structure of the European industry, although this could have been done in two ways. First, there could have been a programme of massive 'accumulation of knowledge' and of productive capacity similar to that induced by the American military and space programmes. Second, there could have been an 'offensive' catching-up strategy, continuously acting upon variables like licensing policies and international transfers of technology, international trade, direct foreign investment, and the size and technological strength of domestic companies, in order to reduce technological and commercial lag times. This has been the Japanese strategy (Dosi [1]): Japanese policy attempted to remove the structural constraints which would have made it unprofitable for the private sector to pursue long-run 'national' objectives. It employed such measures as formal and informal controls on imports and foreign investments, regulations and licences (generally dealt with on a firm-to-country basis), and competition policies acting as a 'stick' for swift adoption of the new technologies. Japanese electronics policy can be summarised in three propositions: a country's position in the international division of labour need not be accepted but can be conquered; what is thought good for the country has to be made profitable for the companies; market competition is a powerful stimulus, as long as it occurs among national companies on the domestic market or with foreign companies on foreign markets. Japan appears to have 'planned', especially through MITI, a long-run strategy of technological catching-up with the US industry, a strategy that has already brought Japan to the technological and commercial forefront in several semi-conductor areas. On the other hand, these ambitious long-run national targets appear consistent with the strikingly aggressive and far-sighted attitude of Japanese companies.

The Japanese approach is significantly different from the European. These differences have deep roots in the nature of the relationship between the state, the companies, and social groups; the greater the degree of social acceptance of some 'rules of the game', the more consistent does companies' behaviour appear to be with a commonly accepted set of national objectives. 'Planning' in Japan does not need to be particularly authoritative, but appears much more as individual behaviour needing to conform with a jointly defined set of objectives. This apparent paradox also emerges in a comparison between German and French electronics policies (and industrial policies in general). If one defines planning as a conscious (*ex ante*) setting of goals, as opposed to the *ex post* harmonisation of behaviour induced by market mechanisms, then probably there has been more planning in Germany than in France. In France, because there has been less common acceptance of rules and targets, and a less conducive industrial structure, planning was more evidently an exogenous authoritative force, while in Germany it appears much more as an endogenous (or even 'market') mechanism.

In Europe, the experience in semi-conductors (and more generally from electronics) suggests that it is very difficult for public institutions to set and implement objectives that do not correspond to tendencies already existing in the private sector. However, 'market mechanisms' do not lead towards a convergence of technological capabilities and industrial strength amongst different countries which started from different technological levels. '*Laissez-faire*' represents an economic environment which, at least in high technologies, appears to suit the winners more than the late-comers. So probably in the next few years the Japanese will come out in favour of a 'liberal' ideology. Conversely, it is symbolic that some representatives of the American semi-conductor industry have started to advocate MITI-style collaboration between companies and government (see [11]). The nearest one gets in Europe to a somewhat instrumental use of market mechanisms (as a powerful *ex ante* stimulus and an *ex post* system of rewards and penalties) is France – where none the less their intervention in electronics has had its pitfalls and failures as mentioned.

Industrial policies towards semi-conductors in Europe suggest that strong 'positive adjustment' policies are often hindered by a somewhat 'short-sighted' attitude on the part of companies. This applies much more to France and the UK than to Germany; the difference is due, not only to cultural and sociological factors, but also to differences in company size, structure, etc. Positive adjustment policies are also hindered by the absence of policy instruments and agencies that can enforce 'far-sighted' objectives which the private sector sees as unprofitable. This absence is greater in the UK than in France and possibly Italy. On the other hand, Italy lacks a committed and efficient public bureaucracy.

With the semi-conductor industry moving towards 'oligopolistic maturity', the role of public policies appears to be changing. The question is no longer just one of a technological lag; it is the question of the place that each country will have in an international micro-electronics-based oligopoly covering a cluster of interrelated industries. The micro-electronics revolution is likely to change the pattern of the old electro-mechanical oligopoly, which has been relatively stable over the past 80 years, and to foster the emergence of a relatively new international structure of supply (Newfarmer [9]). Technology policies would then become a part of a larger set of structural policies, aiming to acquire a significant place in a cluster of inter-linked industries in what the French call *filière-micro-electronique* (Truel [13]). The recent French strategy of building up three electronics 'poles' around Thomson, CGE and St Gobain appears to be a move in this direction.

A cross-country comparison of the success or failure of policies in this field shows also how important institutional differences are. Thus the short-sighted (strongly profit-oriented and risk-adverse) attitude of the French financial system imposed severe constraints on industrial strategies (e.g. the role of Paribas in Thomson strategies, as well as in the UNIDATA affair) – in contrast with the apparently fruitful and far-sighted relationship between the banks and firms in Germany.

In Italy the situation of chronic crisis in the big, and especially in the state-owned, enterprises showed itself in the difficulties and weaknesses of groups like STET and Olivetti. The experience of European electronics policies points to the limitations of technology policies *alone* (which is not by any means saying they are useless). Their degree of success, their scope, and their 'philosophy' come to depend on such matters as the existing structure of the industry, the strategies of the various companies, the institutional framework, etc. This will increasingly be the case. If the trend is towards an integrated micro-electronics-based international oligopoly, then technology policies will have to be conceived together with broader (structural) strategies related to one country's participation in it. The analysis and the assessment of policies has then to be broadened in scope, covering such questions as the relationship between oligopoly, technical progress, and international competitiveness, and the 'rules of the game' in the relationship between the state and big companies.

References

[1] Dosi, G., 'Structural adjustment and public policy under conditions of rapid technical change: the semi-conductor industry in Western Europe', Sussex European Research Paper (forthcoming).

[2] —, *Technical Change, Industrial Structure and Public Policy: the case of the semi-conductor industry* (forthcoming).

[3] General Technology Systems, *Netherlands Micro-electronics Study*, Brantford, 1979.

[4] Grant, R. M. and Shaw, G. K., 'Structural policies in West Germany and the United Kingdom towards the computer industry' (mimeo., City University), 1979.

[5] Jublin, J. and Quatrepoint, J. M., *French Ordinateur*, Paris, Alain Moreau, 1976.

[6] Kuhn, T., *The Structure of Scientific Revolutions*, Chicago University Press, 1962.

[7] Lakatos, I., *The Methodology of Scientific Research Programmes*, Cambridge University Press, 1978.

[8] Nelson, R. and Winter, S., 'In search of a useful theory of innovation', *Research Policy*, vol. 6, January 1977.

[9] Newfarmer, R., 'International oligopoly and uneven development in the international economic order' in *Nordic Symposium on Development Strategies in Latin America and the New International Economic Order*, vol. II, University of Lund, 1979.

[10] Pavitt, K. and Walker, W., 'Government policies towards industrial innovation: a review', *Research Policy*, vol. 5, January 1976.

[11] 'Proceedings of the Rosen Research/Morgan Stanley semi-conductor forum', *Rosen Electronics Newsletter*, 15 July 1980.

[12] Sciberras, E., 'The UK semi-conductor industry' in K. Pavitt (ed.), *Technical Innovation and British Economic Performance*, London, Macmillan, 1980.

[13] Truel, J. M., 'L'industrie mondiale des semi-conducteurs' (doctorate thesis, Université de Paris-Dauphine), 1980.

[14] US International Trade Commission, *Competitive Factors Influencing World Trade in Integrated Circuits*, Washington DC, USGPO, 1979.

[15] Zysman, J., *The French Industry between the Market and the State*, Cambridge Mass., MIT Press, 1974.

[16] —, 'Between the market and the state: dilemmas of French policy for the electronics industry', *Research Policy*, vol. 3, January 1975.

9 The NEB Involvement in Electronics and Information Technology

by W. B. Willott

Electronics and computers, including both hardware and software, have been a major part of the NEB's activities since it was formed. This chapter describes briefly the historical background to this involvement, and illustrates some of the main issues by reference to Inmos.

The Historical Background

The NEB was established in 1975 with a broad remit to develop the UK economy, to promote efficiency and international competitiveness, and to maintain productive employment. In order to achieve some results the NEB had to select a few key sectors on which to concentrate its financial and management resources, bearing in mind that this rather young organisation was also being given a number of major tasks in holding and managing shareholdings transferred to it by government, in particular BL and Rolls-Royce.

At the beginning of 1976 the government transferred to the NEB its 10.1 per cent holding in ICL and its majority shareholding in Ferranti. At the same time, the Department of Industry's Industrial Development Advisory Board referred Data Recording Instruments to the NEB and in February 1976 the NEB acquired a 54 per cent holding. Thus, while the NEB was still at the stage of developing its strategies, it found itself with interests in mainframe computers, small computers, electronic systems, integrated circuit manufacture, and computer peripherals, and this raised the question of whether the NEB should simply seek to manage its shareholdings as an investment house or try to develop a more coherent strategy across the sector.

The broad criteria the NEB set itself for involvement in a particular sector were that the industry should be one with rapidly growing world demand; there should be scope for import saving, evidence of existing or potential UK international competitiveness, and cohesion with existing NEB holdings; and the case should be one in which the NEB could play a direct role (that is the constraints on the industry's development could be eased by microeconomic rather than macroeconomic policy instruments).

From 1976 onwards the NEB held intensive discussions within the computer and electronics industry, with customers and academics, it commissioned consultants' studies, and it studied the strengths and likely developments of the main foreign competitors. The results of these discussions, together with those emerging from the Industrial Strategy SWPs, are summarised in this chapter.

General Trends

The increasing convergence of computers and communications were bringing the computer and its related products and services out of their specialised roles and into general business, and eventually domestic, use; given the declining costs and increasing power of devices, the use of computing techniques would expand faster than hitherto. Micro-electronics, and in particular the micro-processor, would be the driving force behind this expansion in scope and usage.

In computing, market dominance by the traditional US giants, and particularly IBM, had been slightly reduced in the mid-1970s. In terms of equipment and, equally important, in terms of marketing and business strategy, they were slow to move with the emergence of the computer from its specialist function. There was thus a brief opportunity for the UK industry before the US giants could properly deploy their massive financial, technical and marketing resources to capture the new areas of business. In terms of direct government support for the computer and computer service industries, the UK had provided (and still does) significantly less than other major competitors, including the US. In the period 1971–5 the industry estimates that support in the UK was a little over half that in France, a fifth of that in Germany and a tenth of that in Japan.

Industry Structure

With the exception of ICL in mainframe computers and the UK subsidiaries of the major multinationals, the computer industry was weak and fragmented, and even ICL was small by international standards. Many producers were small single-product companies. In the wider electronics field, again apart from the major US and European multinationals, the UK companies with financial resources that were significant on an international scale, like GEC and Plessey, were conglomerates, with resources spread across a wide range of activities from power plant to consumer electronics.

It is a matter of argument whether success leads to large size or vice versa. In France the government has picked individual, cash-rich companies like St Gobain as a vehicle to develop information technology. In the software field, in the UK the largest groups of programmers and designers are to be found in the major applications companies, but otherwise they are in over 500 relatively small, entrepreneurial software houses. The French government, by contrast, saw scale economies as of importance and, with the help of the publicly owned banks, set about rationalisation, so that by 1976 seven of the ten largest European software companies were French.

Major advantages of size in the computer industry are the ability to provide a reliable and sophisticated network of after-sales service, and to offer integrated systems – partly because of the growing interdependence of devices, and partly because computer manufacturers seek to ensure that all their equipment and services are compatible but to prevent compatibility with competitors. In these circumstances the small single-product or service company will usually be at a severe competitive disadvantage.

The NEB's Approach

The competitive disadvantages facing relatively small companies, and the enormous opportunities arising from the trend towards the convergence of communications and computers, suggested that the exploitation of these opportunities required a competitive domestic presence in some or all of the following areas: mainframe computers; mini- and micro-computers; peripherals and terminals; communications; systems; software; semi-conductors. Some of the action required to produce a strategy across these sectors, for example public purchasing policy, was outside the remit and powers of the NEB. However, within the remaining areas the NEB was faced with three options:

(a) to accept that the UK domestic industry was already too far behind its major competitors and to go for international partnerships or inward investment, primarily from the US majors;

(b) to encourage the integration of existing UK companies to secure economies of scale in production and marketing;
(c) to establish 'green field' ventures in the areas not covered by existing UK companies.

These options were not mutually exclusive, and indeed a variety of approaches was adopted. In the case of mainframe computers, ICL was already the largest European manufacturer, with an established company structure and management. The NEB, therefore, confined itself to providing finance, as necessary, and letting the management get on with the job.

In the case of peripherals, the NEB's subsidiary company, DRI, was already the largest independent European-owned manufacturer, but still small by US standards, in a field where scale economies are crucial. The market was therefore increasingly dominated by US companies, who were influencing industry standards in the changing peripherals technology, and it was judged necessary to embark on a joint venture with one of the major US manufacturers, Control Data Corporation, in order to gain access to the new technology and develop sufficient manufacturing volume to remain cost-competitive with US and Japanese competition.

In the field of electronic office equipment the future trend was judged to be away from independent single products towards inter-communicating systems. Although there were a number of UK companies with good competitive products, none had a significant international presence in more than one. In 1976–7 the Office Equipment SWP accepted that the UK industry needed to become more integrated, but concluded that there was no mechanism whereby that could easily be achieved by the industry itself. The NEB did not pursue the possibility of encouraging a major merger of the relevant activities of existing UK companies, since the prospects for voluntary restructuring did not seem very great in practice. Many of the main companies saw their strategies as pointing in different directions. For example, GEC bought a US office machinery company, AB Dick, while Plessey started from its traditional telephone-PABX activities. The NEB therefore set up Nexos as a green field company, both to bring together the products of a number of the smaller suppliers so as to provide a comprehensive product range, and, more importantly, to create an integrated system. It will take several years before the success of a venture of this magnitude can be assessed.

The UK Micro-electronics Industry

Most of the NEB's investments in electronics have been aimed at the application of new technology. However the largest, and most controversial, project has been in the base micro-electronics technology of silicon chips. In the area of electronic components, the growth in total demand and the proliferation of applications has paralleled major advances in miniaturisation. The progression from valves and transistors to integrated circuits on silicon chips using large-scale integration (LSI) and very large-scale integration (VSLI) has led to a dramatic growth in computing power; a small desk-top micro-computer now has the capability of a roomful of electronic hardware of fifteen years ago, and this opens up a vast range of applications, especially in control systems and office electronics.

Until recently this market has been almost totally dominated by US companies, who benefited from the spin-off from the space programme in the 1960s and brought together a high level of technological skill with aggressive selling in a domestic market which was rapidly growing and receptive to new ideas. The companies that managed to secure a substantial share of this market were therefore well placed to dominate the European market, which, typically, followed the US market after a lag of a few years. This dominance, because of a technological lead, was reinforced because, in the case of standard electronic components at least, the learning-curve effect appears very significant and leads to substantial economies of scale. The results of these trends can be seen from the pattern of supply into the UK market. In 1962 UK companies held more than 68 per cent of the domestic market. This share declined steadily during the 1960s, the decline accelerating after the 1968–71 price war which accompanied the entry of companies such as Intel into world markets and the withdrawal of UK companies from the manufacture of standard components. By 1978 US companies supplied 90 per cent of the UK market and the number of significant UK-owned suppliers had been reduced to four: Ferranti, Plessey, GEC and Lucas, the latter two manufacturing mainly for internal use. This position was mirrored elsewhere in Western Europe: total European integrated circuit production in 1979 was $500 million against consumption of $1600 million.

The most recent development has been the growing success of Japanese manufacturers. Recognising the importance of micro-electronics as a fundamental industrial building block, the major companies there, with government help, including $350 million support for R and D, have caught up with American technology and in doing so have developed a formidable R and D strength. Moreover, by applying the characteristic Japanese skills in process development and manufacture, they have been able to compete with the American majors, particularly in selected target areas. Although their share of the overall US integrated circuit market is only about 4 per cent, they have, for example, seized 25 per cent of the US market for 16K MOS (metal-oxide–silicon) memories. Many outside observers see Europe as the future battleground between Japanese and American companies. It is not surprising, therefore, that there has been a rush by European governments to try to capture mobile inward investments by these firms.

However, this poses the question, as it did in the mid-1970s, whether it is sufficient to rely on the availability of micro-chips on the world market, and on satellite production in the UK and Europe. There are a number of disadvantages: it leaves UK users vulnerable if there is a world shortage, as for example when IBM bought heavily in 1978; moreover there may be a degree of spin-off from close contact between end-users and the R and D facilities of the manufacturers. This can be seen as one aspect of the argument on whether the UK should manufacture 'custom' or standard chips, given the size of the UK (or indeed European) market, the limited supply of skilled manpower, and the relative value-added.

The arguments in favour of concentrating on manufacture of 'custom' chips or 'specials' were essentially these. First, certainly the UK market, and possibly the European market, were too small to give adequate scale returns in the face of the already dominant US companies with an established, large and rapidly growing domestic market. Secondly, given the commodity nature of standard chips, past evidence suggested that the competition could be intense and that prices would come tumbling down. Manufacture was, arguably, unlikely to be very profitable and, given that the UK did not seem to be particularly adept or efficient at large-scale manufacture, a UK company was not likely to be very successful. Thirdly, if standard chips were to be made elsewhere it was sensible to buy them as cheaply as possible and then to use UK software skills in maximising value-added in applications. Finally, in chip manufacture itself, there was more value-added, and profits to be made, in manufacturing 'customs', where the individual skill element and the overall efficiency in the end-use were higher.

The contrary arguments were that many of the major technical advances would arise from the development of standard chips, and that access to them would be necessary if end-users and 'specials' manufacturers were to remain competitive with those who had such access. In other words, mere purchase of the chips, or even assembly here, did not transfer technology. Secondly, multinationals (particularly those based in the US) are subject to enormous regulatory and other pressures from their home governments which may make their products or terms less suitable in foreign territories. Thirdly, although the risks are undoubtedly high, given the competitive pressures, and although profit margins are likely to be lower than for 'specials', the volumes are so enormous that total profits are potentially large. It is estimated that 80–90 per cent of total demand will be for standards. Fourthly, each step change in technology or scale of integration provides an opportunity for new entrants, though the entry fees also increase substantially with each step. Table 9.1 shows the changes in rank ordering at each of the three previous steps.

The outcome of this debate was that most UK companies remained 'specials' manufacturers, though GEC, which had the financial resources to manufacture standards, announced in 1978

Table 9.1   Changing production structure illustrated by
            the 'dynamic RAM',[a] 1974–9

	Storage capacity[b]	Rank of company		
		1	2	3
1974	1,000	Intel	American Microsystems	Advanced Memory Systems
1978	4,000	Mostek	Texas Instruments	Intel
1979	16,000	Mostek	NEC	Texas Instruments

[a]A random access memory.
[b]'Bits' of information.

a joint venture with Fairchild (US) to do so at Neston on the Wirral.

Inmos

The NEB had not taken a public stance in this debate, though it had not been convinced by the arguments against standards. The Inmos concept, of an entirely green field venture to get in at the step change from LSI to VSLI, just as Intel had at the introduction of LSI, was the brainchild of Dick Petritz, the original founder of Mostek, and Iain Barron, the founder of Computer Technology, a pioneering UK micro-computer company. They approached the NEB for finance, and found that the NEB was prepared to back them.

It was recognised that the main source of technology would have to be the US, and indeed the bulk of sales (probably 60 per cent or more) would have to be there. However, as part of establishing a complete indigenous UK capability to manufacture standards, an R and D capability would be built up in both the US and the UK, while manufacture would eventually be primarily in the UK. The first products would be memory products, designed in the US, with the first production runs set up there and then transferred to the UK for manufacture. Meanwhile, the UK R and D team would concentrate on micro-processor development, though as part of the process of transferring technology some memory design work would be done here.

To test the commercial feasibility of the proposition, the NEB commissioned independent studies by consultants expert in the semi-conductor industry, both at the outset and before the second half of the investment was committed. The studies confirmed that, although the project entailed considerable risks, there was a reasonable probability of success. Subsequent events have borne out the technical appraisal. The Inmos concept of 'redundancy' (building in at design stage greater capacity than the circuit requires) offers significant advantages in reducing the number of rejections at process stage and in product reliability. The window of opportunity for a new generation of products still remains open: despite claims by a number of manufacturers since 1978, the next generation has proved harder to develop than most people had expected, and the time-scales originally predicted by Inmos have proved valid, so that the company should enter the market with timely products.

The Launch and Subsequent Developments

The NEB approved the Inmos proposal in April 1978. Since the consent of the Secretary of State was required for investments of over £10 million, this was duly sought. The work of the NEDO SWP on UK micro-electronics strategy had not then been finalised and GEC had begun to indicate a preference for a joint venture with Fairchild, although the precise relationship they had in mind was not then clear. In view of these uncertainties it was not until 13 June 1978 that statutory consent was obtained; the formal establishment of Inmos was announced on 22 July 1978 together with the names of the three founder members, Dick Petritz, Iain Barron and Dr Schroeder (formerly director of memory design engineering at Mostek).

During the remainder of 1978 Inmos began to recruit staff and the site for the UK Technology Centre was identified. In March 1979 Inmos acquired its US prototype processing facility at Colorado Springs and began building work on the production site. The location of the first production plant in the UK aroused keen interest around the assisted areas and a consultant's report was commissioned to assess the relative merits of various locations. Despite the attractions of a number of other sites, bolstered by their eligibility for regional grants, Inmos took the view that the production site should be located near to the Technology Centre; industry experience suggested that wide separation of R and D from production led to problems. The NEB had approved the second tranche of equity in principle in July 1979, with the Inmos Corporate Plan. In December 1979 Inmos formally requested the second tranche to enable it to make commitments for the development of the first UK production plant. The new NEB reviewed this, as a priority, and concluded that the company was performing in line with its Corporate Plan. They also accepted the Inmos recommendation that the plant should be located at Bristol. This recommendation was made public by the company in December 1979, and on 2 January 1980 the NEB sought statutory consent for the second £25 million.

Since the initial approval of the Inmos project, there had been a change of government. The incoming Conservative administration had undertaken a review of the whole of the NEB's activities, which culminated in the Secretary of State's statement to Parliament on 19 July 1979 and the new Guidelines published in draft in December of that year.

The timing of the Inmos siting and funding issues inevitably led to the two being linked and created a difficult political problem for the government. A further dimension was that, under the new Guidelines, it became part of the NEB's role to seek private finance for its ventures whenever practicable. With Schlumberger's take-over of Fairchild (following which the joint venture with GEC collapsed) and the involvement of the government, GEC expressed an interest in the Inmos venture in March 1980. During April and May a government decision on the second £25 million was further deferred for exchanges of information and preliminary negotiations with GEC, but on 17 May it was announced that GEC were withdrawing. In view of the time that had elapsed since the Inmos Corporate Plan had been approved by the NEB, the Board decided in June to undertake its own full review of the company, involving independent consultants and a team of independent specialists. This review, which was concluded in July, assessed that the company was still on course, but that the effects of the delay in approving the second £25 million had altered the balance of advantage from Bristol to a site in the assisted areas where regional grants would be available. On 29 July the Prime Minister announced in Parliament that the second tranche of £25 million would be provided for Inmos to build their first UK production plant in South Wales.

Conclusion

Electronics and information technology is an area of very rapid growth, where the structure of the industry in the various sectors concerned does not always suggest that the UK will be able to seize the opportunities in the face of strong overseas competition. This chapter outlines the ways in which the NEB has sought to fill a number of the possible gaps. One example, Inmos, that has been covered at rather greater length, illustrates the ability of the NEB to take risks and to back a radically different course from the received wisdom of the industry – though it will of course take several years to see how successful Inmos will be – and how the political dimension can sometimes interfere with normal commercial decision-making.

10 Policies for Micro-electronic Applications in Industry

by Jim Northcott

This chapter starts by asking whether there is a need for policies to encourage micro-electronic applications and examines the extent to which the existing government schemes are effective. It then makes a number of suggestions – at this stage highly tentative – about ways in which present policies might be improved.

Recently there has been increasing attention to the impact of micro-electronic applications. Little has so far been published, however, on the operation of the main government policy measure in this field, the Microprocessor Application Project (MAP). It was therefore chosen as the subject of the first part of a study by the Policy Studies Institute (PSI) of micro-electronic applications in industry and services. The first report, *Microprocessors in Manufactured Products,* published in November 1980, is based on case studies of the experience and attitudes of 90 companies in manufacturing industry. It is to be followed in 1981 by another which will examine applications in production processes. This chapter is mainly based on that study.

Are Government Policies Needed?
There is fairly general agreement that the potential applications of micro-electronics are very many and varied, and it is therefore a new technology of exceptional importance. It would also seem to be a natural field for development in Britain, on account of its high value-added, low materials, energy and import content, lack of environmental disadvantages, high export potential, and dependence on education and special skills. Moreover, successful adoption of the new technology can make such radical improvements in the performance and attractiveness of products that firms which adopt it can achieve bigger production volumes, higher prices, better pro-

ducts, new markets – in short a rapid and profitable expansion. Conversely, if we fall behind in the new micro-technology, our products will become more difficult to sell in overseas markets, or even at home, and the consequences will be gravely damaging.

The stakes, then, are high; but this is not in itself sufficient reason for the introduction of specific policies to promote micro-electronics if ordinary market forces can be relied on to produce the desired results. The relevant questions are – whether there are signs that we are falling behind in this new field and whether there are special factors which may impede our progress. On neither count is the position reassuring.

The PSI study was not primarily designed to gauge the extent of our international competitiveness and such evidence as it provides is mixed. At one extreme, some firms are not only keeping up with world competition, but in certain product lines are actually setting the pace; at the other extreme, in some product lines no producer in Britain is attempting to compete at all. Between these extremes, some firms are probably keeping up with the best of their overseas competitors, a rather greater number manifestly not, and there are a number of others who hope they are keeping up, but quite possibly may not be. Overall, our leading competitors seem to be ahead in the sense of having more chip-based products already on the market and of pushing their development and sales with more confidence and enthusiasm.

More serious is the presence of a number of special factors which, in the absence of government intervention, would make a successful outcome unlikely.

First, we no longer compete in a free market. The governments of our main competitors, although most of them favour a free market system in general, are giving special support to the development of this new technology. British companies, if left to stand on their own feet, are therefore likely to find themselves at a disadvantage.

Second, this is not an area where the forces of competition can always be relied on to elicit an appropriate response. Many of the firms studied by the PSI expressed concern at what their competitors were doing, or might do, as a major reason for wanting to go ahead. But not all – some are not planning to compete because they are not aware of the scope for applications, or their importance, and some of these are in danger of being knocked out. Others, impressed by what their overseas competitors are already doing with new technology, instead of rushing to manufacture similar or better products here, have decided that it is easier, safer and more profitable to import foreign products instead. It can be argued that, if there are areas in which British firms cannot or will not compete, it is better for them to drop out and instead let the better-value products be imported. However, since the new technology has applications in a very wide range of industries, a major part of our manufacturing would then be at risk.

Third, because the new technology is very different, it can be difficult for a firm with no previous experience to develop it at first; but, once established in this field, a growing number of further applications can be developed with far less trouble, time and expense. This can give a great, sometimes decisive, advantage to the first firm to make a breakthrough. Unfortunately in many industries our leading overseas competitors appear to be well placed to achieve that breakthrough.

Fourth, the fact that the technology is new, fast-changing and difficult means that many firms, although aware of the scope, conscious of the competition and desirous of getting started, are faced with a number of practical difficulties. There are problems in getting to know how to use the new technology, risks of things going wrong in developing it, and difficulties in raising the necessary finance. What is unprecedented about this particular new technology is that it has so many different kinds of application in so many companies which hitherto have had little or no contact with electronics. Hence there is a need for a great many companies to take action. Not surprisingly, many are baffled about where to begin.

Those which do determine to enter this new area find themselves up against a particularly awkward combination of problems – difficulties in building up a design team, in covering the costs of development, re-tooling and launching, in mastering problems with software and input and output devices, in choosing the most appropriate kind of chip and securing supplies of it, in getting approval from the safety authorities, in overcoming scepticism or hostility in customers, parent boards or trade unions.

The MAP Scheme

These special factors seem between them to justify government intervention, but there remains the question of whether the form it has taken is appropriate. The scheme has four parts:

(a) a programme of seminars and publicity to generate a greater awareness of the opportunities and threats;

(b) a programme of crash courses to train more people in the necessary special skills;

(c) a grant of £2000 towards the cost of a consultant's feasibility study of a new application;

(d) a contribution of 25 per cent of the development costs of viable new applications.

In the first $2\frac{1}{4}$ years of the scheme over 130,000 have attended seminars for senior executives in industry, the number of short training courses has grown from 2500 in 1978 to over 30,000 in 1980, over 1600 sponsored feasibility studies have been started, and support has been approved for over 300 new projects. All four parts of the scheme are aimed directly at problem areas which the PSI study suggests are ones of particular difficulty. It is not easy to evaluate their precise impact, but it appears to be considerable in relation to the sums of public money expended – about £7 million on awareness and training, £3.5 million on consultancy and £15 million on development.

The MAP scheme is probably one of the most enterprising and successful industrial support schemes so far undertaken by the Department of Industry. Nevertheless, from the evidence of companies using the scheme, it appears that there are a number of ways in which it could be improved.

Consultancy advice
The support for consultancy is one of the more original and valuable features of the scheme. The trouble tends to be, however, that a firm which has no experience in micro-electronics will often have no experience in choosing or using consultants either. Many of the smaller firms, when confronted with the Department's list of over a hundred consultants, with only a limited amount of information about each, felt unable to make a rational choice between them. Some gave up in bewilderment, some responded to the first consultant who came across them at a meeting or sent them a promotional circular, and some resorted to other methods of selection which were more random and capricious than they would have wished.

Technical consultants vary greatly in the range and quality of their expertise, in the scale of their charges and in their suitability for any particular project. It is not surprising, therefore, that while many firms were satisfied, many others felt that the consultant they had chanced to use was not the most suitable. Conversely, some of the consultants which appeared to have the most to offer received few if any enquiries under the scheme.

Conscious of these problems, the Department brought out a new list of consultants, giving fuller information about each and classifying them by size, organisation, capability, area of operation, and subject and industry specialisation. It also brought out some notes giving general advice on the selection of consultants and offering firms a short list. More recently it has organised a pilot series of special seminars, at the end of which firms are introduced to consultants operating in the area.

These are useful improvements, but they still fall short of what is really needed. What many firms want is advice to guide them directly to the consultant most likely to be suitable. This is something which it is difficult for a government department to provide – the tradition of even-handed treatment is not compatible with recommending one consultant rather than another. On the other hand, advice from commercial sources tends also to be unsatisfactory, since it is unlikely to be disinterested – it is presumed that a consultant will be interested in securing commissions, a hardware supplier in increasing sales of equipment. Many therefore feel that they are still not adequately advised.

Delays in vetting procedures
Another frequent cause of complaint is the delay involved in the vetting procedures. When firms apply for consultancy support, the form they have to complete is commendably brief and simple, but they must none the less expect to wait some weeks for a decision. When they apply for development support the sums involved are larger, the form is necessarily longer and more difficult, and the wait for a decision is longer also – normally a matter of months.

The reason given for the delay is the need to prevent public money being wasted on ineligible projects; further, firms sometimes fail to provide the full information required, and there are staff shortages. However, firms considering adopting the new technology usually wish, and often need, to proceed as quickly as possible. The wait for weeks or months for a decision, combined with uncertainty about the outcome, inevitably reduces the incentive. Since the preparation of the application and the negotiations involve costs to the firm, and also further delays, the incentive is reduced yet more.

The extent to which these factors apply obviously varies greatly between firms and projects. There is reason to believe, however, that many firms regard them as going a substantial way towards offsetting the value of the grants; some deliberately decide not to apply for support.

As regards the benefits to the economy to be expected from the scheme, since one of the effects is likely to be a speeding up of decisions to go ahead with the new technology, it is anomalous for it to be adminstered in a way which slows down the implementation of those decisions. The effects of the delays are usually far from negligible and there must be plenty of cases where the net effect of the scheme is actually to make things happen *later* than if there had been no support.

Thus it seems that the present procedures reduce both the incentive value to firms of the grants, and the benefit to the economy in the form of earlier adoption of the new technology. In these ways they involve a 'waste' of public money that is no less real than the 'waste' involved if quicker vetting procedures required higher staffing levels, or resulted in support being given to a few projects which were not strictly suitable. There is a trade-off to be made between these different kinds of 'waste', and better value for public money would be obtained if the other kinds of 'waste' were also taken into account.

Additionality

Another aspect of the MAP scheme that might repay closer scrutiny is the principle of 'additionality'. The idea is that public money would be 'wasted' if it was used to support things that were going to happen anyway. It is thus a condition of eligibility for development support under this scheme (as under most of the Department's other industry support schemes) that a project would not have gone ahead in the same way without it. This rule is open to a number of objections.

First, it accentuates the delay – firms cannot go ahead at their own risk while awaiting a decision, because this could be taken to indicate that they intend to go ahead anyway. It also adds an extra complexity to vetting procedures and an extra uncertainty about the likelihood of an application succeeding.

Second, it is potentially in conflict with the principle of viability which is also a condition for support. Thus to be certain of eligibility a firm needs to show that the project would be clearly viable *with* a 25 per cent grant but clearly not viable *without* it. Since 25 per cent of the development costs will typically represent a much more modest proportion of the total costs involved in development, tooling up for production and launching a new product line, it may reasonably be wondered just what proportion of projects are genuinely so finely poised as to be eligible on both counts.

Third, 'additionality' does not correspond very well with the realities of how industrial decisions are taken. Some firms are quite definite that they would go ahead with a project anyway, and others equally definite that there would be no question of proceeding except with a grant. There appear, however, to be a greater number of firms for which the issue is much less clear-cut; they have not finally decided whether to proceed or not, and the decision may depend on a number of different factors together – the availability of a grant being only one of them, and probably not the most important at that. A common view is that if they feel a project is worthwhile, they will probably go ahead one way or another, with or without a grant; but if they do get a grant it will help things along, improving the prospects of the project and quite possibly making an earlier start possible. In these circumstances the question of whether a project is genuinely 'additional' does not always appear very meaningful.

At the same time, precisely because the issue is so blurred, many firms maintain they would have no difficulty in presenting their project in such a way as to make it look 'additional'. The 'additionality' requirement therefore encourages firms to be disingenuous in their dealings with the Department: it favours the firm that 'knows the ropes' and maintains a 'martini man' to pull in any hand-outs that may be on offer; and it penalises firms that are open in their dealings, particularly the smaller ones without previous experience in applying for support.

Fourth, the additionality requirement is open to the objection that it channels disproportionate support towards less promising projects. Enterprising and go-ahead firms are punished for starting early and being successful, and denied the extra boost which might turn a promising project into a real winner; firms which come later with less promising projects are encouraged to carry on with them and thereby to dissipate scarce resources on schemes which are much less likely to succeed.

Perhaps the emphasis should be not on more projects but on more results. A few strongly backed projects from the most dynamic firms may make more impact on our international competitiveness than a much larger number of marginal projects from more hesitant firms. Perhaps also the emphasis of the scheme should not be so exclusively on its incentive effects. It is not merely that so many firms deny that cash incentives have any influence on their decision, but the more basic consideration that incentives are concerned with decisions to start, whereas what matters, after all, is not the start but the result.

Thus, on the one hand, there is little value in persuading firms to start new projects unless they can be carried through to a successful conclusion. And, on the other hand, the fact that a firm is prepared to start a project on its own initiative does not necessarily mean that any public money spent on its support will be wasted. Regional development grants (which are not subject to 'additionality') have been found very useful by firms which would have been prepared to move to a development area even without any cash incentive, but later ran into greater difficulties than expected, when, for some of them, the extra cash made the difference between success and failure. In moving into micro-electronics, no less than when moving into development areas, firms often run into unexpected difficulties; so they could well value, or even desperately need, support in projects which originally they felt happy to undertake on their own.

Thus it does not follow that abandoning the principle of 'additionality' would be bound to result in a 'waste' of public money. It is possible that less emphasis on initial intentions and more emphasis on ultimate outcomes, less concern to get the greatest number of projects and more concern to get the greatest total impact, would bring better value for public money.

Levels and forms of support

At present the MAP scheme has standard conditions of eligibility and standard levels of support – £2000 towards the costs of consultants' feasibility studies and 25 per cent of the costs of development work. A scheme of this kind which provides a clear and readily predictable basis for support for the generality of firms which contemplate developing micro-electronic applications is certainly useful. But firms are not all alike, nor are their projects. Some have special characteristics which might merit support at different levels, or in different forms.

There may be occasions, for example, when development support at levels greater than 25 per cent are appropriate. Whatever the impact of 25 per cent, some higher figure, such as 50 per cent, might be expected to have greater impact. It may be that 25 per cent is normally enough to encourage firms to do things they would be rather inclined to do anyway; but substantially higher rates might be needed to persuade them to do something they definitely would not have contemplated otherwise. It may be desirable to offer a firm substantially more than the normal rate in the latter case if the project is thought to be of exceptional importance for the industry or the economy generally, or valuable as a demonstration project, or one which, although it would be likely to go ahead anyway, offers such exceptional prospects that really strong backing seems justified to transform a modest success into a world beater.

Different kinds of project may also need support in different forms. To some firms it may be more relevant to offer loans, interest relief grants, help in securing private finance, the underwriting of private sector loans, or financing on specially favourable terms through organisations such as Finance for Industry. Pre-production orders might be appropriate for certain kinds of new product to bring them through the development stage to successful production; bulk orders might be given for equipment already on the market, to allow economies from large-scale production. There may also be scope for special support for selected pace-setting firms to enable them to act as models for other firms in the same field, or to help them to spread their expertise to their suppliers or customers.

For some firms and projects the most useful kinds of support may be quite different. BSC (Industry) Limited, the Steel Corporation's subsidiary set up to bring new industry to areas where employment in steel is declining, has shown what can be achieved through the use of varied and sometimes unconventional forms of support, such as help with sites, buildings, equipment, materials, transport, subcontractors, recruitment, training, sales, design, technical assistance and expert advice; in fact whatever package, however unusual, is most effective in meeting the particular needs of the company concerned, subject only to the condition that the costs involved are consistent with the results to be expected.

One form of support which is particularly valued is assistance in preparing firms' applications for support. At first sight it might seem incongruous to spend public money on helping firms claim further public money, but the true balance of costs and benefits may often turn out favourably. There are plenty of small firms which can design, make and sell good products, but are much less skilled at preparing applications for government support. If some of these can be enabled to compete effectively in the micro-electronics era through the provision of MAP support the money will not have been wasted; the alternative of leaving them to sink may well be far more expensive in reduced international competitiveness and increased unemployment, while the social damage may be far more expensive still.

Another element in the success of BSC (Industry) has been its ability to talk to people in client firms as one businessman to another. There are many people in industry who are reluctant to apply for grants because differences in background, attitudes and ways of operating make it difficult to establish fruitful working relationships with civil servants. They may be equally reluctant to seek help from commercial organisations whose interests they feel may conflict with their own. For them the ideal source of support would be an organisation run on commercial lines, yet with no conflicting interests, and by people with an industrial background like themselves. The success of BSC (Industry) suggests that this may be an element of some importance which has been missing from most government support schemes.

New Agencies for Development?
The various considerations discussed above have differing implications for the kinds of organisation needed. The ending of 'additionality', and a greater emphasis on getting decisions taken quickly, would make little difference to the administrative organisation. Some of the other issues, however, would require organisational changes.

The present administrative process consists essentially of checking whether particular applicants fall within the defined conditions, and giving the standard amount of aid to those that qualify. However, the provision of higher levels of support for some firms would involve a very different process. It would have to be strongly selective and, if it was not to do more harm than good, this selectivity must operate in an informed and purposeful way. This discrimination between one firm or project and another, through an assessment of the relative scope for different projects and of the likely value of each project to the economy, requires the formulation of a long-term strategy for development to which individual cases could be related. This is far removed from the present requirements and implies a different kind of organisation – more entrepreneurial in flavour than could be contained in a Whitehall department. Similarly the provision of alternative kinds of aid requires considerable flexibility in operation, with the emphasis on originality rather than on consistency in following set rules. Likewise the provision of specific and reasoned advice on the choice of consultants implies positive recommendation of particular consultants, which is hardly compatible with the traditional Whitehall posture of neutrality.

Thus there may be a need for a new organisation, which could give firms specific impartial and expert advice on how to get started; which could provide aid at higher levels and in alternative forms on a selective basis; and which would be perceived by potential users as essentially their sort of organisation. This new kind of agency (or possibly more than one) should be set up outside Whitehall, under the auspices of the Department of Industry, but separate from it; mainly or wholly financed by government, but autonomous in its day to day operations; run on down-to-earth lines, but free from the pressure of commercial interests; staffed by people with high technical expertise, but also with direct experience in industry.

Such an agency might be set up as an off-shoot of one or more of the existing organisations which already have similar roles or methods of operation: for example, the various industry research institutes; the NEDO Sector Working Parties, which have already set a precedent in the Clothing Industry Productivity Resources Agency; the Institution of Electrical Engineers and other professional organisations, which already play a useful part in the awareness and training programme; the National Computing Centre, which already provides many relevant services to industry; or the NEB, NRDC or Finance for Industry, all of which already have experience in selective backing of new-technology ventures.

Alternatively there could be advantages in setting up a new organisation. A possible model is the highly successful VDI Technology Centre in West Berlin. It comes under the auspices of the Union of German Engineers, the professional engineers' authority, and is funded by the Federal government, but its detailed operations are independent of both. It has a professional staff of about thirty, who, in addition to the relevant technical expertise, all have direct industrial experience. They are backed up by library and technical facilities, keep abreast of hardware and software developments, and maintain close contacts with research institutes, technical bodies, consultants, universities and other relevant organisations.

When a firm contacts the centre it is visited by a member of the staff, who discusses the proposal and its prospects, both the technical and the business aspects, and advises on the best course of action. He can suggest a suitable consultant, provide funding where appropriate, and give help and advice when wanted right through the feasibility appraisal and development stages to commercial production. The appeal of the Technology Centre seems to lie in the way it is regarded by user companies. They respect its technical and business competence and regard it as 'their' organisation, able to see their problems from their point of view, neither seeking to sit in judgement on them nor to make a profit out of them.

Such an organisation would not be an alternative to the present Department of Industry MAP scheme, but would be additional to it. The proposal to establish it should not be seen as a criticism of the present scheme, which is already one of the most successful ever run by the Department. The point is rather that the advent of micro-electronic technology presents special problems which require exceptional measures for their solution.

11 Report of the Discussion

by Charles Carter

The conference turned first to consider the justification for government action to support and encourage innovation. No one sought to argue that it was desirable, or even possible, for government to do nothing in this field; after all, it controls large parts of services such as education which are essential to successful innovation. But there was a somewhat ill-defined difference of view about the proper reasons for government action, and in consequence about the nature and extent of that action.

One view, starting from the usual theory of the working of a market economy, saw possibilities that innovation would be sub-optimal because of a divergence between private and social marginal rates of return, or because the financial sector has an excessive aversion to risk. Thus government should intervene, but in a manner intended to improve the working of markets, not to supersede those markets. The assertion that this view was relevant only to static situations was not supported, but the problem in a dynamic setting was one of maximising the present value of future *expected* net returns, and therefore involved issues related to the formation of expectations in situations of considerable uncertainty. It was admitted that the signals on which economic agents act in a market economy might be weak or misleading, and that part of the function of government might therefore be to strengthen those signals, or to improve their relevance by a better dissemination of knowledge. But it was thought that it was unduly pessimistic to suppose that the economic agents in Britain are incapable of responding to market signals in order to maximise returns; it was still reasonable to suppose that where there is opportunity for gain it will be taken.

The alternative view was described as 'structuralist', but it was not very clearly defined. It starts from a belief that markets are so profoundly and inescapably imperfect that measures to improve the efficiency of their working will be totally inadequate. Therefore it is necessary to have a plan for innovation which would induce or compel changes in industrial structure or practice leading to appropriate types and rates of innovation. The example of the changes which have been induced in the Japanese economy was quoted: at the outset of these changes, the Japanese appeared to be doing almost the opposite of what a market economist would have recommended. The structuralists regarded the quality of market signals as likely to be poor, and the possible achievements of a reactive process based on these signals as totally inadequate to deal with the particular problems of the British economy, with its strong tendency to de-industrialisation related to technical backwardness. Some speakers appeared to have doubts about any reliance on 'marginalism', though it was pointed out that there are inevitable decisions to be made about the allocation of resources, and such an allocation, if it is to be optimal, requires consideration of alternative marginal uses.

The idea that governments should seek to improve the working of markets did not lead to any great clarity about *what* they should do. A market economy was seen as having many different decision-makers, reacting to situations in different ways and creating a competition of ideas; therefore government action should recognise this decentralisation of responsibility, and not seek to impose uniformity. In contrast, the structuralist view involves a plan of action, in which particular industries or technical developments are selected for preferential treatment, for instance by subsidy, by special access to finance, by government action in R and D or in training, or by the establishment of new state industries. But the examples of possible action given by the structuralists were of a very modest kind – such as restoring the Selective Investment Scheme, giving rather more money to the general advancement of knowledge, creating a separate industrial civil service, making more constructive use of Sector Working Parties to identify technology gaps and product opportunities, providing even more support to investment in manufacturing industry. Since the basis of the structuralist position is that the problem of inadequate innovation in Britain is extremely serious, and is beyond solution by the constricted workings of a market economy, there was thought by some to be justice in the criticism that a total lack of proportion existed between the ends envisaged and the means proposed.

But the most serious attack on the structuralist position related to a certain vagueness about how one was to create a plan and take the subsequent decisions which would lead to its successful implementation. What grounds existed for supposing that committees of eminent scientists and technologists (probably ill-informed about business), or groups of civil servants (many with no significant experience elsewhere), or Ministers (subject to innumerable sectional pressures) would make wise decisions? Whatever groups of people made the decisions, they would lack a clear set of principles on which to make them (since the principles of a market economy are assumed in advance to be inadequate); there would be a danger of scientists having delusions about grand technological developments, and of planners divorced from industrial responsibility proposing things which cannot realistically be done with available manpower or other resources. Furthermore, the record of the numerous interventions of government to stimulate technical advance is most discouraging, and offers strong support to the view that non-market decisions would be badly made. Inevitably Concorde was mentioned, but also the history of decisions on nuclear power, and the persisting gross imbalance of the government's programmes for the support of R and D.

Interestingly enough, however, the 'marginalists' turned out to be, beneath the skin, believers not so much in the efficacy of restoring and supporting the operation of the market as in the need for profound cultural change. They saw the 'British disease' as having a history of a century or more, and as showing itself in an inadequacy of management and a sourness of industrial relations which no measures would cure in the short run, or even in the medium run. In principle the faults (unless they are supposed to be of genetic origin) should be capable of being reduced by education, in a broad sense of that word; but the effect of this (even if we knew what to do) would be very slow, and plainly many of those present did not see how the problems of the British economy could possibly wait for such a long-delayed relief.

But there were some more hopeful remarks. Thus, it was suggested that, while 'picking winners' in innovation would always be very difficult, something could be achieved simply by increasing the number of projects started, in the expectation that this would increase the number of successes. Government financing agencies could have a part to play in achieving this. Again, some saw the problem as relating to the allocation to sectors of a necessarily limited supply of high ability: our failures in manufacturing industry might be the obverse of our considerable success in certain service industries, and a quite modest reallocation of ability (such as may already be occurring) might produce a more even performance.

It is possible that if, at the end of the first section of the conference, participants had been asked to list the government actions which they would regard as likely to be helpful to successful innovation, the lists prepared would have been rather similar, despite the differing views about the rationale for government action; while at the same time all or nearly all of those present would have been very pessimistic about the prospects of success for the measures they proposed.

Turning to consider the lessons from past UK industrial policy, the conference added weight to the view that the problems were to be found in the inadequacies of management and of industrial relations, aggravated by the influence of politicians, who meddle with and pervert policies for short-term political reasons, and by the lack of a consensus between the Parties on fundamental industrial issues. Certain trends of thought were, in retrospect, seen to have been unhelpful – for instance, the uncritical acceptance in the 1960s that bigger would be stronger; and the recurrent bouts of national arrogance, causing us to go beyond our ability in seeking to make technological leaps, and to ignore the experience of other countries. There were reminders that the picture was not entirely black – for instance, a nationalised industry, coal, had achieved a notable success in mechanisation; and that there was a need for government, through some appropriate agency, to encourage sensible reorganisations in industry. However, there was little said which suggested any hopeful or useful conclusions for the future from the experience of UK industrial policy in the last thirty years. This may not have been a well-considered attitude; it is, after all, easy to conclude that a set of policies which have been followed by so disastrous a decline must have been irrelevant or gravely deficient, but this is being wise after the event.

In discussing Allen's paper on Japan, stress was laid on the fact that the Japanese 'miracle' is a recent one, and that in the 1930s the Japanese economy exhibited many weaknesses (including bad industrial relations). Japan thus shows the possibility of a U-turn, but it offers little help in telling us how to achieve one. In the postwar period, Japan has enjoyed a consensus on objectives (including objectives of a long-term nature), but has had, within its generally conformist society, enough room for Independent and enterprising minds to break in. It has had quite a strong (though partly concealed) planning system, and some limitation of competition, though technical and market rivalry has remained strong, and the large firms have associated with them many small suppliers which have to withstand strong market discipline. Similarly, no great enlightenment came from the discussion of the French experience. France has moved from an elaborate system of central planning to a regime described as 'interventionist liberalism', whose purpose is to toughen the responses of private firms, while at the same time lessening certain hindrances in the public sector, such as the large deficits of nationalised industries, the increasing weight of the social security budget, and the faults of energy policy. But the process of 'toughening' private firms, to make them more flexible and more ready to take risks, involves much dialogue with government, and the strengthening of government intervention by designating a single place from which any public funds may flow. That intervention involves the designation of strategic sectors, achieved (it was alleged) by well-informed guesswork rather than precise reasoning; but the end result is, in a sense, a plan.

At the end of the first day, a plea was again heard for the reintroduction of a 'national plan' for Britain, and for the creation of interventionist agencies of government which would be outside the civil service, would have authority, a non-political status and permanence, and would relate closely to private enterprise. Such agencies could deliberately spend more to correct slow growth, could put out more effort in times of slump, and could carry large projects through their difficult initial periods of high uncertainty. Inevitably, there were countering voices which doubted the existence of any clear objectives which could be reflected in a 'plan', and which questioned whether government would allow the pursuit over a sufficient period of a consistent policy. The lack of consensus, which is seen by many as part of the problem, was illustrated by the day's discussions.

However, in a way which one would like to suppose to be particularly British, a somewhat greater convergence appeared when discussing on the second day a range of particular policies which might be followed. Those doubtful about intervention were eloquent in explaining that of course there must be some government action to stimulate innovation, while the interventionists were assiduous in denying any ambition to do anything very large, ex-

pensive or unusual. There was some discussion of the choice between selective and general policies, and it was suggested that the
problems of making a right exercise of discretion to be selective
justified a preference for general policies, even if in comparison
they involved some moderate sacrifice. Government involvement
needed to be consistent, not only in the sense of avoiding sudden
change but also in having a uniform method of assessment of costs
and benefits; though it had earlier been pointed out that the multi-
ple purposes of government policy made total consistency an un-
attainable ideal. The costs of government policy include the dangers
of sapping the self-reliance of entrepreneurs, and of making possible
cosy arrangements inimical to technical progress, but protected by
tariffs or by rules of government purchasing.

In general, however, there was evidence of support both for
'background' policies, such as improvements in managerial, engineering and technical education, and the promotion of a degree
of competition which is adequately stimulating but not so keen
that it enforces short views; and also for assistance to R and D and
for financial help to innovating firms, perhaps through a body like
the NEB, or by giving guarantees to pension funds so that they can
finance riskier projects. The protectionists appeared to be in a
minority, but in any case argued only for minor selective protection.
Government was seen to need, in any area of its action, a sufficient
involvement to provide genuine familiarity with the problems. It
might then give further help by promoting better intercommunica-
tion between firms.

The conference at this stage noted one grave unsolved problem –
the poor state of industrial relations – and one grievous anomaly,
namely that governments spend far more on preventing industrial
change (by bolstering up dying and incompetent enterprises) than
on promoting innovation. There was a reminder that much of the
discussion repeated what had been said for many years: Ashley in
1902, examining the causes of British technical backwardness, had
recommended improvements in education and the use of protective
measures.

Turning next to consider the specific case of micro-electronics,
the conference noted the appearance of a policy common in agriculture but unusual in the industrial field, namely a deliberate effort
by government to spread new knowledge. The very rapid changes,
both in the scope and cost of micro-electronic technology, and in the
market situation relating to micro-electronic systems, provided a

special case for government to act, at least in a catalytic capacity. It was noted that, in relation to a large part of the basic technology, the adjustment needed by Britain was not to a competitive system of many small scientific firms, but to tomorrow's world in which there would be a new international oligopoly based on the silicon chip. Some speakers doubted if the signals given by the market could possibly be correct or adequate in this industry, given the speed of change and the distorting influence of heavy government expenditure on micro-electronics for defence. Of four major areas of application – electrical and electronic consumer goods, automobiles, capital goods and defence equipment – Britain was weak in the first three; so it was going to take a great effort to maintain any sort of a position in micro-electronic technology. The special problems of doing so were discussed, particular emphasis being given to the slowness of reaction of British businesses and to the lack of a proper educational infrastructure. While there was some expression of appreciation of the measures taken by government, there was a feeling that a confusing variety of government agencies was involved, that the emphasis given to the use of consultants might lead to inadequate attention to problems of executing their ideas, and that the various support schemes were too inflexible.

Discussion of educational policy in relation to innovation ranged widely. It was suggested that the British education system had become too 'soft', for instance in the number of hours of effort per year required of schoolchildren. Its requirements at secondary level allowed too much specialisation, and for a considerable proportion of pupils did not set firm and relevant requirements of attainment. Vocational training was grossly inadequate in quantity and old-fashioned in concept; the rigidities of apprenticeship systems were a particular disadvantage. Engineering and technology had not, until recently, attracted a fair share of talent; engineering courses were ill-related to the needs of industry; and the prestige given to pure science still exercised a harmful distorting influence. Early specialisation, and the unwillingness of non-scientists to seek any familiarity with scientific ideas, perpetuated the problem of the 'two cultures', and in particular caused many among both managers and civil servants to be deficient in their understanding of technological change. Management education was seen as a special problem, despite the great increase in its quantity; it was failing to provide enough managers with a tough analytical approach to problems and an adventurous entrepreneurial spirit. But all of these educational deficiencies were difficult to remove, because of the great power of the educational establishment, the wide discretion given to teachers and their excessive job protection, and the continued dominance of the Oxbridge ethos (though precisely what that was supposed to be was not clear). Perhaps the best way forward would be to increase the number of points at which the educational system has to respond to market forces.

A less satisfactory consideration of R and D policy then followed, partly because of familiar difficulties about the exact definition of words. It was questioned whether the old idea that Britain is 'good at invention but bad at innovation' is in fact true: one contributor saw the problem not as being an excess of work in basic science, but as a gross deficiency in technology and engineering design. The import of ideas by British industry is in fact high (though this of course does not prove that it could not, with advantage, be higher). The recommendations put forward amounted to an increase in the total of R and D expenditure, a transfer from defence to civil activity, and an improvement of systems to spread knowledge and to encourage firms to use new technology. It was pointed out that the discovery and development of new ideas may not be enough; the problems may be downstream, in a lack of vigour in taking them further, related to an unwillingness or inability to shoulder risks and a poor assessment of markets. But it cannot be said that the conference came to any clear or useful conclusions either about the amount or about the distribution of R and D expenditure.

The Chairman then drew together the discussion of the two days, defining 'industrial policy' for the present purpose as those things which are collectively needed to promote innovation, over and above the influences exerted by government through macro-economic policy and its regulation of the general social framework. He reminded the conference that 'collective action' need not always be government action. He drew a distinction between the non-selective forms of action (e.g. in education policy), with a widespread but possibly slow and uncertain effect; and selective help to individual firms or groups of firms, with the associated problem of obtaining a right choice. Pressures of politics and of public accountability, and the absence of any immediate spur from the rewards of success, made government agencies inefficient in making choices of industrial policy. He referred to the dominant problems of inadequate management and faulty relations with trade unions, and to the lack of a general culture or ethos which facilitated innovation. It would be helpful if the private sector had a clearer view of its long-run self-interest, and if entrepreneurs spent less time waiting for government to act, but fostered appropriate action (including collective action) by industry. Where government support is given there is need for checks on efficiency, lest a measure which supports or protects becomes a featherbed on which to slumber.

A final discussion repeated many points made earlier, though with references to the need for the financial sector to be more helpful. Looking back at the two days as a whole, my personal view is that the discussion repeated a familiar tale. The factors which conceivably affect British performance in innovation have been studied many times, and very little is being said now which was not familiar a quarter of a century or more ago. Nor has anyone much in the way of new ideas about what is to be done about it. There has to be an element of government intervention, and the possible forms of that intervention are well known. The main change, compared with discussions in earlier years, is a sharp drop in belief in the wisdom of government, and consequently a diversion of emphasis from creating broad centralised strategic plans to action which supports the market economy, improving its signals and helping it to work better. This, however, shifts attention to the improvement of the quality of business decisions, and of the environment in which they have to be made. Since the ill-success of the economy produces a very unfavourable environment for innovation, a large number of entrepreneurs of extraordinary skill and daring seem to be needed to turn the course of events; government supportive measures will not be effective if applied to reluctant and inefficient firms. How does one find these entrepreneurs quickly enough to avert a collapse of morale and of free political institutions?

Index

Index

additionality, principle of, 10, 218–20

adjustment policies, 122–3, 177

Advanced Computer Technology Project, 186

advisory services, 161–3

Advisory Council for Applied Research and Development (ACARD), 132, 143, 153, 174

American Telegraph and Telephone (ATT), 13

Anglo-American Council on Productivity, 54

antitrust legislation, 7

Association of German Engineers (VDI), 190

Bank of Japan, 74

banks, role of, 131, 149–50

BIPE, 153

British Iron and Steel Federation, 76

BSC (Industry) Limited, 221–2

Brookings Institution, 118

Centre National d'Etudes des Télécommunications, 190

Clothing Industry Productivity Resources Agency, 223

CODIS Committee, 153

collaborative research centres, 160–1

Commissariat à l'Energie Atomique, 190

Commissariat du Plan, 153

competition
Japanese internal, 78–9
limits of, 6–8

perfect, 6–7, 10–11
policy, 42–4, 230
worldwide, 135

Competition Act (1980), 42, 43, 45

computer industry, structure of, 204–5

Confederation of British Industry (CBI), 44, 116, 120, 150

Cotton Yarn Spinners' agreement, 42

Council on Prices, Productivity and Incomes, 45

'creative destruction', 117

credit, availability of, 74, 130–3

Data Processing Programmes (Germany), 125, 126, 186–7

Délégation à l'Informatique, 193–4, 196

demand growth, rate of, 120

Department of Economic Affairs, 46

Department of Education and Science, 54

Department of Employment, 36

Department of Scientific and Industrial Research (DSIR), 54, 59

Department of [Trade and] Industry, 57, 58, 138

diffusion of technology, 1, 120, 125–6

Direction des Industries Electroniques et de l'Informatique (DIELI), 192

Distribution of Industry Act (1945), 40

Donovan Report, 37

Economic Development Committees (EDCs), 45, 46, 48
economic growth, rate of, 8, 117, 118
education, *see also* management, education; vocational training
  direction of, 33, 37, 85, 181, 230
  in special skills, 26, 29, 34, 100–1
  Japanese system of, 79–80
employee participation, 155
Engineering Industry Training Board, 33
enterprise unions, 82, 83
European Commission, 43
European Court of Justice, 43
exchange controls, in Japan, 75
Export–Import Bank (Japan), 74
exports
  composition of British, 90, 147
  Japanese encouragement of, 74

Fair Trade Commission (Japan), 73, 87
Fair Trading Act (1973), 42
Federation of British Industries, 84
Finance for Industry, 221, 223
Finniston Report, 33, 101, 155
firms
  large, research in, 11, 12, 134
  large, share of government funds in, 163, 165
  multi-divisional, 12
  organisation of, in Japan, 72
  small, research in, 11, 12, 22, 116, 121, 134, 153

government intervention, 1
  in Britain, 72, 135, 137–8, 179–80, 229, 233
  in European industry, 186–90
  in Japan, 72–3, 180–1

horizontal policies, 126, 154–6
House of Commons Expenditure Committee, 64
House of Commons Trade and Industry Committee, 122

Income-Doubling Plan (Japan), 73
incomes policy, 44

Industrial Development Advisory Board, 138, 203
industrial financing, in Japan, 74–6
industrial organisation, 10–14
  in Japan, 72
industrial performance, 13, 88, 146
industrial policy
  in Britain, 1–2, 11, ch. 4 *passim*, 75, 102, 117, 123–5, 147–56, 176, 225
  in Europe, 125–6, 182–202
  in Japan, 2, ch. 6 *passim*
  in machine tool industry, 2, ch. 5 *passim*
  objectives of, 91–2, 121–3, 232
industrial relations, 34–6
  in Japan, 82–3, 86
Industrial Reorganisation Corporation (IRC), 39, 46, 49, 56, 57, 60
Industrial Restructuring, Rationalisation and Development Law (Italy), 189, 196–7
Industrial Strategy, 47, 48, 146, 156, 170, 177–8, 204
Industrial Structure Commission, 3, 153–4
Industry Act (1972), 56, 57, 58, 138
Industry Training Boards, 54
Informatisation de la Société, 187
Inmos, 3, 48, 140–1, 144, 192, 195–6, 203, 210–12
innovation
  arguments against, ch. 3 *passim*
  factors affecting, 129–35
  financing, 23, 121, 125
  in advanced industrial societies, 8ff
  in Britain, 24, 27–9
  in machine tool industry, ch. 5 *passim*
  in manufacturing industry, ch. 3 *passim*
  in semi-conductor industries, ch. 8 *passim*
  in unfavourable conditions, 14, 25

in United States, 24
lack of, 2, 22, 92–6
regulation of effects of, 5
role of government in, 4, 8, 26, 37, 52–3, 59–60, ch. 7(V) *passim*
timing of, 23, 135
Institution of Electrical Engineers, 223
invention, at expense of innovation, 32
investing institutions, 131, 132, 142, 151; *see also* banks
investment
  by US in Europe, 185
  from private funds, 19, 131
  from public funds, 19, 158
  incentives, 39–42, 85
  long-term, 15, 86
  management of, 142–3
  rate of, 88–9
  timing of, 4, 23
Iron and Steel Board, 76

Japan Development Bank, 74

knowledge-intensive industries, 70–1

lifetime employment, 82, 83–4
loans, refundable, 125

machine tool industry
  British, performance of, 60–4
  government schemes for, 53–60
  supply of skilled labour in, 65
Machine Tool Industry Research Association (MTIRA), 59
Machine Tool Industry Scheme (MTIS), 57–8, 62, 64, 65
Machine Tool Trades Association, 64
machine tools trial-period schemes, 55, 64
management
  education, 29–30, 181, 231–2
  efficiency, in Japan, 79
  inadequacy, 26, 28–9

manpower policies, 126
Maldague Report, 147
Market Entry Guarantee Scheme, 48, 127
market information, 161–3
market mechanisms, 182
markets
  efficiency of, 2, 4–6, 16
  location of, 22
  size of, 23
measurement, problems of, 4 5
Mechanical Engineering and Machine Tools Board, 59
Medical Research Council (MRC), 121, 143
mergers, control of, 42–3
micro-electronics
  applications in industry, ch. 10 *passim*
  government support for, 124, ch. 8 *passim*, 207, 230–1
Microprocessor Application Project (MAP scheme), 3, 124, 213, 215–22, 224
Ministry of International Trade and Industry (MITI) (Japan), 69, 70, 76, 120, 153, 164, 173, 199–200
  Industrial Committees of, 73
  Agency for Industrial Science and Technology, 80
Ministry of Science and Technology (Japan), 80
Ministry of Technology, 54, 55, 60, 172
Mission pour les Circuits Intégrés, 196
Mitchell Committee, 54, 64
Monopolies [and Mergers] Commission, 42, 44, 76, 78, 154
Monopolies and Mergers Act (1965), 42

National Board for Prices and Incomes (NBPI), 39, 44, 45
National Computing Centre, 223
National Economic Development Council (NEDC), 39, 45, 46, 116, 124

National Economic Development Office (NEDO), 45, 48, 125, 154, 223
National Engineering Laboratory, 59
National Enterprise Board (NEB), 3, 39, 46, 47, 48, 49, 57, 58, 59, 103, 127, 129ff, 153, 180, 192, 196, 203ff, 223, 230
National Plan, 39, 46
National Research Council (Italy), 190
National Research Development Corporation (NRDC), 49, 54, 55, 103, 108, 138, 164, 223
National Science Foundation (US), 9, 11, 162

OECD, 8, 10, 123
Science and Technology Indicators Unit, 98

Pay Board, 44
personal relations
between investor and innovator, 132
in Japan, 81–2
Plan Calcul, 186
Plan Circuits Intégrés, 187, 196
Policy Studies Institute (PSI), 213, 214
politics, impact on NEB, 144
Price Commission, 35, 44, 45
price control, 44
private returns, rates of, 8–10, 179–80, 225
Product and Process Development Scheme, 48, 58, 124, 127, 138, 164
protectionist practices, 102–3, 175–6
public financing, 17–18, 138, 163–4
public purchasing policy, 65–6, 165–8, 190

quality control, 81

regional development grants, 220
regional employment premium, 41

regional policy, 39–42
resale price maintenance, 42
Resale Prices Acts (1964, 1976), 42
research and development (R and D), 1, 90ff
government support for, 7–8, 9, 15, 17, 103ff, 155, 158
in civilian high technologies, 106–7
in defence, 105–6, 111–12, 176, 186, 190
in universities, 108–9
industry-financed, 101–3, 131, 179
Japanese expenditure on, 77–8
policies, 101, 110–11, 190–8
Research and Development Requirements Boards, 59, 108, 125, 127, 138, 164
Restrictive Practices Court, 42
Restrictive Trade Practices Green Paper, 43–4
Restrictive Trade Practices Acts (1956, 1968, 1976, 1977), 42, 43
Ringisei, 81
risk-aversion, 130, 159, 162, 164, 179, 180, 225
risk-sharing, 7, 163, 164–5, 168, 180
Robbins Report, 54
Rothschild Report, 18, 59, 105

Sector Working Parties (SWPs), 48, 127, 171, 204, 226
sectoral policies, 110–11, 126
Selective Employment Tax, 41
Selective Investment Scheme, 48, 127, 171, 226
semi-conductor industry, 182ff
silicon chips, 121, 141, 207–10, 214
skills, lack of, 23, 53
social returns, rates of, 8–10, 36, 179–80, 225
Special Areas Act (1934), 40
specialisation, in British trade, 147
strikes, 36
structural adaptability
in Europe, 191–2
in Japan, 69

structural failure, 116
structuralist view, 118–19, 225–6

task partitioning, 167
tax incentives, 138, 168
   in Japan, 75, 76
Teaching Company Scheme, 162
technical consultants, 216–17
Technological Evolution Fund
   (Italy), 186
technology
   acceleration of change in, 119–21
   advance of, 88–9
   diffusion of, 1, 120, 125–6
   import and export of, 97–100
   transfer of, 157, 162
Technology Agreements, 120, 127
Tokyo Round, 191
trade
   policies, 177
   theories of, 98, 157

trade union obstruction, 25, 34–6,
   86
Trades Union Congress (TUC),
   120, 122, 127
Treaty of Rome, 43

UNESCO, 33
Union of German Engineers, 190,
   223
US Department of Justice, Antitrust Division, 13

VDI Technology Centre (Germany), 162, 190, 223–4
Venture Capital Company (Germany), 164
vocational training, 66, 79, 101,
   154–5, 179

Warner Report, 60, 65–6
Wilson Committee, 130–1, 142